workbook in physics for science and engineering students

workbook in physics for science and engineering students

SECOND EDITION

FREDERICK J. BUECHE
Professor of Physics
University of Dayton

McGraw-Hill Book Company

New York St. Louis San Francisco Auckland Düsseldorf
Johannesburg Kuala Lumpur London Mexico Montreal New Delhi Panama
Paris São Paulo Singapore Sydney Tokyo Toronto

Workbook in Physics
for Science and Engineering Students

ISBN 0-07-008839-X

1234567890 DODO 798765

This book was set in Univers Medium by Allen-Wayne Technical Corp.
The editors were A. Anthony Arthur and Frances A. Neal;
the cover was designed by Anne Canevari Green;
the production supervisor was Thomas J. LoPinto.
R. R. Donnelley & Sons Company was printer and binder.

contents

preface

Ideally, each student taking a course in general physics would meet periodically with a tutor. The tutor would question him to ascertain his level of understanding of the subject matter and would guide him to further understanding. In addition, the tutor would drill the student in the use of the principles that he is learning, point out his mistakes, and show the proper approach to be taken. Unfortunately, such a tutorial system is seldom available, and the teacher of the course has only limited time to help students individually and supervise drill exercises. The author has written this workbook in an effort to compensate partly for this lack of direct teacher-student interaction. Although it would be folly to think that any written guide could fully substitute for a private tutor, the author feels that the student who uses this supplement wisely will benefit much.

It is suggested that the student proceed in the following way. First, he should study thoroughly the pertinent sections of the textbook, *Introduction to Physics for Scientists and Engineers* 2d ed. (occasionally cited in this workbook as "Bueche"), or a comparable text. When he feels he has acquired a reasonable understanding of the text material, he should then turn to the workbook. Without looking at the answers or methods of solution, he should tackle in sequence the questions and problems covering that material. If the student understands the principles behind the question or problem, its solution will usually be possible in no more than several minutes. The answer should then be checked against that given in the workbook, and the presented method of solution should be examined. If the wrong answer is obtained or if the problems cannot be solved after a few minutes' thought, the given solution should be looked at closely to discover what weakness in theory or technique is responsible for the trouble. If necessary, reference back to appropriate sections in the text should be made. Finally, the student should go on to the solution of the homework problems assigned by the instructor.

Of course, all this should be carried out at a leisurely pace, on a daily schedule tuned to the lectures in the course. If study is delayed until a few days before each test, the author can only wish the student well and expect the worst. However, as a feature of a regular study program, a pretest review of the questions and problems in the workbook should prove of considerable value.

Frederick J. Bueche

workbook in physics for science and engineering students

1 physics and measurement

1 What is meant by the statement "Physics is an experimental science"?

2, Give the names of the basic units of length, mass, and time.

3 How is the unit of length defined?

4 What is the present definition of the second?

5 How is the mass of an object defined?

6 What is the significance of the symbol mks? SI?

7 Does an object always have the same mass and length?

q

1
questions
1-13

8 What is the relation of derived units to mass, length, and time units?

9 List the abbreviation prefixes for the factors 10^9, 10^6, 10^3, 10^{-2}, 10^{-3}, 10^{-6}, 10^{-9}, 10^{-12}, and 10^{-15}.

10 Estimate the number of atoms placed side by side which would make a row 1 cm long.

11 A layer of gas one atom thick is adsorbed on a flat metal surface. About how many gas atoms cover an area of 1 cm^2?

12 The number of atoms in 1 kg atomic mass of an element is called Avogadro's number, N_A, 6.02×10^{26}. Find the mass of a carbon atom. The atomic mass of carbon is 12, that is, 12 kg of carbon contains N_A carbon atoms.

13 Write the following in the form $a \times 10^b$: 251, 0.167, 5471, 0.0006201, 1000.

1 Physicists measure the behavior of nature, interpret their measurements, and predict the results of new measurements. Questions and answers which are not subject to experimental test are outside the province of physics.

2 Meter, kilogram, second.

3 One meter is exactly 1,650,763.63 times larger than the wavelength of the orange light emitted by krypton 86.

4 One second is the time taken for 9,192,631,770 vibrations of a certain type associated with the Cs 133 atom.

5 The unit of mass is the kilogram, the mass of a particular object kept near Paris. Other masses are determined by comparison.

6 The three letters stand for meter, kilogram, and second, the basic units of the unit system designated in this way. It is more correctly known as the International System (SI).

a

1

answers

1-13

7 No. Its mass and length vary as its speed relative to the measurer changes.

8 All derived units can be expressed in terms of mass, length, and time units. For example, the unit of area is m^2. That of speed is m/sec, and so on.

9 Giga, mega, kilo, centi, milli, micro, nano, pico, and femto.

10 A typical atom is about 2×10^{-10} m in diameter. Therefore, the number is about $1 \times 10^{-2}/2 \times 10^{-10} = 0.5 \times 10^{8} = 5 \times 10^{7}$.

11 Assuming an atomic diameter 2×10^{-10} m, a square centimeter will have $\frac{1}{2} \times 10^{8}$ atoms on each edge. The number will be 0.25×10^{16} atoms.

12 There are 6.02×10^{26} carbon atoms in 12 kg of carbon. The mass of an atom is $(12/6.02) \times 10^{-26}$ kg or about 2×10^{-26} kg.

13 See Appendix 3 of Bueche to obtain 2.51×10^{2}, 1.67×10^{-1}, 5.471×10^{3}, 6.201×10^{-4}, 1×10^{3}.

14 Measure the height of this page using a ruler graduated in millimeters and estimate the error in your measurement.

15 If the answer to problem 14 were 19.97 ± 0.02 cm, what would this symbolism mean and why could not the answer be written as 20 ± 0.02?

16 The combined mass of 20 identical screws is 3.16 ± 0.04 g. Find the mass of a single screw.

17 A cube is measured to be 2.00 ± 0.02 cm on each edge. Find its volume.

18 Add the following lengths: 2.0×10^{-4} cm, 3.16×10^{-3} cm, and 0.00513 cm.

19 Evaluate the following:

$$\frac{3.2 \times 10^{-19} \times 500}{1.6 \times 10^{-27}}$$

20 Give a dimensional argument to show that the following formula is not correct:

$$v = ae^{-t/a}$$

where

v = speed

a = distance

t = time

14 □ 25.40 ±0.01 cm

This is interpreted to mean that the true size lies between 25.39 and 25.41 cm.

15 The true size is between 19.95 and 19.99 cm. The designation 20 ± 0.02 is meaningless since we are not told the main number accurately enough to give meaning to the error estimate.

16 □ $m = (3.16 \pm 0.04\ \text{g})/20 = 0.158 \pm 0.002$ g. To check this, notice that the mass might have been as large as 3.20/20 = 0.160 g and as small as 3.12/20 = 0.156 g, which agrees with the limits of error found.

17 □ $V = (2.00 \pm 0.02)^3 = 2^3\,(1 \pm 0.01)^3$

$= 8(1 \pm 0.03 + 0.0003 \pm 0.000001) \cong 8(1 \pm 0.03)$

$= 8.00 \pm 0.24\ \text{cm}^3$

18 Write all to the same power of ten and add:

$2.0 \times 10^{-4} + 31.6 \times 10^{-4} + 51.3 \times 10^{-4}\ \text{cm} = (2.0 + 31.6 + 51.3) \times 10^{-4}$

$= 84.9 \times 10^{-4}$ cm

19 Rewrite as

$$\frac{3.2 \times 10^{-19} \times 5.0 \times 10^{2}}{1.6 \times 10^{-27}} = \frac{3.2 \times 5}{1.6} \times 10^{10} = 10 \times 10^{10} = 1.0 \times 10^{11}$$

20 When one has e^x, the quantity x must always be a dimensionless number. In this case $x = t/a$, which has the units of time/distance and is therefore not a pure number. Even if the exponent were changed, the units on the left would be those of v, namely m/sec, while those on the right would be the units of the distance a. Since the units are wrong, the equation cannot be correct.

2 directed quantities; vectors

1 What is (a) a vector quantity and (b) a vector?

2 What is a scalar quantity?

3 Give two different ways of showing that a quantity F is a vector quantity.

4 How does one find the resultant of several vectors graphically? For example, of the following:

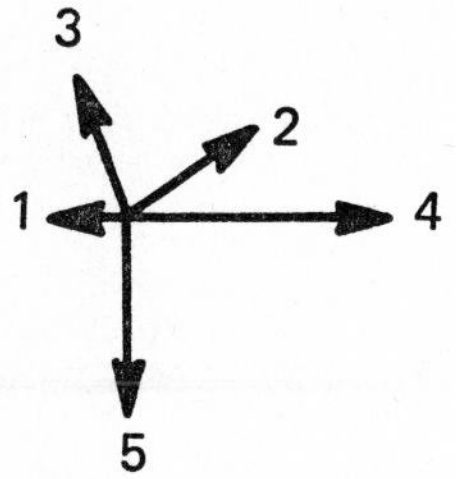

q
2
questions
1-8

5 What is meant by splitting a vector into its x and y components?

6 What is meant by the following?
$\mathbf{F} = -3\mathbf{i} + 4\mathbf{j}$

7 What is the result of multiplying a positive scalar by a unit vector?

8 What must be true about the components of two vectors if the vectors are to be equal?

1 (a) A quantity which has both magnitude and direction and obeys the associative and commutative laws.

(b) The arrow whose length represents the magnitude of a vector quantity and whose direction represents the direction of the quantity.

2 A quantity having no direction associated with it.

3 □ **F**; $\vec{F}$

4 One adds them *tip* to *tail* as shown. We arbitrarily start with vector 4. Notice that the direction of the resultant **R** is from beginning point to end point.

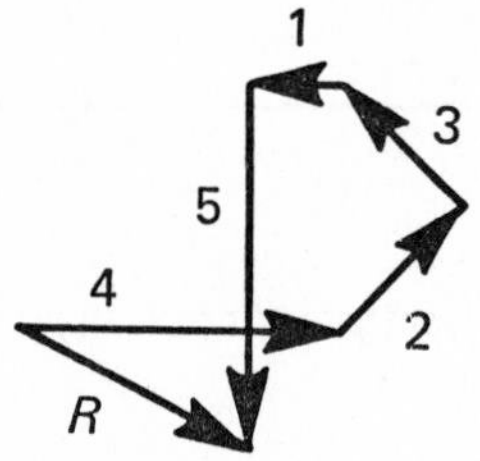

5 The effective x and y portions of the vector (its components) are shown. In this case both F_x and F_y are negative.

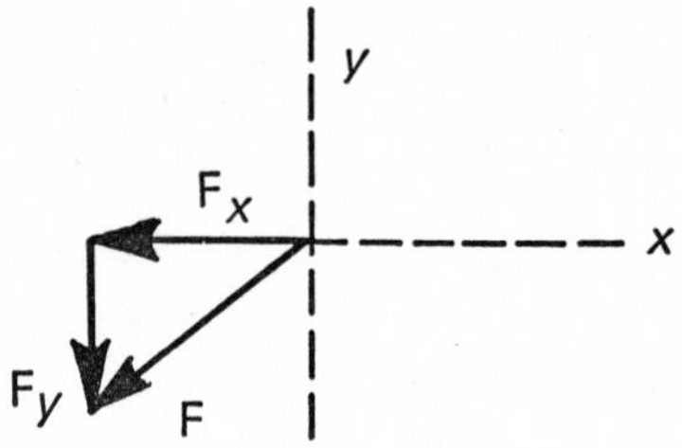

6 The x component of **F** is -3 and its y component is 4. The vector is as shown.

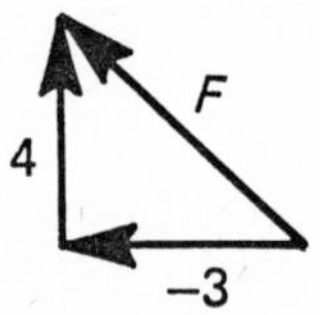

7 It yields a vector in the direction of the unit vector and with a magnitude equal to the scalar.

8 Their components must be equal, respectively.

a

2
answers
1-8

9 What is the commutative law as applied to vectors?

10 What is the associative law as applied to vectors?

11 In figure 2.1 (*a*), the numerical value of sin θ is ______, of cos θ is ______, and of tan θ is ________.

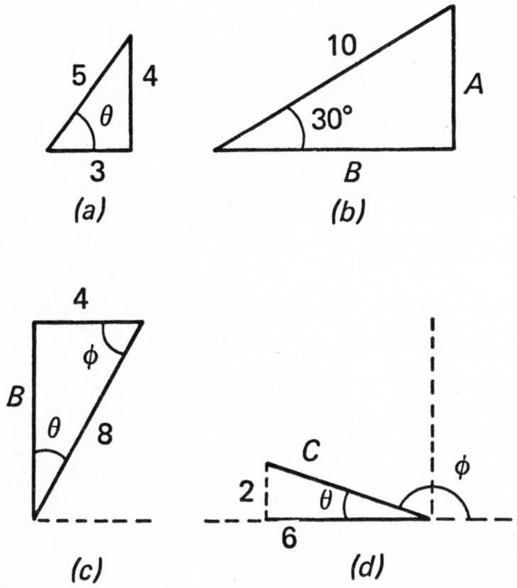

figure 2.1

12 From the tables we find that the value of sin 30° is________, while cos 30° is ________, and tan 30° is ________.

13 In figure 2.1 (*b*), the length of A is ________ units and the length of B is ________ units.

14 In figure 2.1 (*c*), the angle θ is________° while the length of B is________ units.

15 In figure 2.1 (*c*), having found θ, the value of ϕ is $90° - \theta$ or ________°.

16 In figure 2.1 (*d*), the value of tan θ is ________ and thus θ is approximately ________°.

17 In figure 2.1 (*d*), the length of C is________ units.

9 $F_1 + F_2 = F_2 + F_1$. The order of adding the vectors does not change the result.

10 The grouping of the vectors does not change the sum.
$(F_1 + F_2) + F_3 = F_1 + (F_2 + F_3)$

11 □ 0.80; 0.60; 1.33

12 □ 0.50; 0.87; 0.58

13 □ 5; $5\sqrt{3} \cong 8.7$

14 □ 30; $4\sqrt{3} \cong 6.9$

15 □ 60

16 □ $\frac{1}{3}$; 18.4

17 □ $2\sqrt{10} \cong 6.3$

a

2
answers
9-17

18 Having found θ in figure 2.1(d), we know ϕ is 180° - θ or ________°.

19 Refer to figure 2.2. The x component of the 10-unit vector is ____________ units, and its y component is __________ units. (b) For the 15-unit vector, the x component is ________ units and its y component is __________ units. (c) Using the results of (a) and (b), the x and y components of R are __________ units and __________ units, respectively. (d) The magnitude of R is __________ units, and tan θ equals __________ from which θ is found to be __________°.

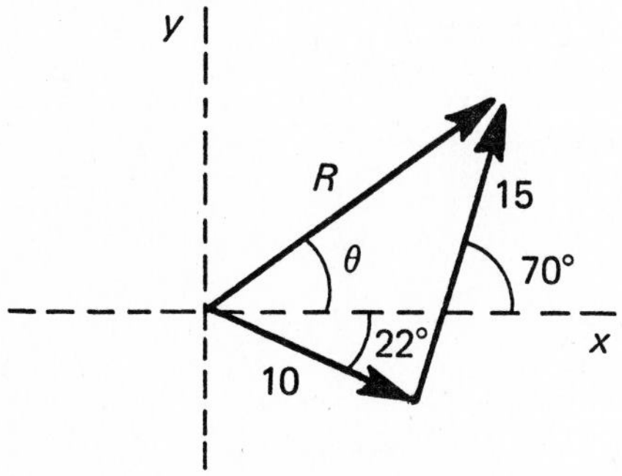

figure 2.2

2
questions
18-20

20 Refer to figure 2.3. The x components of the 7-, 10-, and 5-unit vectors are _____ units, __________ units, and __________ units, respectively. (b) The y components of the 7-, 10-, and 5-unit vectors are __________ units, __________ units, and __________ units, respectively.

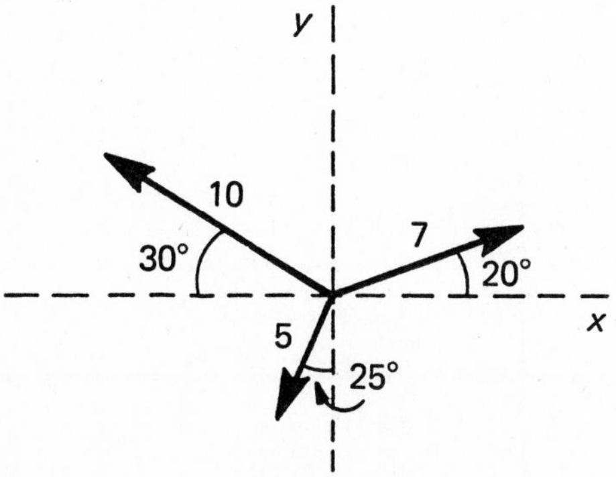

figure 2.3

18 □ 162

19 (a) 9.3; -3.7
(b) 5.1; 14.1
(c) 14.4; 10.4
(d) 18.0; 0.72; 36

20 (a) 6.6; -8.7; -2.1
(b) 2.4; 5.0; -4.5

21 A man walks 2 miles due south. He turns east 30° and walks 2 more miles. He now makes a right-angle turn toward the north and walks 1 mile. What is his final position relative to his starting point?

22 Three dogs simultaneously grab at the same bone. The first dog pulls with a force of 50 lb in a direction due west. The second dog pulls with a force of 12 lb 30° east of north, and the third pulls with a force of 25 lb 30° east of south. What is the magnitude and direction of the force needed to hold the bone motionless?

23 Two boys wish to erect a ramp. One has a board 5.0 ft long; the other has a board 1.5 ft long. If the second boy has his board at an angle of 25° with the horizontal, what is the angle between the two boards if they join at their top ends? What is the distance between the two boards along the ground?

24 What vector must be added to a vector **3i** - 2**j** + 4**k** to give a vector 8**i**?

21 $\mathbf{R} = (-2\mathbf{j}) + (1.0\mathbf{i} - 1.74\mathbf{j}) + (0.87\mathbf{i} + 0.50\mathbf{j})$

$\mathbf{R} = 1.87\mathbf{i} - 3.24\mathbf{j}$

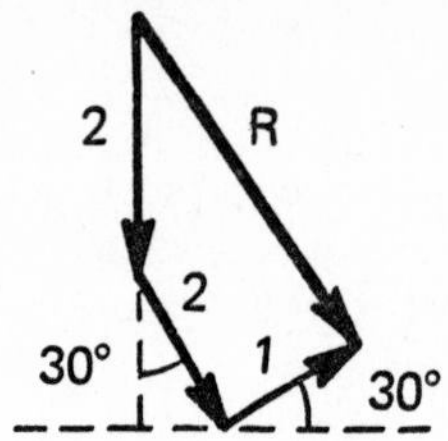

$\tan^{-1}\theta = -\dfrac{3.24}{1.87}$

$R = 3.7 \qquad \theta = -60°$

22

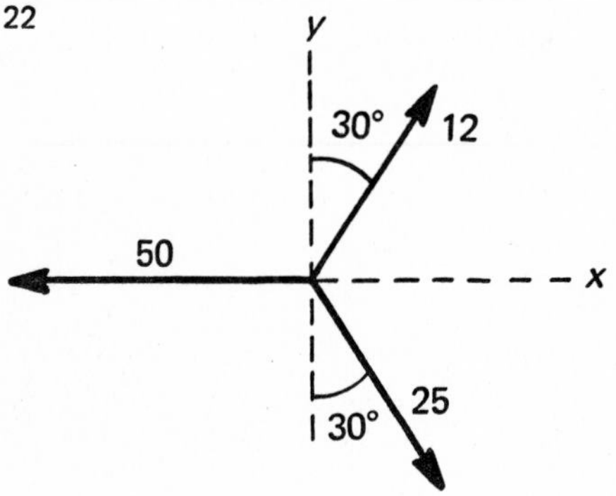

$R_x = 6.0 - 50 + 12.5 = -31.5$
$R_y = 10.4 - 21.7 = -11.3$
$R = 33.5$ at $\theta = 200°$
The force in question is equal and opposite.

33.5 lb at 20°

23

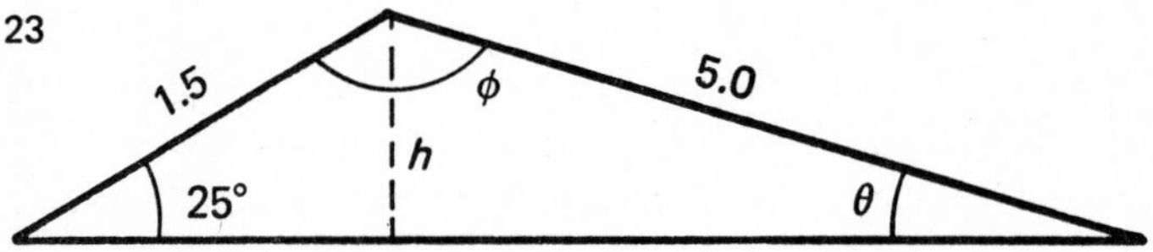

$h = 1.5 \sin 25° = 0.634$

$\sin\theta = \dfrac{0.634}{5} = 0.127$

$\theta = 7°$ $\phi = 65 + 83 = 148°$
Distance = 6.3 ft

24 Call the vector $A\mathbf{i} + B\mathbf{j} + C\mathbf{k}$. Then
$(3\mathbf{i} - 2\mathbf{j} + 4\mathbf{k}) + A\mathbf{i} + B\mathbf{j} + C\mathbf{k} = 8\mathbf{i}$
$(3 + A)\mathbf{i} + (B - 2)\mathbf{j} + (C + 4)\mathbf{k} = 8\mathbf{i}$
The components of two equal vectors are equal. Therefore
$3 + A = 8$ or $A = 5$
$B - 2 = 0$ or $B = 2$
$C + 4 = 0$ or $C = -4$
$5\mathbf{i} + 2\mathbf{j} - 4\mathbf{k}$

25 Find the resultant of the following vectors:

$2\mathbf{i} + 6\mathbf{j} - 3\mathbf{k}$

$8\mathbf{i} - 2\mathbf{j} + 2\mathbf{k}$

26 The wind blows south at 50 mph. An airplane which can travel at 150 mph relative to the air moves at top speed due south. What is its velocity relative to the earth?

27 Suppose the plane of the previous problem flies east as fast as it can. What now is its velocity relative to the earth? Write your answer in component form.

28 In what direction must the plane of problem 26 be aimed if it is to go straight east above the earth? (Assume that it moves at its top speed.)

25 ☐ $\mathbf{R} = 10\mathbf{i} + 4\mathbf{j} - \mathbf{k}$

26 The plane's speed will be 150 + 50 = 200 mph relative to the ground.

27 Taking east as x and north as y, its velocity is $\mathbf{v} = 150\mathbf{i} - 50\mathbf{j}$.

28 The plane must head at an angle θ shown such that the northward component is 50 mph, thereby canceling the wind's effect.

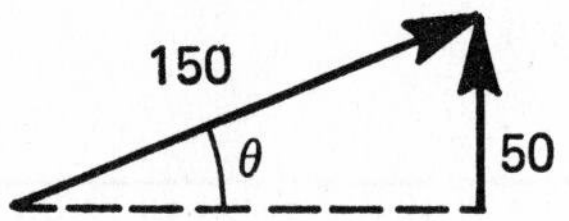

$$\sin\theta = \frac{50}{150} = 1/3$$

from which $\theta = 19°$.

a

2
answers
25-28

3
bodies at rest

1 What do we mean by the weight of a body?

2 State the first condition for equilibrium of a body.

3 State both the vector and component equations summarizing the first condition for equilibrium.

4 What is the meaning of the word torque as applied to equilibrium in a plane?

1 The pull of gravity upon the body.

2 For a body to be in equilibrium, it is necessary (although not sufficient, in general) that the vector sum of the forces acting on the body be zero.

3 $\Sigma \mathbf{F} = 0$

$\Sigma F_{xn} = \Sigma F_{yn} = \Sigma F_{zn} = 0$

4 Torque τ is defined to be (lever arm) X (force). The lever arm is the length of a perpendicular dropped from the pivot point for measuring torques to the line of the force.

a

3

answers

1-4

5 What is the lever arm for each of the forces shown in the figure?

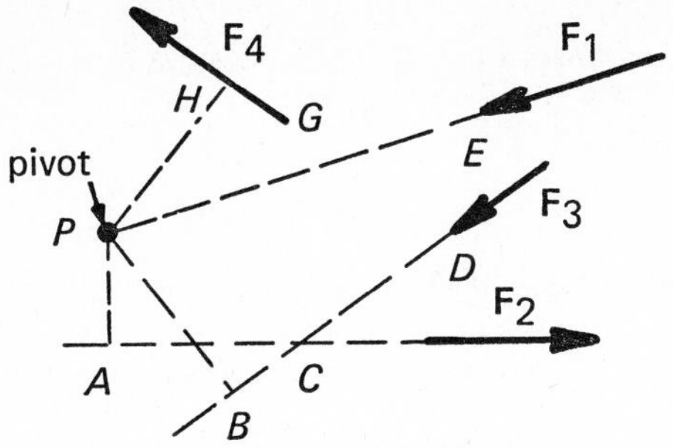

6 State the second necessary condition for equilibrium of a body.

7 Is the choice of a pivot point for writing the torque equation critical?

8 Define center of gravity.

9 Refer to the figure. All the forces acting on the bodies are shown.

(a) The body shown in part __________ is in equilibrium. (b) in part *(a)* of the figure, the value of the unbalanced force is __________ lb. (c) The sum of the vertical forces in part *(a)* is __________. (d) What is the tension in the cord in part *(b)*? What force does the cord exert on the block? On the ceiling? (e) In part *(c)* a force of __________ lb must be exerted to the (right or left?) if the cart is to be in equilibrium.

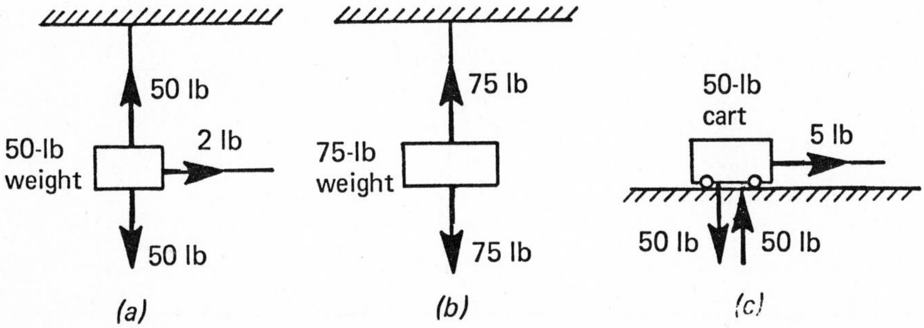

q

3 questions 5-9

5 For F_1, F_2, F_3, F_4, respectively, they are $0; PA; PB; PH$.

6 The sum of the torques acting on the body must be zero (taking counterclockwise torques positive and clockwise torques negative):

$$\Sigma\tau_n = 0$$

7 If the sum of the forces acting on the body is zero and if the sum of the torques is zero about one pivot point, it will be zero about all pivot points. Therefore its choice is not critical. However, it is more convenient to choose it at some places than others.

8 It is a point at which a force equal to the weight of a body may be considered to act so as to duplicate the torque resulting from the pull of gravity.

9 (a) b
(b) 2 lb
(c) zero
(d) 75 lb; 75 lb; 75 lb
(e) 5 lb, left

10 Refer to the figure. (a) The pull of gravity on the block is __________ lb in a direction __________. Taking *up* as a positive, the forces in the y direction on the junction are __________. (b) The forces in the x direction are __________. (c) Since the block does not move, $\Sigma F_x = 0$. Combining this fact with the answer to (b) yields the equation __________. (d) Solving the equation in (c) for T_1 gives T_1 = __________. (e) Since $\Sigma F_y = 0$, the following equation results: __________. (f) Combining the results of (d) and (e) gives T_2 = __________ and T_1 = __________.

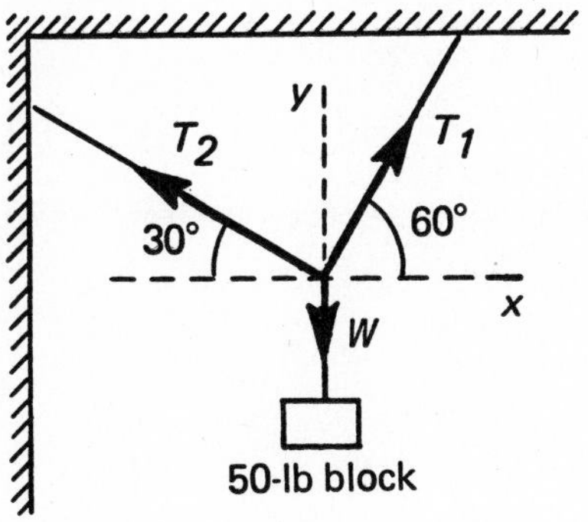

11 For the uniform 20-lb bar shown in the figure, taking the pivot as shown, (a) the torque due to the 40-lb force is __________ ft-lb; (b) the lever arm for the 20-lb force is __________ ft and the torque due to this force is __________ ft-lb; and (c) the torque due to the 50-lb force is __________ ft-lb. (d) The resultant torque due to the 20-, 40-, and 50-lb forces is __________ ft-lb. (e) In order for the bar to remain in equilibrium, P should be __________ lb since its lever arm is __________ ft.

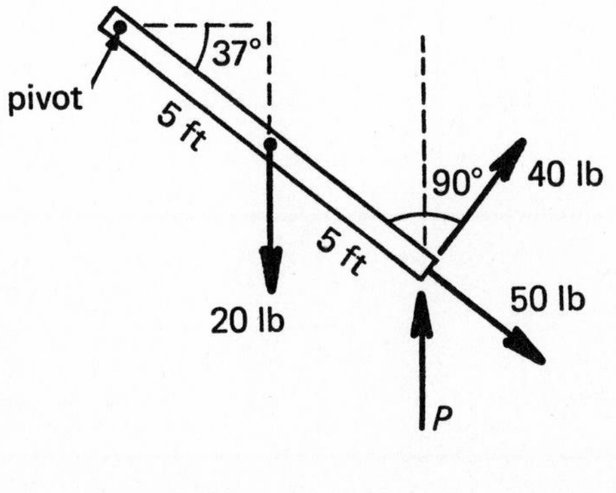

q

3
questions
10-11

10 (a) 50; down; $0.87T_1$; $0.50T_2$; -50
(b) $0.50T_1$; $-0.87T_2$
(c) $0.50T_1 = 0.87T_2$
(d) $1.7T_2$
(e) $0.87T_1 + 0.50T_2 = 50$
(f) 25 lb; 43 lb

11 (a) 400
(b) 4; -80
(c) zero
(d) 320
(e) -40; 8

a

3
answers
10-11

12 Find the tensions in the ropes shown below.

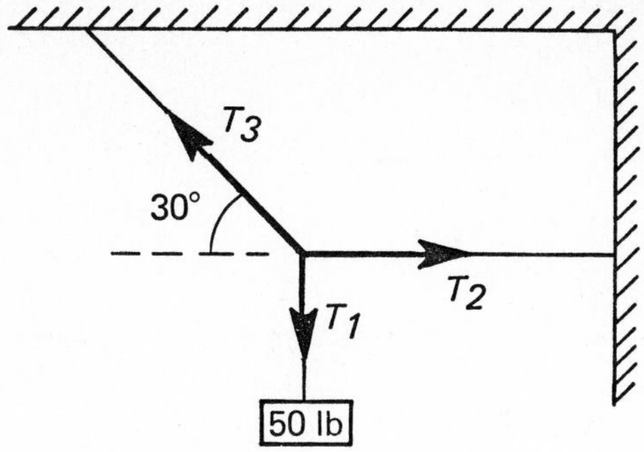

13 A uniform 2-lb mirror hangs from two cords as shown. Find the tensions in the cords as well as the magnitude of the force **P** needed to hold it as shown.

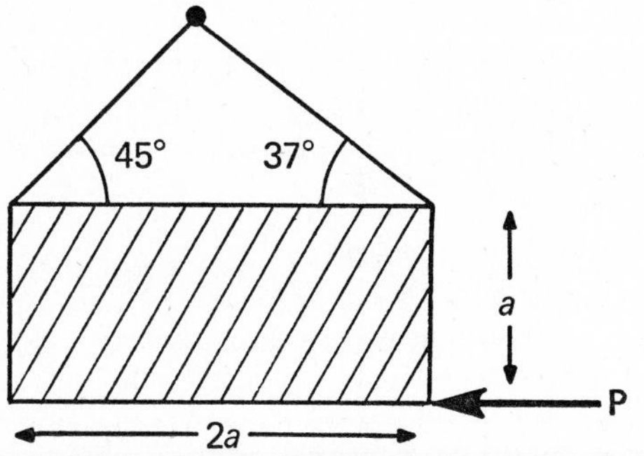

14 A block weighing 50 lb is hung from the ceiling on a uniform chain weighing 10 lb. What is the tension at the top of the chain? At the midpoint of the chain? At the block?

q

3
questions
12-14

12 ☐ $T_1 = 50$ lb
Isolate the rope junction.
$-T_1 + T_3 \sin 30^\circ = 0 \quad \Sigma F_y = 0$

or $T_3 = \frac{50}{0.5} = 100$ lb
$T_2 - 0.87\, T_3 = 0 \quad \Sigma F_x = 0$
or $T_2 = 87$ lb

13 Draw the forces acting *on the mirror* together with their components as shown.

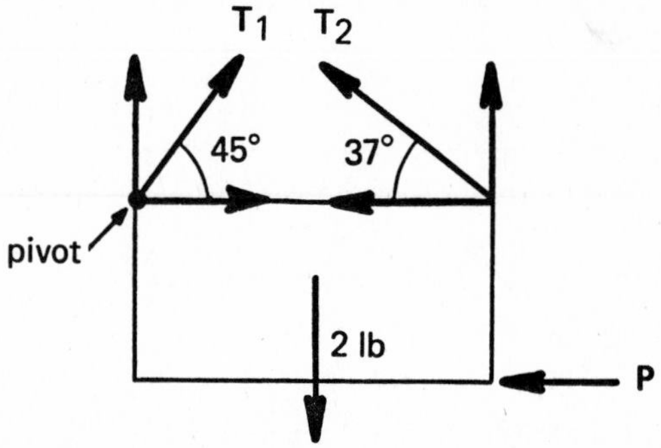

$\Sigma F_x = 0$ gives $0.71T_1 - 0.80T_2 - P = 0$
$\Sigma F_y = 0$ gives $0.71T_1 + 0.60T_2 - 2 = 0$
Taking torques about the point shown (using components)
$(0.6T_2)(2a) - 2(a) - P(a) = 0$
(The other force goes through the axis and causes no torque.)
Solve simultaneously: $T_1 = 1.52$; $T_2 = 1.54$;
$P = -0.15$ lb
The negative sign tells us P is opposite to direction shown.

a

3
answers
12-14

14 ☐ 60 lb; 55 lb; 50 lb
In the first case, the weight supported is that of block plus chain. In the second case, the block and half the chain are being held up.

15 If the beam shown below is uniform and weighs 10 lb, find the tension in the cable and the force components at the wall.

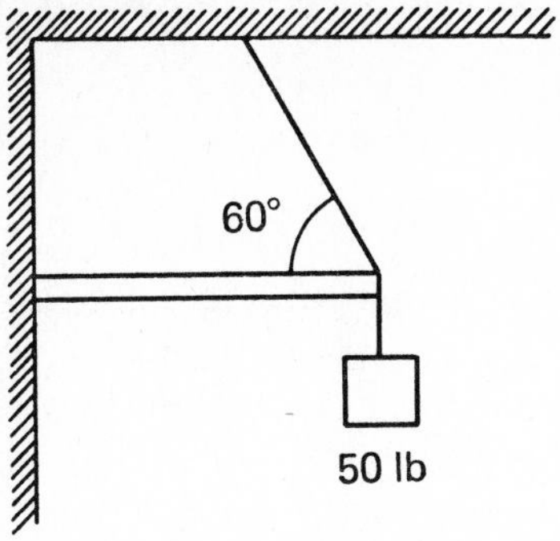

16 For the system shown below, find the tensions a, b, and c as well as the value of the weight W.

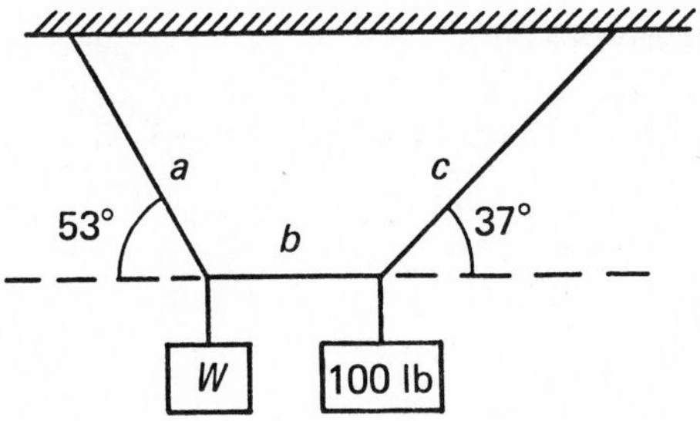

3
questions
15-17

17 For the 40-lb body shown below which has its center of mass as indicated, where must the force P be applied and what must be its value to keep the body in equilibrium?

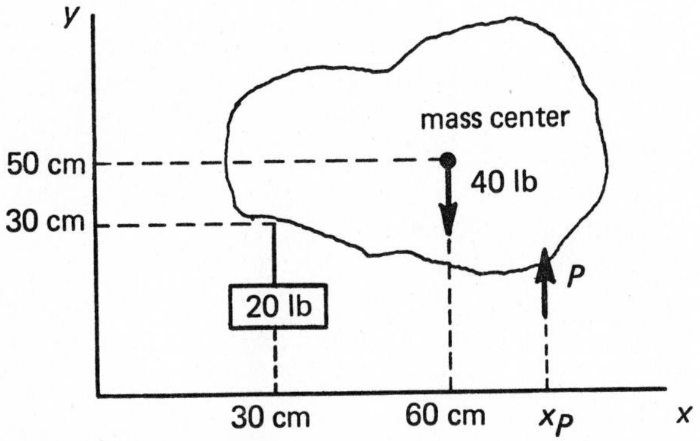

15 $\Sigma F_x = 0$
$H - 0.5T = 0$
$\Sigma F_y = 0$
$V + 0.87T - 10 - 50 = 0$

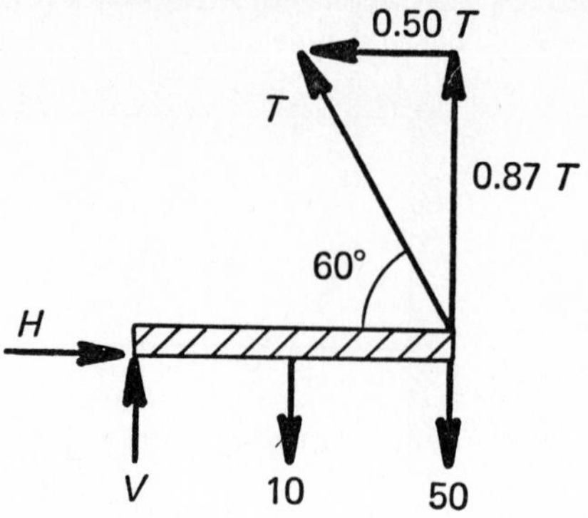

$\Sigma \tau = 0 \qquad -10\left(\frac{L}{2}\right) - 50L + (0.87T)L = 0$

Solving gives

$T = 63$ lb; $H = 32$ lb; $V = 5$ lb

16 Isolate first the junction on the right.

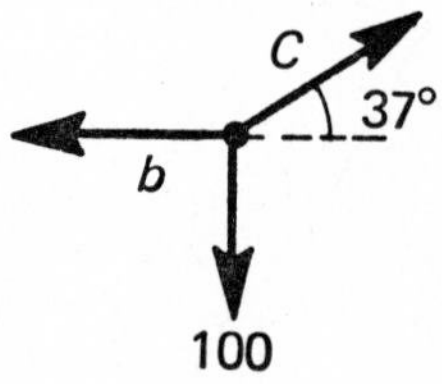

$0.60C - 100 = 0$

$\therefore C = 167$ lb

$0.80C - b = 0$

$\therefore$ b = 133 lb

Isolate next the left junction.

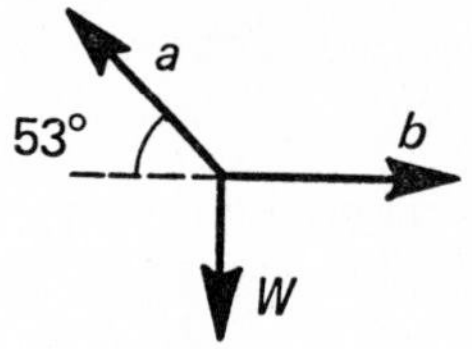

$-0.60a + b = 0$

$a = \dfrac{133}{0.60} = 222$ lb

$0.80a - W = 0$

$W = 177$ lb

17 Isolate the body and write

$\Sigma F_y = 0; -20 -40 + P=0$

$\therefore P = 60$ lb

Take torques about the origin of coordinates.

$P(x_p) - (40)(60) - (20)(30) = 0$

from which

$x_p = 50$ cm

a

3
answers
15-17

4
uniformly accelerated motion

1 What is the definition of average velocity?

2 What is the definition of average speed?

3 A man runs 30 m east and then 40 m north, all in a time of 20 sec. Find his average velocity and his average speed.

4 What is the distinction between average velocity and instantaneous velocity?

5 An object moves along the x axis according to the following equation for its x coordinate.

$$x = x_0 + \beta t^2$$

Find its instantaneous velocity at the time t_0 by use of differentiation.

1 Velocity is a vector in the direction of a displacement $\Delta \mathbf{r}$. In terms of $\Delta \mathbf{r}$ and the time Δt taken for the displacement to occur, the average velocity **v** is

$$\mathbf{v} = \frac{\Delta \mathbf{r}}{\Delta t}$$

2 Speed is a scalar. If a distance Δs is traveled in a time Δt, then the speed is $\Delta s/\Delta t$.

3 ☐ Velocity = 2.5 m/sec at 53° north of east
Speed = 3.5 m/sec
From its definition, $\Delta \mathbf{r}$ is as shown in the figure. Therefore

$$\mathbf{v} = \frac{50 \text{ m}}{20 \text{ sec}} = 2.5 \text{ m/sec}$$

with $\theta = 53°$
But $\Delta s = 30 + 40 = 70$ m so
Speed = 70 m/20 sec = 3.5 m/sec

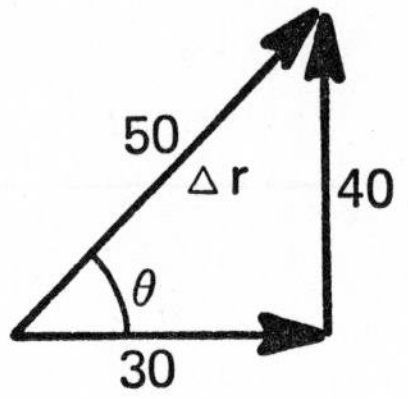

a

4 The velocity and speed defined above are the average values for the time Δt. In the limit of $\Delta t \to 0$, these quantities are the instantaneous values. The instantaneous values are the velocity and speed as the object passes a given point.

5 ☐ $v = 2\beta t_0$ in the $+x$ direction

4
answers
1-5

$$v = \frac{dx}{dt} = \frac{d}{dt}(x_0 + \beta t^2) = 2\beta t$$

and inserting the value $t = t_0$ gives $v = 2\beta t_0$.

6 Repeat the previous problem with

$x = x_0 - \beta t^3 \quad (\beta > 0)$

7 The equation of motion of an object along the x axis is

$x = x_0 + \beta t$

Find its average velocity in the time interval

$3 \leqslant t \leqslant 10$ sec

8 A ball moves with constant speed along a circle of circumference 2.0 m. If it makes one revolution in a half second, what is (a) its average velocity and (b) its average speed during one revolution? What are (c) its instantaneous speed and velocity?

9 Define average acceleration $\bar{a}$ and instantaneous acceleration a.

10 A wheel rolling initially with a velocity v = 10 m/sec in the x direction comes to rest in 4.0 sec. What is its average acceleration?

11 A ball moving with a velocity 20**i** m/sec strikes a wall and reverses its direction so its new velocity is −20**i** m/sec. Assuming a time of contact of 3×10^{-4} sec, find the average acceleration of the ball during the contact time.

q

4
questions
6-11

6 ☐ $\mathbf{v} = -3\beta t_0^2\mathbf{i}$ where **i** is a unit vector in x direction

$$v = \frac{dx}{dt} = 0 - 3\beta t^2$$

Substitute $t = t_0$. The negative sign tells us the velocity is in the $-x$ direction.

7 ☐ $\bar{\mathbf{v}} = \beta\mathbf{i}$
Since $\bar{v} = \Delta x/\Delta t$, we require Δx, which is given by $\Delta x = x_{10} - x_3 = 7\beta$.
But $\Delta t = 10 - 3 = 7$ sec. Therefore $\bar{v} = 7\beta/7 = \beta$. In this case, the instantaneous and average speed are the same. Can you show it?

8 (a) Since the ball returns to its original position, $\Delta r = 0$ and so $\bar{v} = 0$.

(b) For one revolution $\Delta s = 2.0$ m and $\Delta t = \frac{1}{2}$ sec so average speed = 4m/sec.

(c) Instantaneous speed and velocity are equal numerically. Since the ball moves at constant speed, its average speed is equal to the instantaneous speed. Thus, $|\mathbf{v}| = 4$ m/sec; **v** is tangential to the circle.

a

9 If in a time Δt the velocity of an object changes by $\Delta\mathbf{v}$, then

$$\bar{\mathbf{a}} = \frac{\Delta\mathbf{v}}{\Delta t}$$

and

$$\mathbf{a} = \lim_{\Delta t \to 0} \frac{\Delta\mathbf{v}}{\Delta t} \equiv \frac{d\mathbf{v}}{dt}$$

4
answers
6-11

10 ☐ -2.5 m/sec^2 in the $+x$ direction
$\Delta v = 0 - 10$ m/sec $= -10$ m/sec
$\Delta t = 4.0$ sec
$\bar{a} = \Delta v/\Delta t = -2.5$ m/sec^2
This may be thought of as an acceleration of 2.5 m/sec^2 in the $-x$ direction.

11 ☐ $-\frac{4}{3} \times 10^5\mathbf{i}$ m/sec^2

$\Delta\mathbf{v} = -20\mathbf{i} - (20\mathbf{i}) = -40\mathbf{i}$ m/sec
$\Delta t = 3 \times 10^{-4}$ sec

$$\bar{\mathbf{a}} = \Delta\mathbf{v}/\Delta t = -\frac{4}{3} \times 10^5\mathbf{i} \text{ m/sec}^2$$

12 Show that if the time taken for the ball to stop in the previous problem is 1.5×10^{-4} sec, the average acceleration is the same during stopping and rebounding.

13 The graph of the speed of a car moving along a straight road is shown. Find its instantaneous accelerations at t = 2, 5, 8, and 12 sec.

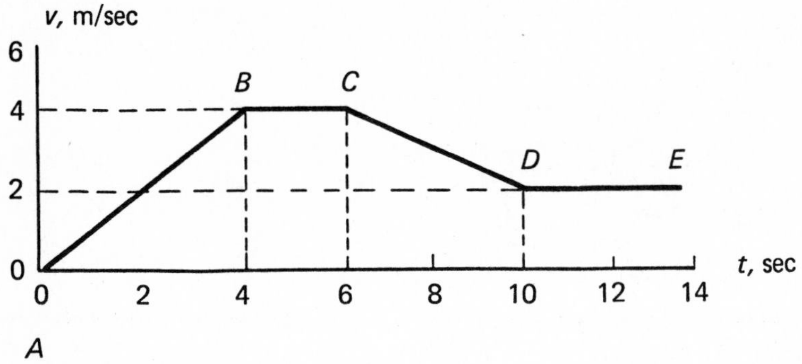

14 A ball is thrown straight up in the air with initial speed 20 m/sec. Plot graphs showing its speed, height, and acceleration as functions of time.

q

4
questions
12-14

12 During stopping, $\Delta \mathbf{v} = 0 - (20\mathbf{i}) = -20\mathbf{i}$ m/sec so

$$\overline{\mathbf{a}} = -20\mathbf{i}/1.5 \times 10^{-4} = -\frac{4}{3} \times 10^{+5}\mathbf{i} \text{ m/sec}^2$$

During rebounding

$\Delta \mathbf{v} = -20\mathbf{i} - 0 = -20\mathbf{i}$ m/sec

so

$$\overline{\mathbf{a}} = -\frac{4}{3} \times 10^5 \mathbf{i} \text{ m/sec}^2$$

13 □ 1 m/sec^2; 0; $-\frac{1}{2}$ m/sec^2; 0

Since the velocity is not changing in regions BC and DE, the acceleration is zero in these regions. In region AB the acceleration is constant and so
a = (4 m/sec) ÷ 4 sec.
In region CO, the instantaneous and average accelerations are also identical and
a = (-2 m/sec) ÷ 4 sec.

14

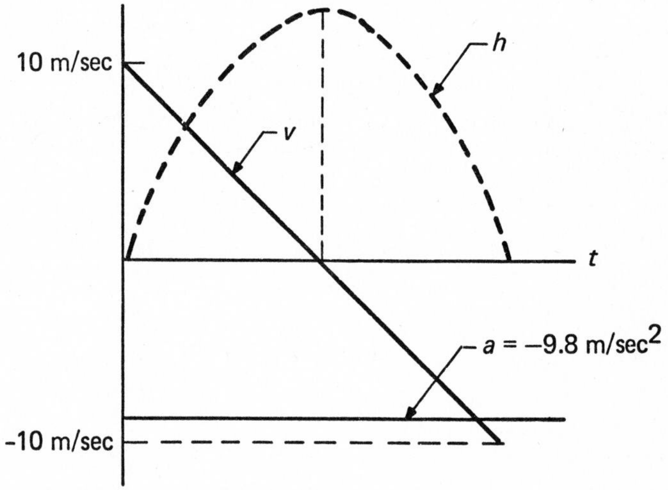

Since $h = \dfrac{v^2 - v_0^2}{2a}$

$$h_{max} = \frac{-v_0^2}{2a} \cong 20 \text{ m}$$

a

4
answers
12-14

15 A car starting from rest achieves a speed of 3.0 m/sec at a time of 9.0 sec after starting. What was its average acceleration and how far did it go?

16 A train moving at a speed of 30 m/sec slows down to 10 m/sec in 30 sec. For the 30-sec interval, find (a) how far the train went, (b) deceleration of train, and (c) how far the train had gone before its speed was reduced to 20 m/sec.

17 When an object is thrown straight up with an initial speed v_0, (a) how high is it when its speed is $\frac{1}{2}v_0$? (b) What fraction of its total time rising is spent in getting to this point?

18 A ball is thrown straight up with a speed 15 m/sec from the top of a 20-m high building. How fast is the ball going just before it strikes the ground?

19 Two boys are standing on the penthouse floor of an apartment building. The first boy drops a vase out the window. Two seconds later the second boy throws another vase downward out the window. Both vases hit the ground at the same instant. If the vases dropped 400 ft, what was the initial velocity of the second vase? What was the final velocity of each vase?

15 ☐ 0.33 m/sec²; 13.5 m

By definition,

$$\bar{a} = \frac{v - v_o}{t - t_o} = \frac{3 \text{ m/sec}}{9 \text{ sec}} = \frac{1}{3} \text{ m/sec}^2.$$

If we assume constant acceleration,

$$\bar{v} = \frac{1}{2}(v_o + v) = 1.5 \text{ m/sec; whence } x = \bar{v}t = 13.5 \text{ m}.$$

16 ☐ 600 m; 0.67 m/sec²; 375 m

Assume uniform deceleration.

For part (a): known: v_o = 30 m/sec, v = 10 m/sec, and t = 30 sec. Also $\bar{v}$ = 20 m/sec. Use $x = \bar{v}t$ to find x = 600 m. Use $a = \frac{v - v_o}{t}$ to find a = -0.67 m/sec². For part (c): v_o = 30 m/sec; v = 20 m/sec, and a = -0.67 m/sec². Use $v^2 - v_o^2 = 2ax$ to give x = 375 m.

a

17 ☐ $0.038 v_o^2$; $\frac{1}{2}$

Take *up* as positive.

(a) Use $v = \frac{1}{2} v_o$, a = -9.8 m/sec² and $v^2 - v_o^2 = 2ay$ to find $y = 0.038 v_o^2$.

(b) Since the object loses equal amounts of speed in equal amounts of time, it loses half its speed in half its rise time.

4
answers
15-19

18 ☐ 24.8 m/sec

Take *down* positive. Only the net displacement from the top of building down to ground concerns us. Known: v_o = −15 m/sec, y = 20 m, and a = 9.8 m/sec². Use $v^2 - v_o^2 = 2ay$ to find v = 24.8 m/sec.

19 ☐ 85 ft/sec; 160 ft/sec; 180 ft/sec

Take *down* positive. Consider the first vase and find its time of flight and speed just before hitting. Known: $v_o = 0$, a = 32 ft/sec², y = 400 ft. Use $y = v_o t + \frac{1}{2}at^2$ to find t = 5 sec and $y = \bar{v}t$ with $\bar{v} = \frac{1}{2}(v + v_o)$ to find v = 160 ft/sec. Consider next the second vase. Known: t = 3 sec, y = 400 ft, a = 32 ft/sec². Use $y = v_o t + \frac{1}{2}at^2$ to find v_o = 85 ft/sec. Then use $v = v_o + at$.

20 A car is cruising along a road at 50 ft/sec. At a certain instant the driver spies a train beginning to move toward the road from a railroad station. The driver believes he can beat the train without changing his speed. If the railroad track and the road are at right angles to each other and the train has an acceleration of 5 ft/sec^2, will the driver live to tell the story? The car is initially 400 ft from the crossing, while the station is 230 ft from the crossing.

21 A freight train travels through a station at a uniform speed of 27 ft/sec. A passenger train just begins to move out of the station as the first train passes. If the second train has a uniform acceleration of 0.25 ft/sec^2, when will the two trains be side by side?

22 A projectile moving at a speed of 100 m/sec leaves the earth at an angle of 37° to the horizontal. Where is it, relative to the starting point, when it is 150 m high?

23 The speed of a certain object is shown in the graph. Find its average value in the interval from t = 2 sec to t = 8 sec.

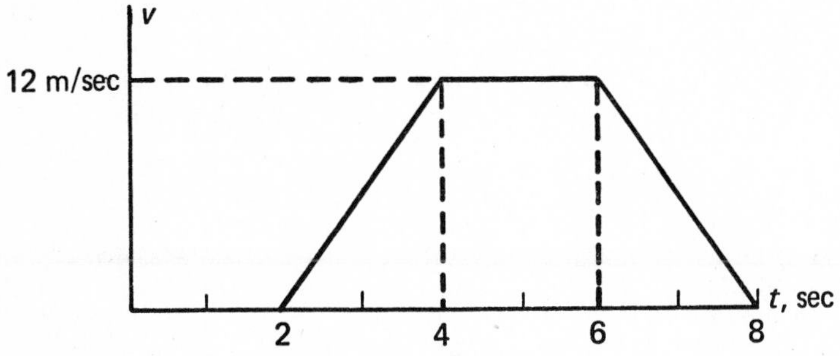

4
questions
20-24

24 The speed of a certain particle is given in meters per second by $v = 80 - 4t$ for $t \leqslant 20$ sec.
Find the average value of v in the interval $0 \leqslant t \leqslant 20$ sec.

20 ☐ Yes

The time the driver will have is

$$t = \frac{400}{50} = 8 \text{ sec}$$

During this time, the train will move a distance

$$x = v_0 t + \frac{1}{2} at^2 = 160 \text{ ft}$$

Since the train had to move 230 ft before reaching the crossing, they will not collide.

21 ☐ 216 sec

Distance gone by first = distance gone by second

(27 ft/sec) $t = 0 + \frac{1}{2}$ (0.25 ft/sec^2)t^2 from which t = 216 sec.

22 ☐ 280 and 704 m

In the vertical problem, v_{oy} = 60 m/sec, a = -9.8 m/sec^2, and y = 150 m. Use

$y = v_0 t + \frac{1}{2} at^2$ to find t = 8.7 and 3.5 sec. One answer represents going up, the other, coming down. In the horizontal problem $x = \bar{v}_x t$ = (80 m/sec)t = 700 and 280 m. Notice $\bar{v}_x = v_{ox}$ since there is no x acceleration.

a

4
answers
20-24

23 ☐ 8 m/sec

As shown in the text, the average of a function is the area under its curve divided by the horizontal interval. In the present case, area = 48 m and the interval is 6 sec. Therefore, $\bar{v}$ = 8 m/sec.

24 ☐ 40 m/sec

This is most easily done by integration.

$$\bar{v} = \frac{\int_0^{20} (80 - 4t)\, dt}{20} = \frac{1600 - \frac{1}{2} 4 \cdot 400}{20} = 40 \text{ m/sec}$$

Can you show this by graphical methods?

5
laws of motion

1 What does Newton's first law predict for the motion of a spaceship in outer space, assuming that its means of propulsion is shut off?

2 What does Newton's third law tell us about the force exerted on the earth by a satellite circling the earth?

3 If the same resultant force is exerted on two different masses, m_1 and m_2, what will be the ratio a_1/a_2 of the two accelerations?

4 Fill in the blanks with the proper units for F, m, or a.

F	$= m \cdot a$
_______	= kg • (m/sec^2)
_______	= _______ • (cm/sec^2)
_______	= slug • (______)

q

5
questions
1-8

5 The mass of an object which weighs W at a position where its gravitational acceleration is g is __________. An object which weighs 1 N on earth has a mass of __________ kg and weighs __________ dyn.

6 A force $\mathbf{F} = F_x\mathbf{i} + F_y\mathbf{j}$ acts on an object of mass m. Find the acceleration of the mass.

7 An object of mass m is subjected to a constant force F for t seconds and to no force thereafter. Assuming the object to start from rest, find its speed $2t$ sec after the force is decreased to zero.

8 A 2-kg object is accelerated from rest by a force $\mathbf{F} = 5\mathbf{i} - 3\mathbf{j}$ N. Find its displacement after 4 sec.

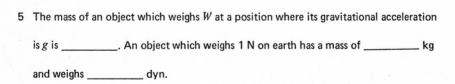

1 The spaceship will continue to move with the same velocity (i.e., in a straight line) unless acted upon by some external force.

2 The satellite pulls on the earth with a force equal and opposite to the force with which the earth pulls on the satellite.

3 ☐ $a_1/a_2 = m_2/m_1$

Since $F = m_1a_1$ and $F = m_2a_2$, we have $m_1a_1 = m_2a_2$.

4 newton = kg• (m/sec^2)

dyne = g• (cm/sec^2)

pound = slug• (ft/sec^2)

5 ☐ W/g ; 1/g; 10^5

The first two answers come from $F = ma$ with F replaced by W and a replaced by g. The last answer is found from $F = ma$ as follows:

$$1\text{ N} = (1\text{ kg})\ (1\text{ m/sec}^2)$$
$$= (10^3\text{ g})\ (10^2\text{ cm/sec}^2)$$
$$= 10^5\ (\text{g})\ (\text{cm/sec}^2) = 10^5\text{ dyn}$$

a

5
answers
1-8

6 ☐ $(1/m)\ \sqrt{F_x^2 + F_y^2}$

$a_x = F_x/m$ and $a_y = F_y/m$

So $\mathbf{a} = (F_x/m)\mathbf{i} + (F_y/m)\mathbf{j}$

and $a = (1/m)\ \sqrt{F_x^2 + F_y^2}$

7 ☐ Ft/m

For the first t seconds, $a = F/m$, $v_0 = 0$, and $t = t$. Using $v = v_0 + at$ gives $v = Ft/m$. According to Newton's first law the speed will not change after the force is made zero so the final speed will remain constant at the value given above.

8 ☐ 23 m

Consider each component separately. In the x direction, $a_x = 2.5$ m/sec^2, $v_0 = 0$, and so $x = v_0t + \frac{1}{2}at^2$ gives $x = 20$ m. In the same way, $y = 12$ m. The displacement is $\sqrt{x^2 + y^2}$.

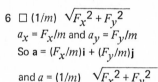

9 A 5-kg box can be pulled at constant speed across a level floor if a force of 20 N is applied to the box at an angle of 37° above the horizontal. Find the friction force retarding its motion. What is the friction coefficient between box and floor?

10 For a certain weather balloon having a mass of 8 kg, the buoyancy force is 90 N. Assuming no friction, how long would it take the balloon to reach a height of 100 m after being released?

11 A 5-kg box sits on a 37° incline. Upon its release, it slides a distance of 400 cm in 10 sec. Find how large a friction force retards its motion. What is μ in this case?

12 A 10-kg block sits on a 53° incline. If the friction force is 20 N, with how large a horizontal force must one push on the block to have it (a) slide down the incline at constant speed, (b) slide up the incline at constant speed, and (c) slide up the incline with $a = 0.5\ \text{m/sec}^2$? In practice, f would be different in the three cases. Why?

9 ☐ 16 N; 0.43

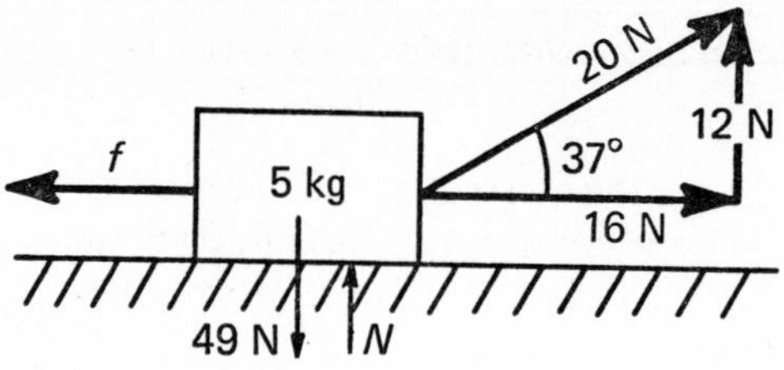

The box is at equilibrium (i.e., not accelerating) so $\Sigma F_x = 0$. The two x forces are +16 and $-f$. Therefore the friction force f must be 16 N. Also, $\Sigma F_y = 0$ and so $12 - 49 + N = 0$, or $N = 37$ N. Then $\mu = f/N = 16/37 = 0.43$.

10 ☐ 11.7 sec

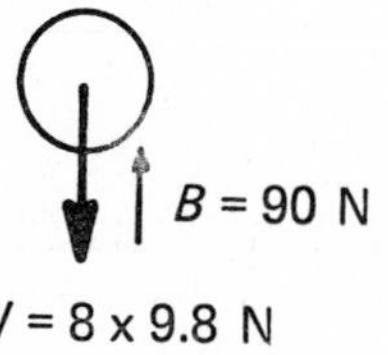

Writing $\Sigma F_y = ma_y$ gives $a_y = 1.45\ \text{m/sec}^2$.

Using $y = v_0 t + \frac{1}{2}at^2$ gives $t = 11.7$ sec.

11 ☐ 29.0 N; 0.74

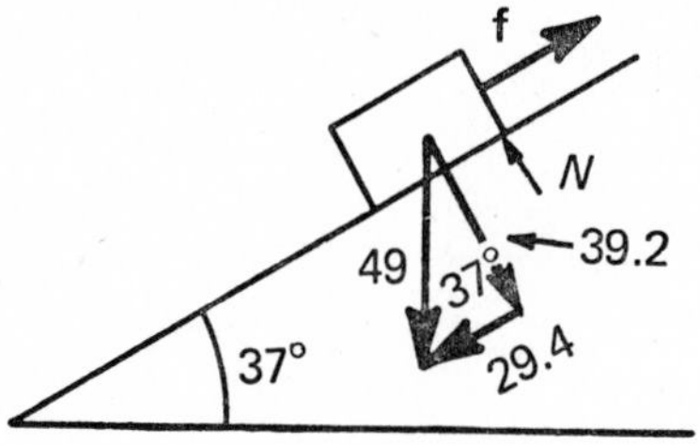

First find its acceleration from its motion:

$x = v_0 t + \frac{1}{2}at^2$ gives $a = 0.08\ \text{m/sec}^2$

Then using $\Sigma F_x = ma$ one has $29.4 - f = (5)\ (8 \times 10^{-2})$. So $f = 29.0$ N.
From $\Sigma F_y = 0$, the normal force = 39 N.
Then $\mu = 29/39$.

12 ☐ 97 N; 163 N; 172 N

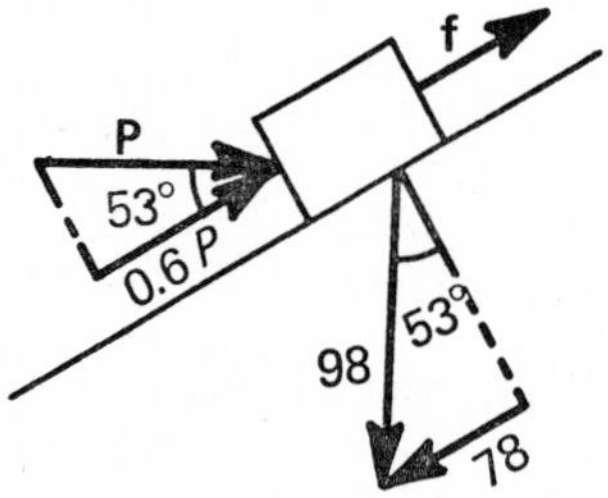

(a) If the block is sliding down, **f** will be up as shown. Since $a = 0$, we have $0.6P + f - 78 = 0$ from which $P = 97$ N.
(b) In this case, the block is going up so **f** will be directed down. Then $0.6P - f - 78 = 0$ from which $P = 163$ N.
(c) In this case
$0.6P - f - 78 = (10)(0.5)$ or $P = 172$ N.

13 A proton ($m = 1.67 \times 10^{-27}$ kg) is shot at a sheet of material with speed 7.0×10^6 m/sec. After emerging from the sheet its speed is 5.0×10^6 m/sec. If the sheet is 0.010 mm thick, find the average retarding force experienced by the proton.

14

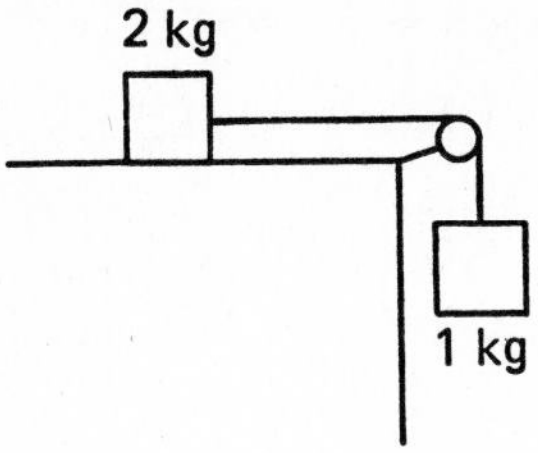

Starting from rest, the 1-kg block falls 90 cm in 3.0 sec. How large is the friction force retarding the motion of the 2-kg block? What is μ for the 2-kg block?

15

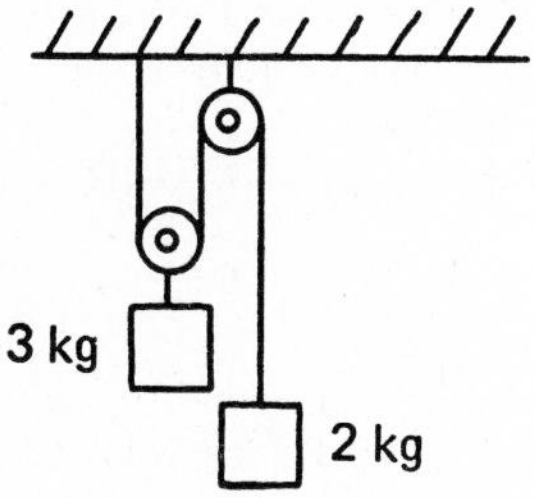

Assuming the pulleys to be massless and frictionless, find the direction of motion and acceleration of the 3-kg mass.

16

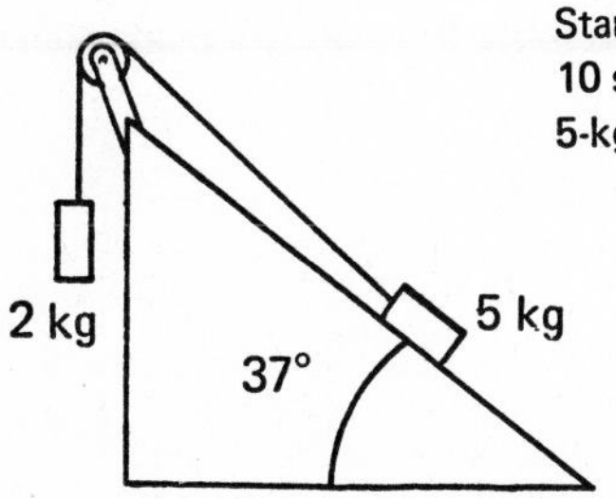

Starting from rest, the 2-kg mass rises 500 cm in 10 sec. How large is the friction force acting on the 5-kg mass? What is μ for the 5 kg on the incline?

q

5
questions
13-16

13 □ 2×10^{-9} N

First find the acceleration by use of $v^2 - v_0^2 = 2ax$. This gives $a = -1.2 \times 10^{18}$ m/sec^2. Substitution in $F = ma$ gives $-F = (1.67 \times 10^{-27})(1.2 \times 10^{18}) = 2.0 \times 10^{-9}$ N.

14 □ 9.2 N; 0.47

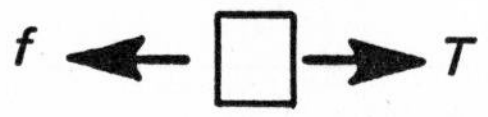

$$T - f = 2a$$
$$9.8 - T = 1a$$
$$9.8 - f = 3a$$

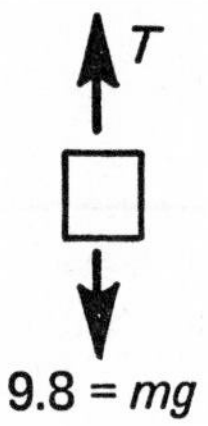

To find a, use $y = v_0 t + \frac{1}{2} at^2$ which gives

$a = 0.2$ m/sec^2. Substitution above gives $f = 9.2$ N.
The normal force on the 2-kg block is 19.6 N.
Therefore $\mu = 9.2/19.6 = 0.47$.

15 □ Upward; 0.89 m/sec^2

The tension in the rope will be T throughout. Assume the 3 kg to have a downward acceleration a.

$29.4 - 2T = 3a$

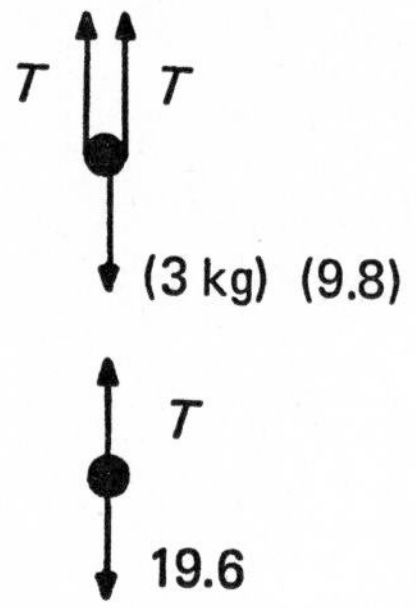

The 2-kg mass will move twice as fast as the 3-kg mass so its acceleration is $2a$. Under our assumption, it will move upward.

$T - 19.6 = (2)(2a)$

Solving simultaneously gives

$a = -0.89$ m/sec^2.

16 □ 9.1 N; 0.23

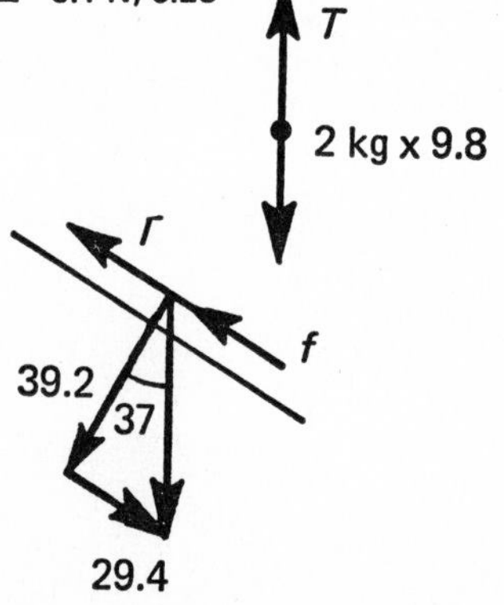

The 2-kg mass rises so $T - 19.6 = 2a$

For the 5-kg mass $29.4 - T - f = 5a$

Solving simultaneously gives

$f = 9.8 - 7a$.

Find a from the motion problem.

$$x = v_0 t + \frac{1}{2} at^2 \rightarrow 5 = \frac{1}{2}(a)(10)^2$$

$a = 0.10$ m/sec^2

This gives $f = 9.1$ N.

The normal force = 39.2 N and so

$\mu = 9.1/39.2 = 0.23$.

17

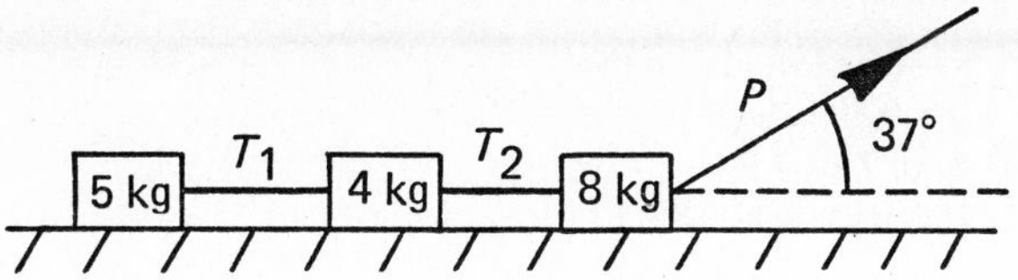

For the system shown, $T_1 = 4$ N. Ignoring friction, find P.

18 A ball on the end of a string hangs from the ceiling of a boxcar which is accelerating at 2.0 m/sec^2. At what angle to the vertical does the string hang? Assume the boxcar to be moving horizontally.

19 A certain spring is so constructed that a force F will stretch it a distance x given by $x = F/100$ where x is in centimeters and F is in newtons. An 8-kg mass hangs from the end of the spring in an elevator. Find x for the case when the elevator is (a) at rest, (b) accelerating upward at 2 m/sec^2, and (c) accelerating downward at 2 m/sec^2.

20 The x displacement of a particle of mass m is given by $x = x_0 + 20t + 30t^2$ cm where t is the time in seconds. Find the force applied to the particle.

17 □ 17 N

We apply $F_x = ma_x$ to each block.
For 5 kg, $T_1 = 5a$ or $a = 0.80$ m/sec^2.
For 4 kg, $T_2 - T_1 = 4a$ or $T_2 = 7.2$ N.
For 8 kg, $0.8P - T_2 = 8a$, from which $P = 17$ N.

18 □ 11.4°

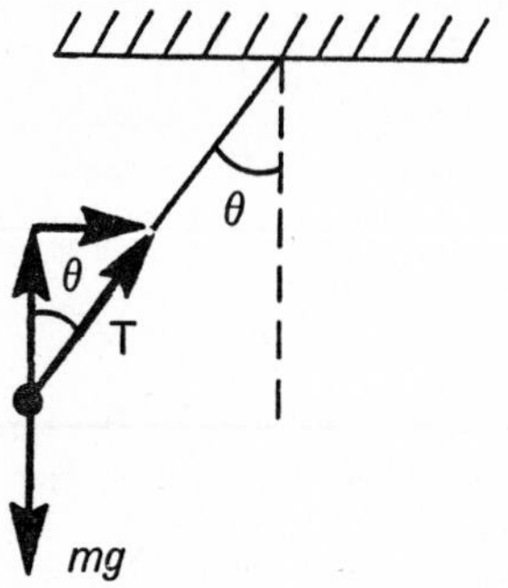

The ball must experience an unbalanced force in the direction of acceleration. It is caused by the horizontal component of **T**. Therefore $F = ma$ gives $T \sin\theta = m(2)$. But $T\cos\theta = mg$. Therefore $\tan\theta = 2/g \cong 0.20$, from which $\theta \cong 11.4°$.

19 □ 0.78 cm; 0.94 cm; 0.62 cm

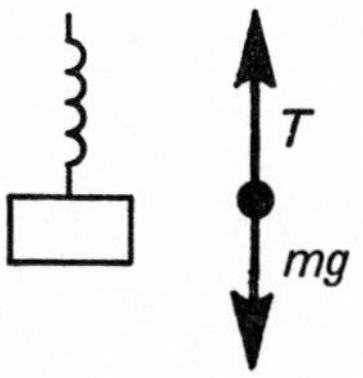

The force exerted by the block on the spring (the block's apparent weight) is equal to the force exerted by the spring on the block. Writing $F = ma$ gives
(a) $T - 78.4 = 0$ so $x = 78.4/100 = 0.784$ cm
(b) $T - 78.4 = 8(2)$ so $x = 94.4/100 = 0.944$ cm
(c) $78.4 - T = 8(2)$ so $x = 62.4/100 = 0.624$ cm.

20 □ 0.60m N

The force is given by $F = ma$.
But $a = dv/dt$ and $v = dx/dt$.
We have
$v = dx/dt = 20 + 60t$ cm/sec
and
$a = dv/dt = 60$ cm/sec^2 = 0.60 m/sec^2
Therefore $F = 0.60m$ N and F is constant.

6
relativistic effects

1 What basic experimental facts was Einstein trying to interpret when he developed his special theory of relativity?

2 What is an inertial reference frame?

3 Can one decide between the following two cases: a system is standing still or it is moving with constant velocity > 0?

4 Can one determine whether a system is accelerating by taking measurements which only involve the system in question?

5 For motion along a straight line, in nonrelativistic mechanics (galilean relativity), an object at a distance x_0 from observer A is at a distance $x' = x_0 - vt$ from observer B, who is moving with constant speed v relative to A. Draw a figure showing the directions involved and state where B was when $t = 0$.

6 For the situation depicted in the previous problem, if A measures the distance from A to the object to be x_0, how large will B measure this distance to be? Show that when $v \ll c$, the result reduces to that given by classical physics.

7 For the situation of problem 5, if observer A measures the distance from A to O he obtains the value x_0. What value does observer B measure for the distance B to O? Show that for $v \ll c$, this agrees with the classical result.

8 A spaceship has an end-to-end length of 60 m when at rest on the earth. If the spaceship now takes off and speeds past the earth with a speed of $0.80c$, how long will it be measured to be by a man on the earth? By a man in the spaceship?

1 The speed of light and the basic laws of physics are the same for observers in all inertial reference frames.

2 A reference coordinate axes system which is not accelerating with respect to the fixed stars.

3 Since the laws of physics applied within a closed system isolated from outside objects are independent of the velocity of the closed system, one cannot determine its velocity without reference to outside systems. As a result, only velocities relative to surrounding objects or systems can be found.

4 Yes. For example, a pendulum will not hang straight down when accelerated in a direction other than the vertical direction.

5

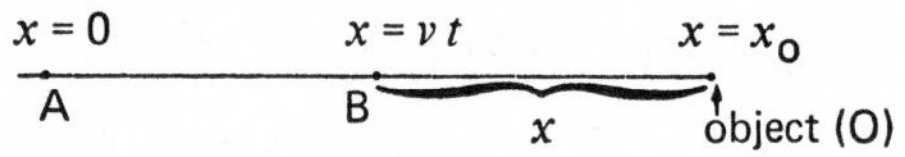

When $t = 0$, A and B were both at the origin.

a

6 □ $x_0\sqrt{1-\beta^2}$ with $\beta = v/c$

This follows directly from the fact that B will consider the distance from A to O to be the length of a moving rod whose rest length is x_0. It therefore shows the Lorentz contraction. As $\beta \to 0$, this measured distance approaches x_o.

6
answers
1-8

7 □ $(x_0 - vt)/\sqrt{1-\beta^2}$

This distance would be $x_0 - vt$ for observer A. The x coordinate measured by the moving observer is larger by the factor $1/\sqrt{1-\beta^2}$ since, according to the stationary observer, the moving observer's measuring sticks are shortened. If $\beta \to 0$, this reduces to $x_0 - vt$, which agrees with the classical result.

8 □ 36 m; 60 m
For the man on earth, the Lorentz contraction causes it to measure

$$L = 60\sqrt{1-\beta^2} = 60\sqrt{1-0.64} = 36 \text{ m}$$

Since the man in the spaceship cannot tell he is in motion without reference to things outside the ship, the length must not have changed for him.

9 As the spaceship of the previous problem passes the earth at $v = 0.80c$, an observer on the earth watches and times a pendulum in the ship which the spaceman claims is vibrating at 3 vib/sec. How fast does the earthman say the pendulum is vibrating?

10 According to an observer on the earth, a rocket ship is approaching the earth at a speed of $0.80c$ and is 2 light years away. How long should it take the ship to reach the earth according to (a) the earth observer and (b) a man in the ship?

11 Two identical 20-year-old twins carry identical pocket watches which they synchronize on earth just before one of the twins takes off in a spaceship for a long voyage in space. When the space twin returns to the earth, he claims to be only 30 years old while his earth brother is 60 years old. How fast was the spaceship moving relative to the earth?

12 Show that a sphere of radius a passing a stationary observer with velocity v will be measured to be an ellipsoid by that observer, the axes of the ellipsoid being a, a, and $a\sqrt{1-\beta^2}$. This does not mean an observer would *see* it as an ellipsoid. He must correct his raw observational data in order to take account of the fact that light from different portions of the object has to travel different distances to his eye. What he *sees* at any instant is various parts of the object as they were at various times in the past. [For a discussion of this, see an article by V.T. Weisskopf in *Physics Today,* **13** (9) September, 1960.]

13 Observer A has two synchronized clocks a few miles apart on the earth. A spaceship flies parallel to the earth's surface with a strong searchlight sending a light beam straight down to the earth. When the ship passes over each of the two clocks, the light activates photocells which stop the clocks. In this way, A times the ship to take 5.00×10^{-6} sec. An observer in the spaceship, using his own clock, times the same trip by use of two searchlights at the clocks on earth. He finds the time to be 3.00×10^{-6} sec. How fast was the ship moving relative to the earth?

9 ☐ 1.8 vib/sec

Since the spaceman's clocks run too slowly by the time dilation factor, $\sqrt{1-\beta^2}$, the time for one vibration is actually $\frac{1}{3}/\sqrt{1-\beta^2}$ sec = 1/1.8 sec. Its frequency is therefore 1.8 vib/sec. Notice that the pendulum is a clock and it has slowed by the dilation factor.

10 ☐ 2.50 years; 1.50 years

According to the earthman, $t = x/v = 2c/0.80c = 2.50$ years. The spaceship clocks run slower than those on earth by a factor $\sqrt{1-\beta^2} = 0.60$. Therefore the 2.50 years of earth time will be equivalent to 1.50 years as measured by the spaceship clocks.

11 ☐ $0.968c$

According to the man on earth, 40 years had elapsed. The spaceship clocks registered only 10 years. Therefore the time dilation factor is 1/4.

$0.25 = \sqrt{1-\beta^2}$

$\beta^2 = 1.0000 - 0.0625 = 0.9375$

Therefore

$v/c = \sqrt{0.9375} = 0.968$

a

6
answers
9-13

12 Assume that the motion occurs along the x axis. A point on the surface of the stationary sphere has coordinates x_0, y, and z with respect to the center such that $x_0^2 + y^2 + z^2 = a^2$.

When moving, an observer on the earth will measure the x coordinates of points on the sphere to be

$$x_0\sqrt{1-\beta^2} = \sqrt{(a^2 - y^2 - z^2)(1-\beta^2)}$$

Therefore the equation of the surface measured is $x^2 = (a^2 - y^2 - z^2)(1-\beta^2)$ or

$$\frac{x^2}{a^2(1-\beta^2)} + \frac{y^2}{a^2} + \frac{z^2}{a^2} = 1$$

which is the equation of an ellipsoid with the axes $a\sqrt{1-\beta^2}$, a, and a.

13 ☐ $0.8c$

By use of the light beams, delay in signaling between ship and clocks is canceled out. The time dilation factor is therefore 3/5 and so $1 - \beta^2 = 0.36$ from which $v = 0.8c$.

14 According to a man (B) in a spaceship traveling toward the earth at $v = 0.8c$, he is sending light pulses to the earth in his line of flight at intervals of 2.00 sec. What is the interval between pulses as measured by a man (A) on the earth? This is an example of the *doppler effect*.

15 A heavy nucleus moving at a speed of $0.8c$ relative to the laboratory shoots an electron from itself in the line of its flight. If the speed of the electron is $0.9c$ relative to the nucleus, how fast is it going as measured in the laboratory?

16 Two particles travel in opposite directions toward each other with velocities $\pm 0.8c$ relative to the laboratory. How fast does one of the particles appear to be going as measured by the other particle? Does it matter which particle one uses as reference?

17 Repeat the previous problem if one has a velocity $0.8c$ and the other a velocity $-0.9c$.

18 A spaceship moving with speed $0.8c$ relative to A on the earth sends out a pulse of light. How fast does the light pulse appear to move according to A?

19 When a certain nuclear particle (the mu-meson) is at rest, its average lifetime is about 2.0×10^{-6} sec. On the average, how far will a mu-meson travel at a speed of $0.90c$ during its lifetime?

q

6
questions
14-19

14 □ $\frac{2}{3}$ sec

Two effects exist. First, because of time dilation, A says the pulses are sent out at intervals of $2.00/\sqrt{1-0.64} = 10/3$ sec. Second, between pulses the ship moves a distance $(10/3)(0.8c)$ towards the earth. This means the second pulse travels this much distance less than the first and so it reaches the earth $(8c/3)/c$ sec earlier than it should. Therefore the time between pulses as measured by A is

$$\frac{10}{3} - \frac{8}{3} = \frac{2}{3} \text{ sec}$$

15 □ $0.9883c$

This requires use of the relativistic velocity addition formula (Eq. 6.7 in Bueche):

$$u = \frac{u' + v}{1 + (u'v/c^2)} = \frac{0.9c + 0.8c}{1 + 0.72} = 0.9883c$$

16 □ $0.976c$

In this case $u = -0.8c$, $v = 0.8c$ in the velocity addition equation (Eq. 6.7 or the equation just above it in Bueche):

$$u' = \frac{-0.8c - 0.8c}{1 + (0.8)(0.8)} = -0.976c$$

a

6
answers
14-19

17 □ $0.988c$

Follow the same procedure as for problem 16 except $u = -0.9c$ and $v = 0.8c$.

18 □ c

By the basic postulates of relativity, the speed of light is always c. This also follows if one substitutes $u' = c$ in the velocity addition formula.

19 □ 1260 m

Because of the time dilation effect, its laboratory lifetime will be

$2.0 \times 10^{-6} / \sqrt{1 - 0.81} = 4.6 \times 10^{-6}$ sec

Then

$x = (0.90 \times 3 \times 10^8)(4.6 \times 10^{-6}) = 1.26 \times 10^3$ m

7
momentum

1 What is the momentum **p** of a body of mass m and velocity **v**? How is it related to the external force **F** acting on the body? What is meant by impulse?

2 A 50-g ball moving at 20 m/sec strikes a wall and rebounds with the same speed but reversed in direction. Find the impulse it exerts on the wall.

3 Estimate the force exerted by the ball on the wall in the previous problem.

4 It is desired to accelerate an object of mass 8.0 kg so that its velocity along a line is changed from v_0 to v_f. What impulse is needed to do this?

5 A force specified as follows

$F = 0 \qquad t < 0$

$F = 3.0\ \text{N} \qquad 0 \leqslant t \leqslant 0.50\ \text{sec}$

$F = 0 \qquad t > 0.50\ \text{sec}$

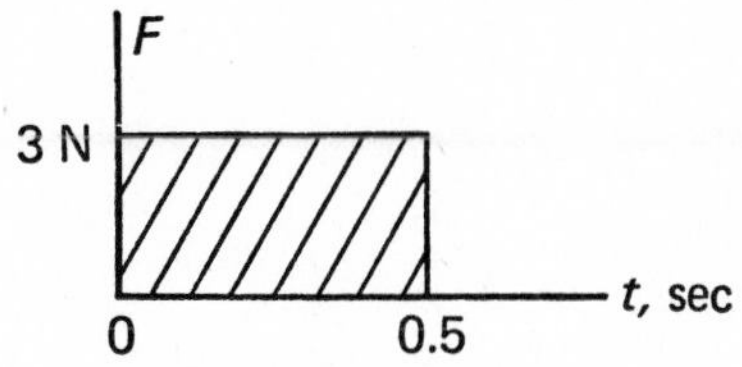

acts on an object.

Find the change in momentum caused by the force.

6 A 7-kg gun is accidentally discharged as it lies at rest on a smooth table. The exiting bullet has a speed of 150 m/sec and a mass of 30 g. Find the recoil speed of the gun.

7
questions
1-6

1 ☐ $\mathbf{p} = m\mathbf{v}$, $\mathbf{F}\ \Delta t = \Delta\mathbf{p} = \Delta(m\mathbf{v})$

The impulse $\mathbf{F}\ \Delta t$ measures the effect of force $\mathbf{F}$ acting on the object for a time Δt.

2 ☐ Impulse = 2.0 kg-m/sec = 2.0 N-sec

By definition, impulse = $\Delta mv = m\ \Delta v$

But Δv = (-20 m/sec) - (20 m/sec) = -40 m/sec and so

Impulse = - (0.050 kg) (40 m/sec)

3 ☐ ~ 2 X 10^4 N

One must assume something about the time of contact. Assume the ball is compressed by 0.10 cm. The time taken for the ball to stop is, from $x = \bar{v}t$, with $\bar{v}$ = 10 m/sec, 1 X 10^{-3}/10 = 10^{-4} sec. The ball is in contact twice this long. Therefore, from the impulse given above, $\bar{F} = \dfrac{2.0 \text{ N-sec}}{10^{-4} \text{ sec}} = 2 \times 10^4$ N

a

4 ☐ $8(v_f - v_0)$ kg-m/sec

We can make use of impulse = $\Delta(mv) = mv_f - mv_0$. Therefore, impulse = $m(v_f - v_o)$.

7

answers

1-6

5 ☐ 1.50 N-sec

As shown in the text, the change in momentum is the area under the curve. It is $\Delta(mv)$ = (0.50 sec) (3.0 N) = 1.50 N-sec

Or one could use the relation

$$\Delta(mv) = \int_0^{0.5} F\,dt = \int_0^{0.5} (3.0)\,dt = 1.50 \text{ N-sec}$$

6 ☐ 0.64 m/sec

There is no unbalanced horizontal force on the system consisting of gun and bullet. Therefore the horizontal momentum must be zero after the firing since it was zero before. As a result

$$0 = (7.00 - 0.03)\ V + (0.03)\ (150)$$

so V = -0.64 m/sec

7 In the previous problem, why is it allowable to neglect the fact that in any practical situation air friction and friction with the table would impede the motions of bullet and gun?

8 An object of mass m has an initial velocity given by $\mathbf{v}_0 = 20\mathbf{i}$ and a final velocity $\mathbf{v} = 20\mathbf{j}$. Find the impulse to which the object was subjected.

9 Suppose that a man stands at one end of a boxcar, the mass of man plus boxcar being M. He throws a ball of mass m with velocity $\mathbf{v}$ toward the other end, a distance L away. The ball hits the other end and comes to rest in the car. Assuming no friction in the boxcar wheels, describe the motion of the boxcar.

10 Two nitrogen atoms approach each other with velocities $v_0\mathbf{i}$ and $-v_0\mathbf{i}$. They collide in such a way that the velocity of one atom after collision is $0.50v_0\mathbf{i} - 0.80v_0\mathbf{j}$. Find the velocity of the other atom after collision. (Assume $v_0 \ll c$.)

11 Water is being poured into a beaker at the rate of 2.0 g/sec with a speed of 8.0 cm/sec. The beaker is sitting on a scale at the time. By how much does the reading of the scale differ from the weight of the beaker plus water?

12 Three particles of equal mass come toward the origin of coordinates with velocities $v_0\mathbf{i}$, $v_0\mathbf{j}$, and $-v_0\mathbf{i}$. After collision at the origin, two of the particles remain at rest. Find the velocity of the third particle.

7 The friction forces would slow the bullet and gun. However, this slowing occurs as the bullet and gun move away. The initial speeds of the bullet and gun just after the discharge would not yet be affected by the friction forces.

8 ☐ $-20m\mathbf{i} + 20m\mathbf{j}$; $20m\sqrt{2}$

Impulse $= \Delta m\mathbf{v} = m\mathbf{v} - m\mathbf{v}_0 = -20m\mathbf{i} + 20m\mathbf{j}$

The magnitude of the impulse is thus $20m\sqrt{2}$.

9 ☐ Initial $V = -(m/M)v$; it stops after $\frac{L}{v}$ sec.

The momentum of the system (ball, man, and car) is zero before throwing. Therefore, equating momentum before and after throwing,

$0 = M\mathbf{V} + m\mathbf{v}$

gives the boxcar speed $\mathbf{V} = -(m/M)\mathbf{v}$. It continues with this speed for a time L/v at which time the ball hits the wall. Again equating momentum before and after collision,

$M(\mathbf{V}) + m(\mathbf{v}) = (M + m)\mathbf{V}'$

where $\mathbf{V}'$ is the car's velocity at the end. Substitution of $\mathbf{V} = -(m/M)\mathbf{v}$ gives $\mathbf{V}' = 0$.

a

7
answers
7-12

10 ☐ $-0.50v_0\mathbf{i} + 0.80v_0\mathbf{j}$

The law of conservation of momentum tells us that the total final momentum must be zero. Then, since the masses are equal, the final velocities must be equal and opposite.

11 ☐ 0.016 g

The scale not only supports the weight but also supplies the impulse needed to stop the water. Taking the impulse for a time Δt we have

$F\Delta t = \Delta(mv) = (0.0020\,\Delta t)\,(v)$

since the water stopped in time Δt is $0.0020\,\Delta t$.

Solving for F gives $F = 1.6 \times 10^{-4}$ N. But 1000 g weighs 9.8 N so this is equivalent to the weight of 0.016 g.

12 ☐ $v_0\mathbf{j}$

From the conservation of momentum $mv_0\mathbf{i} + mv_0\mathbf{j} - mv_0\mathbf{i} = 0 + 0 + m\mathbf{v}$.
Hence $\mathbf{v} = v_0\mathbf{j}$.

13 How large an impulse is needed to stop an electron which is moving with a speed of $0.80c$? (The rest mass of an electron is 9.1×10^{-31} kg).

14 It is proposed to support a 70-kg man by strapping a tank of compressed air on his back and ejecting air downward through a nozzle. How fast must the air be ejected in order to support the man if 20 g is to be ejected each second?

15 An electron moving at a speed $0.20c$ strikes a proton which is at rest. The two particles combine into one. What is the speed of the resultant particle (a hydrogen atom) after collision? (The electron rest mass is 9.1×10^{-31} kg and the proton's is 1.67×10^{-27} kg.)

16 A 2.0-kg block rests over a small hole on a table. As a joke, a man beneath the table shoots a 10.0-g bullet through the hole into the block where it lodges. How fast must the bullet be going if the block rises 1.30 m above the table top?

17 A horizontal stream of water is aimed onto a window in a house. If the water in the stream is moving at 5.0 m/sec and 30 g of water hits the window each second, estimate the force exerted upon the window by the water.

18 A cube of iron has a volume b^3 and a mass of 20 kg when at rest on the earth. Find its density (mass/volume) as measured by a man on earth as it speeds by at $0.90c$. (You may assume that one face of the cube is parallel to the earth's surface.)

13 □ 3.6×10^{-22} N-sec

Since the electron is moving with relativistic speed, its momentum will not be $m_0 v$ but will be $m_0 v/\sqrt{1-\beta^2}$. Because of the impulse, all this momentum is lost. So

$$\text{Impulse} = \frac{m_0 v}{\sqrt{1-\beta^2}} = \frac{m_0 v}{0.60}$$

14 □ 3.4×10^4 m/sec

The impulse given to the ejected gas is equal to its momentum change, $v(\Delta m)$, where Δm is the mass of gas ejected and v is its speed. An equal and opposite (upward) impulse will be exerted on the man. Therefore, the upward force on the man is $F\,\Delta t = v(\Delta m)$ or $F = v\dfrac{\Delta m}{\Delta t}$

But $\Delta m/\Delta t = 0.020$ kg/sec and F is to be equal to the weight of the man, 686 N. Solving for v gives $v = 3.4 \times 10^4$ m/sec.

15 □ 3.3×10^4 m/sec

Momentum before = momentum after $\dfrac{9.1 \times 10^{-31}\,(0.20c)}{\sqrt{1-0.04}} = 1.67 \times 10^{-27} v$

where we assume that the final $v \ll c$. Solving yields $v = 3.3 \times 10^4$ m/sec. We see that $v \ll c$ and so our assumption is justified.

a

16 □ 1000 m/sec

7
answers
13-18

First find the speed of the block after collision from a motion problem. Use $v^2 - v_0^2 = 2ay$. Then $0 - v_0^2 = -(19.6)(1.30)$ so $v_0 \cong 5.0$ m/sec.
Now apply momentum conservation to the collision.
Momentum of bullet before = momentum of both after
$0.010V = (2.01)(5.0)$ from which $V \cong 1000$ m/sec.

17 □ 0.15 N

Let us assume the water does not rebound so that $\Delta mv = v\,\Delta m$.
Then the impulse is $F\,\Delta t = v\,\Delta m$ so that $F = v(\Delta m/\Delta t)$.
But $\Delta m/\Delta t = 0.030$ kg/sec and so $F = (5)(0.030) = 0.150$ N.

18 □ $105/b^3$

The measured dimensions of the object will be $b \times b \times (b\sqrt{1-\beta^2})$ due to the Lorentz contraction.
Its mass, however, will increase to an amount $20/\sqrt{1-\beta^2}$. Therefore the density will be

$$\frac{\text{Mass}}{\text{Volume}} = \frac{(20/b^3)}{(1-\beta^2)} = \frac{105}{b^3}$$

19 From the definition of relativistic force, show that in general the force F is *not* equal to $m_0 a/\sqrt{1-\beta^2}$. In other words, one cannot simply replace m_0 by the relativistic mass in $F = m_0 a$.

20 Show that, if an applied force causes only a change in direction of the momentum but not its magnitude, then $F = ma$ provided that the relativistic mass is used. *(Notice*: This is a special case.)

q

7
questions
19-20

19 By definition, $\mathbf{F} = d(m\mathbf{v})/dt$ where $m = m_o/\sqrt{1 - \beta^2}$ with $\beta = v/c$. If we carry out the differentiation,

$$\mathbf{F} = m\frac{d\mathbf{v}}{dt} + \mathbf{v}\frac{dm}{dt}$$

$$= m\mathbf{a} + \mathbf{v}\frac{dm}{dt}$$

Now $\dot{m}$ involves **v** and **v** changes with t so the last term is not zero. Therefore, $\mathbf{F} \neq m\mathbf{a}$ where m is the relativistic mass.

20 From the previous problem,

$$\mathbf{F} = m\mathbf{a} + \mathbf{v}\frac{dm}{dt}$$

But if mv is constant, then since $m = m_o/\sqrt{(1 - v^2/c^2)}$, both m and v are constant in magnitude. As a result, the last term is zero and so $\mathbf{F} = m\mathbf{a}$. Recall that $\mathbf{a} = \Delta\mathbf{v}/\Delta t$ can be nonzero even if the magnitude of **v** is constant.

a

7
answers
19-20

8
work and energy

1 What is the physicist's definition of work?

2 What is the meaning of the scalar product **A** · **B**?

3 A bead sliding on a straight wire travels a distance of 40 cm before coming to rest. If the friction force opposing the bead's motion is 0.010 N, how much work does the friction force do on the bead in stopping it?

4 A man pushes a box along the floor with constant speed by pushing on it with a force **P** which makes an angle of 37° to the horizontal. A friction force of 20 N opposes the motion. Find **P** and the work the man does in pushing the box 3.0 m.

5 What is the definition of power? Distinguish between average and instantaneous power.

6 Plot a graph of F versus y for an object of mass m being lifted slowly through a height h, starting from y_0. Use the graph to find the work done in the process and show that it agrees with **F** · **r**. Repeat for the object being lowered from $y_0 + h$ to y_0. Show that the work done in the complete process is zero.

1 When an unbalanced force **F** acting on a body causes a displacement $\Delta\mathbf{r}$, then the work done is

$$\Delta W = \mathbf{F} \cdot \Delta\mathbf{r}$$

2 By definition $\mathbf{A} \cdot \mathbf{B} = AB \cos\,\theta$ where θ is the angle between the two vectors **A** and **B**.

3 ☐ -4×10^{-3} J

By definition, $W = \mathbf{F} \cdot \mathbf{r} = Fr \cos\theta$. In this case, the force is in a direction opposite to the displacement so $\theta = 180^\circ$. Therefore $W = (0.010)(0.40)(-1) = -4 \times 10^{-3}$ J. The negative sign tells us the friction force caused the bead to lose energy. This energy appears as heat energy.

4 ☐ 25 N; 60 J

Since the box moves at constant speed, the sum of the horizontal forces must be zero. Therefore $P \cos\theta = 20$ N where $\theta = 37^\circ$. Then $P = 20/0.80 = 25$ N. By definition $W = \mathbf{P} \cdot \mathbf{r}$. But **r** is 3.0 m horizontal and so $W = P(3) \cos(37^\circ) = 60$ J.

5 ☐ Power $= \dfrac{\text{work done}}{\text{time taken}} = \dfrac{\Delta W}{\Delta t}$

If $\Delta t \to 0$, then the above relation gives instantaneous power. Otherwise, it is average power.

6

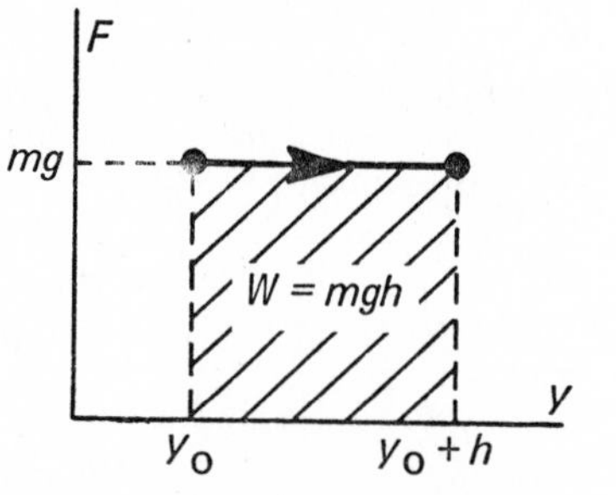

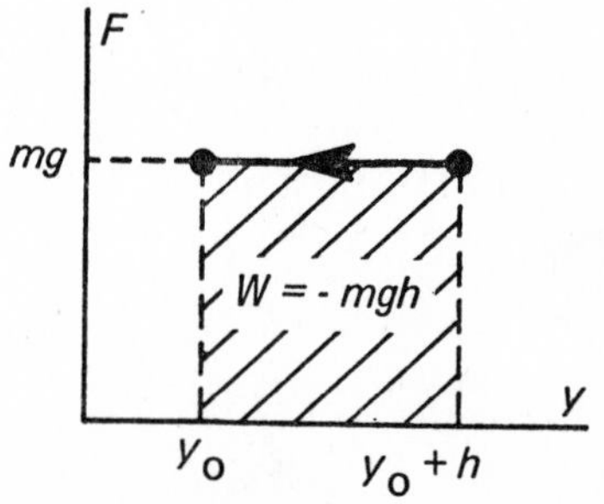

$W_1 = \mathbf{F} \cdot \mathbf{r} = mgh$

$W_2 = \mathbf{F} \cdot \mathbf{r} = -mgh$

$W_1 + W_2 = 0$

7 If a spring is stretched an amount x, the force required to hold it at this stretched position is $F = kx$ where k is a constant. Draw a graph showing F versus x as the spring is stretched from an elongation $x = 0$ to an elongation x_0.

(a) Use the graph to find the work done in the process.
(b) Find the work done by integration of the work equation.

8 How much work is needed to stop a 1000-kg car which is moving at a speed of 20 m/sec?

9 For the car of the previous problem, how large a force would be required to stop it in a distance of 3.0 m?

10 In a certain gun, a 20-g bullet is accelerated from rest to 100 m/sec in a distance of 40 cm. Find the average force on the bullet.

7 □ $\frac{1}{2}kx_o^2$

The area of the shaded triangle is $\frac{1}{2}(kx_o)x_o$ and so the work is $\frac{1}{2}kx_o^2$. Or, by definition of work

$$W = \int_{x=0}^{x=x_o} F_x dx = \int_0^{x_o} kx\,dx = k\int_0^{x_o} x\,dx = \left[\frac{1}{2}x_o^2 - 0\right]k = \frac{1}{2}kx_o^2$$

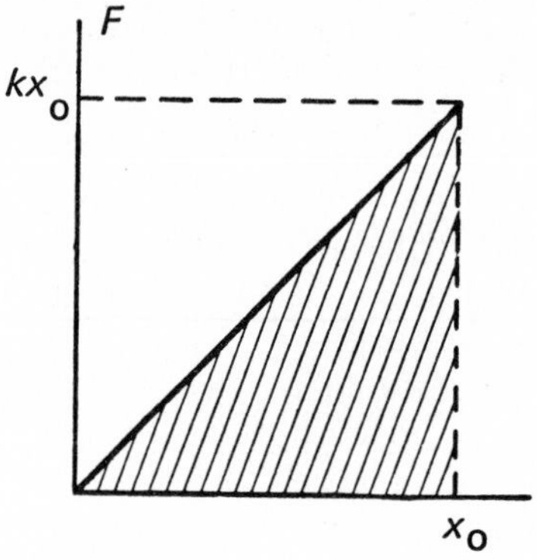

a

8 □ 2 X 10^5 J

This is most easily answered by energy considerations. Using the fact that the kinetic energy will all be used up doing work, one has:

Initial K = work done

$\frac{1}{2}(1000)\ (20)^2$ = work = 2 X 10^5 J

9 □ 6.7 X 10^4 N

The work needed to stop the car was found to be 2 X 10^5 J. This will be equal to $F_x x$ where x = 3 m. Therefore $3F_x$ = 2 X 10^5 so F_x = 6.7 X 10^4 N.

10 □ 250 N

The bullet acquires kinetic energy as the force does work on it. From the work–energy theorem,

Work done = gain in K

$F(0.40) = \frac{1}{2}(0.020)\ (10^2)^2$

One could also use $F = ma$ to solve this.

11 Give the definition and an example of each of the following: (a) conservative force, (b) nonconservative force, and (c) field.

12 Using energy concepts prove that, in the absence of friction, an object has the same speed at the same height while going up and coming down.

13 A car is at rest on a sloping driveway. By accident, a small child releases the brake of the car. How fast will the car be moving when it reaches the street? The street is 2.0 m below the original level of the car.

14 If the speed of the car in the previous problem is actually 3.0 m/sec, how large was the friction force f which retarded its motion? The distance rolled by the car is 5.0 m and the car's mass is 1000 kg.

11 (a) A force such that the work done by it in a vector displacement is independent of the path by which the displacement is effected (gravitation). (b) The work done is not independent of path for a given displacement (friction). (c) A region in which the force in question exists (the earth's gravitational field).

12 Make use of the conservation of energy,

$K + U_g$ = (const) for this system. Substituting,

$$\frac{1}{2} mv^2 + mgh = \text{(const)} = C$$

so

$$v = \sqrt{(2C - 2\,mgh)\,/\,m}$$

Therefore the speed v depends only on height h and has identical values for motion going up or down. Can you show $C = \frac{1}{2} mv_0{}^2$ where v_0 is the speed at $h = 0$?

a

8

answers

11-14

13 □ 6.3 m/sec

Ignoring friction and using the conservation of energy, we write

$$(U_g + K)_{\text{start}} = (U_g + K)_{\text{end}}$$

$$mgh_1 + 0 = mgh_2 + \frac{1}{2} mv^2$$

or

$$g(h_1 - h_2) = v^2/2$$

Placing in $g = 9.8$ m/sec^2 and $h_1 - h_2 = 2.0$ meters gives $v = 6.3$ m/sec.

14 □ 3100 N

$$(U_g + K)_{\text{start}} + \text{energy input} = (U_g + K)_{\text{end}} + \text{energy output}$$

$$mgh_1 + 0 + 0 = mgh_2 + \frac{1}{2} mv^2 + fs$$

$$(10^3)\,(9.8)\,(2.0) = \frac{1}{2}\,(10^3)\,(9)\ + f(5)$$

from which $f = 3100$ N.

15 A car of mass m is moving at a speed of 20 m/sec when it starts coasting (i.e., its motor is turned off) up a 37° incline. How far will it move before it stops?

16 A 1000-kg car starts at rest at the bottom of an incline. Twenty seconds later it is moving with a speed of 30 m/sec and is at a point 20 m higher than its starting point. Find the average power expended on the car. Ignore friction forces.

17 A rubber ball is dropped onto a cement floor from a height of 2.0 m. It rebounds to a height of 1.6 m. What fraction of its energy did it lose in the process of striking the floor? Where did most of this energy go?

15 ☐ 34 m

Ignoring friction forces, the law of conservation of energy gives

$(U_g + K)_{start} = (U_g + K)_{end}$

Since it stops at the end, $K_{end} = 0$ and the above relation becomes

$$0 + \frac{1}{2} m(400) = mgh + 0$$

so

$$h = \frac{200}{9.8} = 20.4 \text{ m}$$

Since $d = h/\sin 37°$, $d = 34$ m.

16 ☐ 43 hp

First find the work done on the car by use of

$(U_g + K)_{start}$ + work input = $(U_g + K)_{end}$ + work output

$$0 + 0 + W = mgh + \frac{1}{2} mv^2 + 0$$

But power = $W/\Delta t$ and so

$$P = 10^3 \frac{[(9.8)(20) + 450]}{20} \text{ watts} = \frac{32{,}300}{746} \text{ hp}$$

a

8

answers

15-17

17 ☐ 0.20

Loss in energy = $(U_g)_{start} - (U_g)_{end}$

$$= mgh_1 - mgh_2$$

$$\text{Fraction loss} = \frac{mgh_1 - mgh_2}{mgh_1}$$

$$= \frac{0.4}{2.0} = 0.20$$

Energy was lost as friction within the ball as it distorted upon contact.

18 A ball is suspended as a pendulum from a 4.0-m-long string. The string is pulled aside until it makes a 60° angle to the vertical and is released. (a) Find the ball's speed as it goes through the zero position. (b) If the string breaks as the ball goes through its zero position, where would the ball strike the floor, 2.45 m below? (c) Repeat (b) if the string breaks when the string makes a 37° angle and the ball is rising.

19 Two adjacent hills along the path of a roller coaster have heights of 20 and 30 m. If a cart is moving at a speed of 10 m/sec as it coasts over the lower hill, can it reach the top of the other hill? If not, how high does it get?

20 A 20-g bullet is shot into a 1.50-kg block sitting on a flat table. The bullet lodges in the block and causes the block to slide 40 cm along the table. If the friction force between block and table is 0.50 N, how fast was the bullet moving?

18 ☐ 6.3 m/sec; 4.5 m from zero position; 6.5 m

Taking the zero level at the bottom of the pendulum path,

$$(U_g + K)_{top} = (U_g + K)_{bottom}$$

$$mg\ (4.0 - 4.0 \cos 60°) + 0 = 0 + \frac{1}{2} mv^2$$

from which $v = 6.3$ m/sec. (b) When the string breaks, the ball is a free projectile with $v_x = 6.3$ m/sec and $v_y = 0$. Since $y = 2.45\ m$, $y = \frac{1}{2}gt^2$ gives $t = 0.71$ sec and $x = 4.5$ m. (c) In this case, $(U_g + K)_{top} = (U_g + K)_{bottom}$ gives

$$mg\ (4.0 - 4.0 \cos 60°) + 0 = mg\ (4.0 - 4.0 \cos 37°) + \frac{1}{2} mv^2$$

from which $v = 4.85$ m/sec.

Now $v_x = v \sin 53°$ and $v_y = v \cos 53°$. Working the projectile problem yields $x = 4.1$ m to which 4.0 sin 37° must be added.

a

19 ☐ No. $h_2 = 25.1$ m

For the two hilltops, ignoring friction, $(U_g + K)_1 = (U_g + K)_2$

$$mg\ (20) + \frac{1}{2} m\ (10)^2 = mg\ (30) + \frac{1}{2} mv^2$$

8

answers

18-20

Solving shows that v_2^2 is negative so the cart cannot reach the top (v_2 is imaginary). To find how high it went, $v_2 = 0$. Therefore, using the same equation as above,

$$mg\ (20) + \frac{1}{2} m\ (10)^2 = mgh$$

from which $h_2 = 25.1$ m.

20 ☐ 39 m/sec

Consider first the motion of the block after the collision. Calling its initial speed v $(U_g + K)_{start}$ + input = $(U_g + K)_{end}$ + output gives

$$\frac{1}{2}\ (1.52)v^2 = (0.50)\ (0.40)$$

from which $v = 0.51$ m/sec. Now consider the momentum conservation during collision.

$$(0.020)v = (1.52)(0.51)$$

giving the bullet's speed $v = 39$ m/sec.

21 How fast must a proton be going to have an energy of 10^6 eV (i.e., 1 MeV)? Repeat for an electron.

22 When 1 g of water cools from its boiling point to its freezing point, it gives off about 420 J of heat energy. By how much does its mass change because of this loss in energy?

23 Hydrogen burns in the presence of oxygen to form water. The heat energy given off in the formation of 1 g of water is about 1.3×10^4 J. How much more do the reactants weigh than 1 g of the products?

21 □ $0.046c$; $0.94c$

The particles will have speeds near that of light. Since 1 eV = 1.6×10^{-19} J we have

$$K = mc^2 - m_0c^2 = 1.6 \times 10^{-13} \text{ J}$$

Since $m = \dfrac{m_0}{\sqrt{1 - v^2/c^2}}$

one can solve for v^2/c^2 obtaining

$$\frac{v^2}{c^2} = 1 - \left(\frac{m_0c^2}{m_0c^2 + 1.6 \times 10^{-13}}\right)^2$$

Putting in the rest masses 9.1×10^{-31} and 1.67×10^{-27} kg for electron and proton, respectively, gives the result.

22 □ 4.7×10^{-12} g

According to the Einstein relation,

$$\Delta E = (\Delta m)c^2$$

$$420 = (\Delta m)(9 \times 10^{16})$$

so that

$$\Delta m = 4.7 \times 10^{-15} \text{ kg}$$

23 □ 1.4×10^{-10} g

Using the Einstein relation

$$\Delta E = (\Delta m)c^2$$

$$1.3 \times 10^4 = 9 \times 10^{16} (\Delta m)$$

from which $\Delta m = 1.4 \times 10^{-13}$ kg.

24 Find the mass of a 1 GeV electron (1 GeV = 10^9 eV).

q

8
question
24

24 □ $1950m_0$

We have $K = mc^2 - m_0c^2$.

Therefore

$$(1.6 \times 10^{-19})(10^9)\,\text{J} = (m - m_0)(9 \times 10^{16})$$

from which

$$m = m_0 + 1.78 \times 10^{-27} \cong 1.78 \times 10^{-27}\ \text{kg} = 1950m_o.$$

a

8
answer
24

9
motion of systems

1 What is the center of mass of a system of masses?

2 Why is the center of mass of a system an important quantity?

3 Does the law of conservation of momentum hold true for motion of the mass center?

4 How does one compute the momentum of a system of particles?

5 How does one compute the energy of a system of particles?

6 What may one say about any collision or explosion within a system?

7 What is meant by Hooke's law?

8 Draw a graph showing the distortion x of a spring as a function of the applied force F_{app} in a region where the spring is hookean.

a

9

answers

1-8

1 An average position of the combined masses composing the system. Precisely, its x, y, and z coordinates are given by relations such as the following:

$$x_{cm} = \frac{\Sigma x_i m_i}{\Sigma m_i}$$

where the m_i are the masses constituting the system and x_i are their coordinates.

2 The motion of the mass center obeys Newton's second law, $\mathbf{F} = d(M\mathbf{v})/dt$ where $\mathbf{F}$ is the resultant external force on the system of mass M and $\mathbf{v}$ is the velocity of the mass center.

3 Yes. This follows directly from $\mathbf{F} = d(M\mathbf{v})/dt$. If $F = 0$, then $M\mathbf{v}$ is a constant.

4 Momentum is a vector and so the total momentum is the vector sum of the momenta of the masses constituting the system.

5 Energy is a scalar. The total energy of a system is the algebraic sum of the energies of the particles constituting the system.

6 The momentum of the system is always conserved, provided one considers an instantaneous collision and refers to conditions just before and just after collision.

7 A system is said to obey Hooke's law if an applied force F_{app} causes a distortion of the system x such that $F_{app} = kx$ with k being a constant.

8

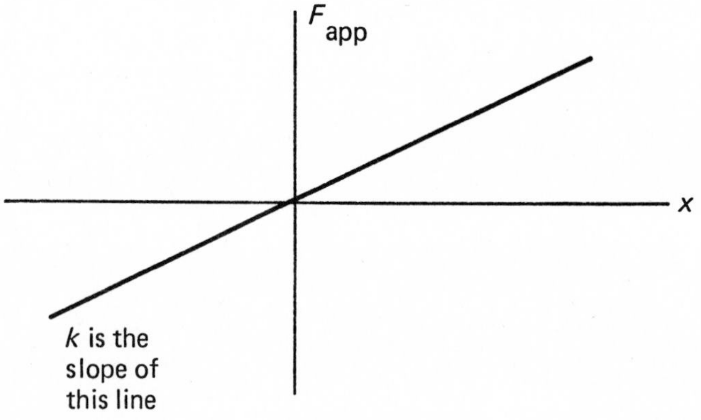

9 Draw a graph showing how the energy stored in a spring varies with the length of the spring in the hookean region. Assume the zero load length of the spring to be L_0.

10 The potential energy curve for an electron near the surface of a metal can be drawn approximately as shown. Draw the force experienced by the electron in this region.

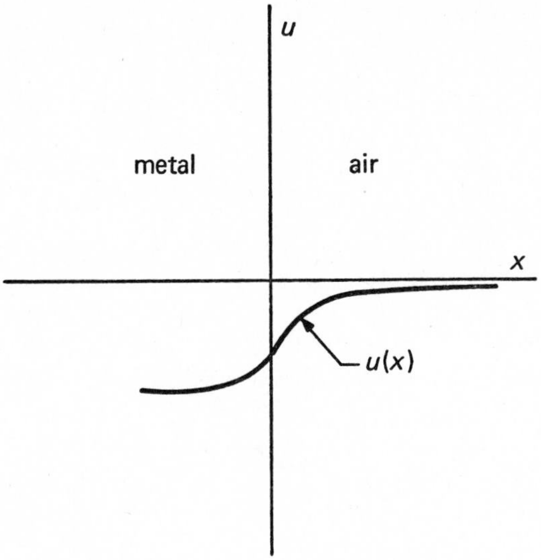

11 Find the position of the center of mass of the three masses shown below.

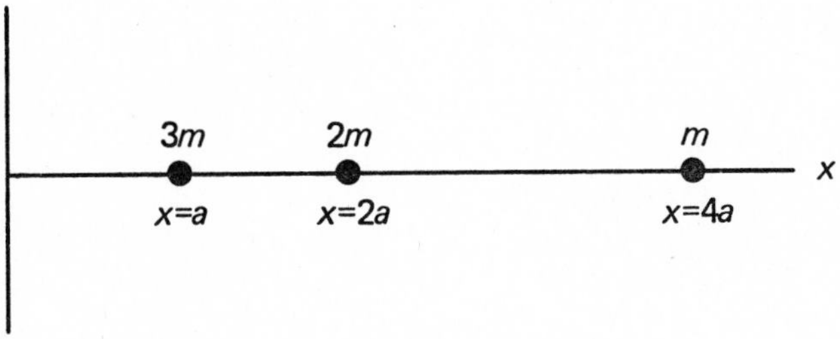

9

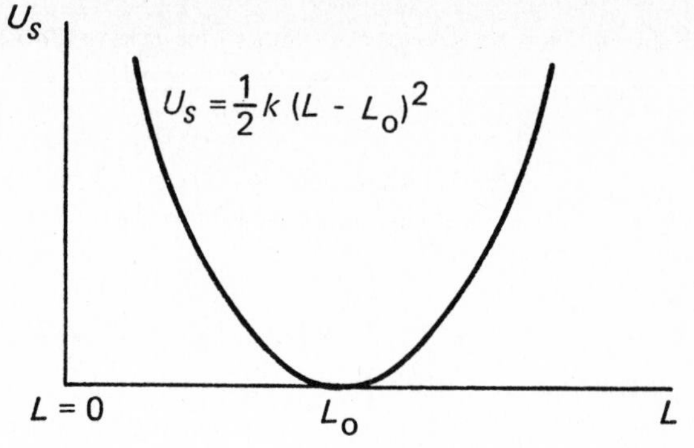

10

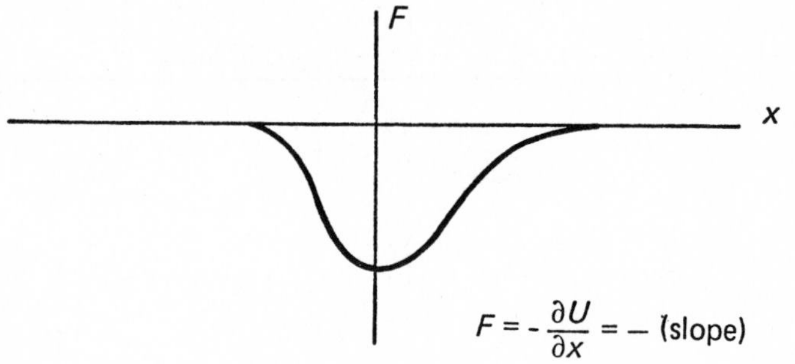

a

9
answers
9-11

11 $\square\ x = \frac{11}{6}a$

By definition

$$x_{cm} = \frac{\Sigma m_i x_i}{\Sigma m_i}$$

$$= \frac{m(3a + 4a + 4a)}{6m} = \frac{11}{6}a$$

12 A uniform board is cut into the shape shown. Find the position of the center of mass.

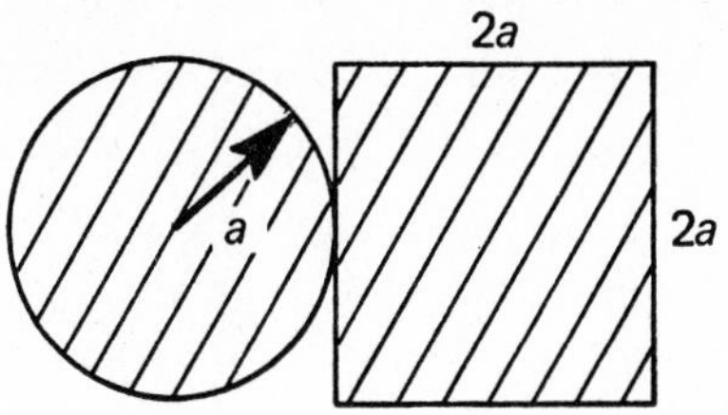

13 Find the center of mass of a nonuniform rod whose mass per unit length varies as $\lambda = e^{-kx}$ with the ends of the rod being at $x = 0$ and $x = L$.

q

9
questions
12-13

12 ☐ $0.12a$ to the right of the point of contact between circle and square.

Centers of mass of circle and square are at the center of each. Treat these as two separate masses.

Mass of circle $= \pi a^2 m_o$

Mass of square $= 4a^2 m_o$

where m_o is the mass per unit area.

$$x_{cm} = \frac{(\pi a^2 m_o)(-a) + (4a^2 m_o)a}{(\pi a^2 m_o + 4a^2 m_o)}$$

$$= 0.12a$$

13 ☐ $x_{cm} = \dfrac{1}{k} - \dfrac{L}{e^{kL} - 1}$

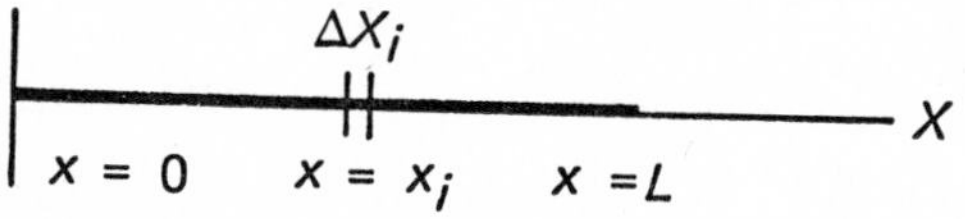

Split the rod into small segments. Each segment of length Δx_i has a mass $m_i = \lambda\,(\Delta x_i)$.

Then $x_{cm} = \dfrac{\Sigma m_i x_i}{\Sigma m_i} = \dfrac{\Sigma(\lambda\,\Delta x_i)x_i}{\Sigma(\lambda\,\Delta x_i)}$

Placing in the value given for λ and letting $\Delta x_i \longrightarrow 0$ so that the sum becomes an integral

$$x_{cm} = \int_0^L x e^{-kx}\,dx \Big/ \int_0^L e^{-kx}\,dx$$

Evaluating these integrals by use of integral tables gives the result above.

14 Find the center of mass of the uniform wire shown below.

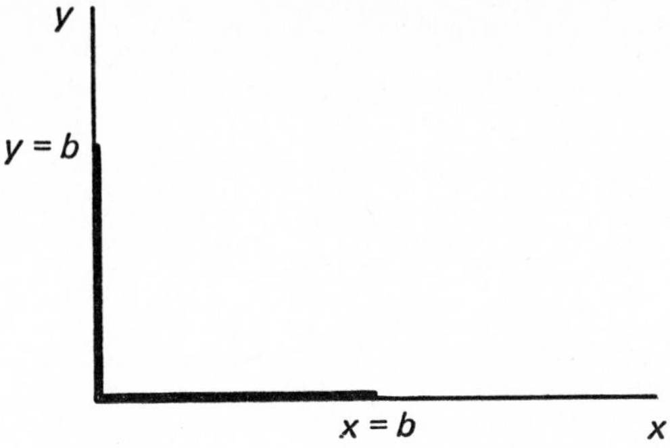

15 Suppose that an explosion occurred on the earth so that the earth split into two fragments, one of mass $M/3$ and the other of mass $2M/3$. Find the radius of the orbit of the larger piece about the sun if the smaller piece has an orbital radius $0.40R_o$ where R_o is the original orbit radius of the earth about the sun.

16 Two particles of mass m_1 and m_2 move along a line towards each other with velocities $\mathbf{v}_1 = -20\mathbf{i}$ m/sec and $\mathbf{v}_2 = +30\mathbf{i}$ m/sec. After collision, mass 2 has a velocity of $-10\mathbf{i}$ while mass 1 has a velocity of $40\mathbf{i}$. Find out as much as you can about m_1 and m_2. Assume a perfectly elastic collision.

14 ☐ At the point $\frac{b}{4}, \frac{b}{4}$

The center of mass of each segment is at the center of the segment. Therefore, the system behaves like two equal masses at $\frac{b}{2}, 0$ and $0, \frac{b}{2}$.

$$x_{cm} = \frac{m\frac{b}{2}}{2m} = \frac{b}{4}$$

$$y_{cm} = \frac{m\frac{b}{2}}{2m} = \frac{b}{4}$$

15 ☐ $1.30R_o$

Since the explosion caused no new external forces to act on the system, the mass center must still be in an orbit with $r = R_o$.

From the diagram, the coordinate of the mass center, R_o, is

$$R_o = \frac{0.40R_o\,(M/3) + R\,(2M/3)}{M}$$

from which $R = 1.30R_o$.

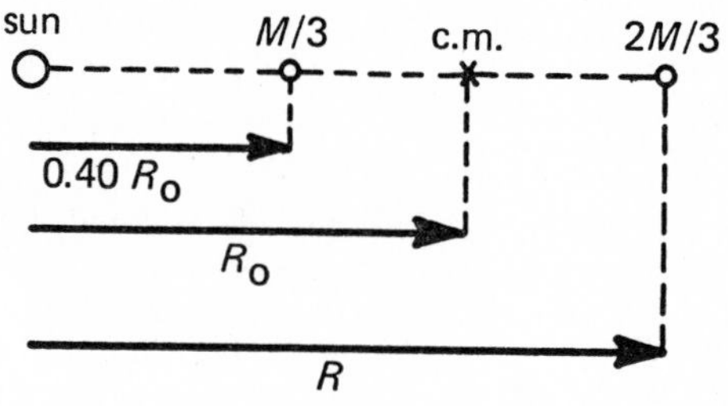

16 ☐ $\frac{m_1}{m_2} = \frac{2}{3}$

From the law of conservation of momentum, momentum before = momentum after

$$-20m_1 + 30m_2 = +40m_1 - 10m_2$$

From the law of conservation of energy

$$\frac{1}{2}m_1\,(400) + \frac{1}{2}m_2\,(900) = \frac{1}{2}m_1\,(1600) + \frac{1}{2}m_2\,(100)$$

These two equations can be simplified and solved simultaneously for m_1 and m_2 to give the results above.

17 A helium nucleus undergoes a perfectly elastic head-on collision with a lithium nucleus. (In atomic mass units, the helium nucleus has a mass of 4.0 while that of lithium is 6.0.) The initial velocities are $-2 \times 10^5 \mathbf{j}$ m/sec and $3 \times 10^5 \mathbf{j}$ m/sec for He and Li, respectively. If the velocity of the Li nucleus is $-1 \times 10^5 \mathbf{j}$ m/sec after collision, what is the final velocity of the He nucleus?

18 In the previous problem, if only $\frac{2}{3}$ of the kinetic energy is retained after collision, wnat are the final velocities of the two particles?

17 □ 4×10^5 m/sec

From the law of momentum conservation

$$(4.0 \text{ amu})(-2 \times 10^5 \text{m/sec}) + (6.0)(3 \times 10^5) = (4.0)v + (6.0)(-1 \times 10^5)$$

Notice that, since mass occurs in each term, its units cancel out in the equation and so any single mass unit may be used. From energy conservation (again mass units cancel):

$$\frac{1}{2}(4)(4 \times 10^{10}) + \frac{1}{2}(6)(9 \times 10^{10}) = \frac{1}{2}(4)v^2 + \frac{1}{2}(6)(10^{10})$$

Factor the last equation to give

$$4(2 - \frac{v}{10^5})(2 + \frac{v}{10^5}) = -6(8)$$

and from the first equation

$$-4(2 + \frac{v}{10^5}) = -6(4)$$

Combining the two equations gives v. Actually, v can be determined directly from either equation.

a

9

answers

17-18

18 □ -0.57×10^5 m/sec; 3.35×10^5 m/sec

Only the energy equation changes. It becomes

$$\frac{2}{3}\left[\frac{1}{2}(4)(4 \times 10^{10}) + \frac{1}{2}(6)(9 \times 10^{10})\right] = \frac{1}{2}(4)v_H{}^2 + \frac{1}{2}(6)v_L{}^2$$

while the momentum equation is

$$(4)(-2 \times 10^5) + (6)(3 \times 10^5) = 4v_H + 6v_L$$

Solving these two equations simultaneously gives two sets of answers:

$v_H = 3.35 \times 10^5$ and $v_L = -0.57 \times 10^5$ m/sec

and

$v_H = -1.3 \times 10^5$ and $v_L = 2.6 \times 10^5$ m/sec

The second set of answers must be discarded since it presupposes the two nuclei can pass through each other.

19 A radium nucleus (m = 226 amu) moving with velocity $2.000 \times 10^5\mathbf{i}$ m/sec emits an α particle (a helium nucleus, m = 4.0 amu) with speed $1.0 \times 10^7\mathbf{i} + 1.2 \times 10^7\mathbf{j}$ m/sec. Find the velocity of the nucleus after the emission.

20 A proton (m = 1.0 amu) and an α particle (m = 4.0 amu) undergo a collision as a result of which both are left at rest. What can be said about their original motions before collision?

21 Suppose that the proton and α particle of the previous problem had final velocities $8 \times 10^6\mathbf{i}$ and $3 \times 10^6\mathbf{j}$ m/sec, respectively, after collision. Assuming kinetic energy to be conserved in the collision, what were the initial velocities of the particles? The α particle was originally moving along the y axis.

22 A 2.0-kg block is attached to the end of a spring (k = 300 N/m). If the spring is stretched 20 cm and released, find the initial acceleration of the block.

19 ☐ $(2.3\mathbf{i} + 22\mathbf{j}) \times 10^4$ m/sec

From the conservation of momentum

$$226\,(2 \times 10^5 \mathbf{i}) = 222\mathbf{V} + 4\,(1 \times 10^7 \mathbf{i} + 1.2 \times 10^7 \mathbf{j})$$

Solving, we obtain the answer above.

20 They were moving in opposite directions along a straight line. Their momenta were opposite in direction and equal in magnitude. If their velocities were non-relativistic, their velocities were inversely proportional to their masses. This all follows from the fact that momentum is conserved in the collision.

21 ☐ $v_p = (8\mathbf{i} + 4.8\mathbf{j}) \times 10^6$ m/sec;

$v_\alpha = 1.8\mathbf{j} \times 10^6$ m/sec

Writing the x and y momentum conservation relations gives:

$$v_{xp} = 8 \times 10^6$$

$$v_{yp} + 4v_{y\alpha} = 4(3 \times 10^6)$$

The conservation of kinetic energy gives

a

9

answers

19-22

$$(v_{xp}^2 + v_{yp}^2) + 4(v_{y\alpha}^2) = 64 \times 10^{12} + 4(9 \times 10^{12})$$

These three equations can be solved for the three unknowns, v_{xp}, v_{yp}, and $v_{y\alpha}$. The results are given above. The two spurious results represent no collision.

22 ☐ 30 m/sec^2

The force needed to stretch the spring is

$$F = (300 \text{ N/m})(0.20 \text{ m}) = 60 \text{ N}$$

When released, this is the unbalanced force exerted on the block by the spring. Using $F = ma$ gives

$$a = \frac{F}{m} = 30 \text{ m/sec}^2$$

23 For the spring and block of the previous problem, repeat to find a when the block is at 15 cm if a friction force of 25 N exists.

24 A block is dropped from a height h above the end of a vertical unstretched spring. It strikes the spring, compresses it, and then rebounds with the spring in contact with it. Find the speed of the block as it rebounds through the original position of the end of the spring.

25 If the spring of the previous problem has a spring constant k, how far will it compress?

26 A block and spring are placed on a flat table. The block is pushed back against the spring, compressing it 20 cm. When released, the block moves 70 cm before coming to rest. How large is the friction force between block and table? (k = 30 N/m)

23 □ 35 or 10 m/sec^2

At 15 cm, the tension in the spring is $F = kx = (300)(0.15) = 45$ N. The friction force opposes the motion while the 45-N force always pulls towards the equilibrium position. Therefore, if the block is moving towards the equilibrium position, the friction force opposes F, otherwise it aids. Writing $F = ma$ gives $(45 \pm 25) = 2a$ so $a = 35$ or 10 m/sec^2.

24 □ $\sqrt{2gh}$

The spring force being conservative, it does zero work on the block over the closed path. Hence, the block returns with its original speed; namely, the speed $v = \sqrt{2gh}$ it gained in free fall.

25 □ $\frac{mg}{k}\left(1+\sqrt{1+\frac{2kh}{mg}}\right)$

Using energy considerations and taking the compressed position as the end state,

$$(U_g + K + U_s)_{start} = (U_g + K + U_s)_{end}$$

$$mgh + 0 + 0 = mg(-x) + 0 + \frac{1}{2}kx^2$$

Notice that the final position of the block is x below the zero level, the equilibrium position. Solving for x gives

$$\frac{mg}{k}\left(1 \pm \sqrt{1+\frac{2kh}{mg}}\right)$$

Why must we choose the + sign?

26 □ 0.86 N

Using energy considerations,

energy in spring at start = energy lost to friction work.

Notice that the intermediate kinetic energy is not needed. We merely say where the energy originally stored in the spring goes.

$$\frac{1}{2}(30)(0.04) = f\ (0.70)$$

which gives $f = 0.86$ N.

a

9
answers
23-26

27 The potential energy of a certain particle is given by $U = 30x^2 - 20y^2$. Find the force acting on the particle.

q

9
question
27

27 □ $-60x\mathbf{i} + 40y\mathbf{j}$

We know that $F_x = \dfrac{-\partial u}{\partial x}$ and

$$F_y = \frac{-\partial u}{\partial y}$$

Therefore

$F_x = -60\,x$ and $F_y = 40_y$

The vector force on the particle is

$$\mathbf{F} = -60x\mathbf{i} + 40y\mathbf{j}$$

a

9
answer
27

10 rotational motion

1 What are the three units for measuring angles and how are they related?

2 If one represents a rotation as a vector, in what direction is the vector chosen? In particular, in what directions are the rotation vectors for the following cases?

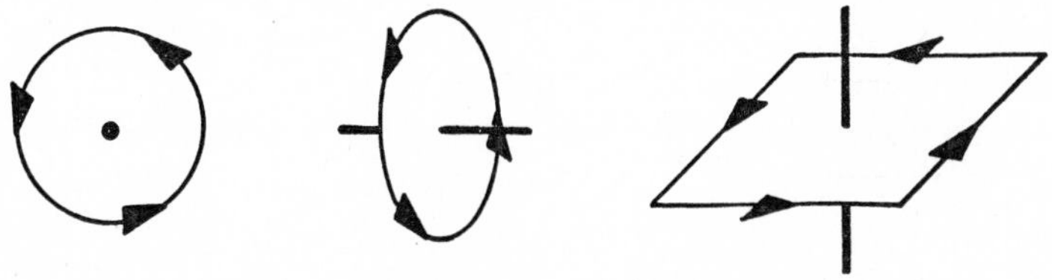

3 Why is it not possible to represent large rotation angles by vectors unless the rotation axes are always parallel or antiparallel?

4 Does the restriction in problem 3 also apply to instantaneous rotational velocity vectors and rotational acceleration vectors?

5 Define angular velocity and angular acceleration.

6 List the five angular motion equations with their linear motion counterparts. What restriction applies to them?

7 Give an example to clarify the meaning of tangential speed and tangential acceleration. How are they related to angular quantities?

8 Why is a particle which is moving around a circle at constant speed accelerating?

1 Radian, degree, and revolution. 2π radians = 360 degrees = 1 revolution.

2 In the direction of the right-hand screw motion. Out of the page; to the right; upward.

3 If the rotation axes are not parallel or antiparallel, the "vectors" representing large rotations do not commute.

4 No. These quantities are defined in terms of infinitesimal changes in angle, and they always obey the common laws of vectors.

5 If an angle changes by $\Delta\theta$ in a time Δt, then the angular velocity $\omega = \Delta\theta/\Delta t$. If the angular velocity changes by $\Delta\omega$ in a time Δt, then the angular acceleration $\alpha = \Delta\omega/\Delta t$.

6 ☐ $\theta = \omega t \longrightarrow x = vt$

$$\alpha = \frac{(\omega - \omega_0)}{t} \longrightarrow a = \frac{(v - v_0)}{t}$$

$$\overline{\omega} = \frac{1}{2}(\omega + \omega_0) \longrightarrow \overline{v} = \frac{1}{2}(v + v_0)$$

$$\omega^2 = \omega_0^2 + 2\alpha\theta \longrightarrow v^2 = v_0^2 + 2ax$$

$$\theta = \omega_0 t + \frac{1}{2}\alpha t^2 \longrightarrow x = v_0 t + \frac{1}{2}at^2$$

The last three are restricted to α constant.

a

10
answers
1-8

7 Consider a wheel of radius r rotating on its axis. A point on its rim moves a circumferential distance, which is given by $s = r\theta$ when the wheel rotates through an angle θ. The point has an instantaneous speed, the tangential speed, given by $v_T = r\omega$, where ω is the angular speed. The point has an acceleration perpendicular to the radius called the tangential acceleration. It is the rate of change of v_T and is given by $a_T = r\alpha$ where α is the angular acceleration. *In these relations, all angles must be in radians.*

8 Acceleration is defined as change in *velocity* (not speed) per unit time. Since the direction of the particle's velocity changes as the particle moves around the circle, it is accelerating. The direction of the change in velocity is towards the center of the circle and so the acceleration is directed radially inward. To distinguish this from the tangential acceleration, we call it the radial acceleration.

9 What is the centripetal force?

10 Express the following angles in radians and degrees: 30°, 490°, $\pi/4$ rad, and 6π rad.

11 A large wheel initially rotating at 0.40 rev/sec is subjected to a retarding friction force which stops it after it turns 8.0 rev. Find the time taken for it to stop and its deceleration.

12 A wheel which is 80 cm in diameter winds a belt. If the motor which rotates the belt starts the wheel from rest and accelerates it uniformly to a speed of 2.0 rev/sec in 20 sec, what is α and what length of belt is wound in this time?

13 In one model of the hydrogen atom (the Bohr model) an electron is pictured rotating in a circle (0.50×10^{-10} m radius) about the positive nucleus of the atom. The centripetal force is furnished by the electrical attraction of the positive nucleus for the negative electron. How large is this force if the electron is moving with a speed of $(2.3)(10^6)$ m/sec? (The mass of an electron is 9×10^{-31} kg.)

9 It is the force which causes the change in direction of velocity referred to in problem 8. It causes the radial acceleration and is directed toward the center of the circle. Its magnitude is

$$F = \frac{mv_T^2}{r} = m\omega^2 r$$

10 ☐ $\frac{\pi}{6}$; 2.72π; $45°$; $1080°$

$360° \longrightarrow 2\pi$ rad. By proportion

$$\frac{30°}{360°} = \frac{x}{2\pi}$$

so $x = \pi/6$ rad. Similarly,

$$\frac{\pi/4}{2\pi} = \frac{x}{360}$$

from which $x = 45°$.

a

10
answers
9-13

11 ☐ 40 sec; 10^{-2} rev/sec^2

Assume uniform deceleration. We know that $\theta = 8.0$ rev, $\omega_0 = 0.40$ rev/sec, and $\omega = 0$. Then $\bar{\omega} = 0.20$ rev/sec, and from $\theta = \bar{\omega}t$ one finds $t = 40$ sec. Using $\alpha = (\omega - \omega_0)/t$ gives $\alpha = -1 \times 10^{-2}$ rev/sec^2.

12 ☐ 0.10 rev/sec^2; 50 m

We know that $\omega_0 = 0$, $\omega = 2.0$ rev/sec, and $t = 20$ sec. From its definition

$$\alpha = \frac{\omega - \omega_0}{t} \quad \text{so } \alpha = 0.10 \text{ rev/sec}^2.$$

To find the length of belt, we must know the angle through which the wheel turned. $\theta = \bar{\omega}t = 20$ rev. Then since $s = r\theta$, we find $s = (0.40 \text{ m})(40\,\pi \text{ rad}) = 16\pi$ m. Notice that θ had to be changed to radians for use in the relation $s = r\theta$.

13 ☐ 9.5×10^{-8} N

The centripetal force is given by mv^2/r. Placing in the numbers, one has

$$F = \frac{9 \times 10^{-31}\,(5.3 \times 10^{12})}{0.50 \times 10^{-10}} = 9.5 \times 10^{-8} \text{ N}.$$

14 A certain disk oriented horizontally starts from rest and begins to rotate about its axis (vertical) with an acceleration of 0.50 rev/sec^2. After 20 sec, a 3.0-g mass attached to the disk at a distance of 40 cm from its center breaks loose from the wheel. How large was the force holding it in place?

15 A child is playing on a swing which is 3.0 m long. He finally succeeds in swinging high enough to "loop the loop." How fast is he going as he goes over the top?

16 A certain thread will break if the tension in it exceeds 2.0 N. It is used to hold a 50-g mass rotating in a circle of 40-cm radius. At what speed (in rev/sec) can the mass rotate before the string breaks (a) if the circle is horizontal and (b) if the circle is vertical?

17 A 20-cm-radius wheel starts from rest at the top of a 3.0-m incline. If it accelerates uniformly and reaches the bottom after 4.0 sec, what was its angular acceleration?

18 The angle through which a certain wheel turns is the following function of time. $\theta = 1 - ct^4$ rad with c a constant. Find ω and α for the wheel.

q

10
questions
14-18

14 ☐ 4.7 N

We first find the rotational speed of the wheel using $\omega = \omega_0 + \alpha t = 0 + (0.50)\ (20) = 10$ rev/sec. Changing this to rad/sec, the linear speed of the mass is

$$v_T = r\omega = (0.40)\ (20\pi) = 25 \text{ m/sec}$$

The mass breaks loose because the force needed to hold it in a circular path exceeds the force available. The force is

$$\frac{mv_T^2}{r} = \frac{0.003\ (625)}{0.40} = 4.7 \text{ N}$$

15 ☐ 5.4 m/sec

To just complete the circle, the gravitational force on the child should just furnish the centripetal force required at the top, mv^2/r. This gives $mg = mv^2/r$ from which

$$v = \sqrt{gr} = \sqrt{29.4} = 5.4 \text{ m/sec}$$

a

16 ☐ 1.59 rev/sec; 1.38 rev/sec

The horizontal case is simple since the tension in the thread need furnish only the centripetal force. Therefore, $2.0 = m\omega^2 r = (0.050)\ (\omega^2)\ (0.40)$ from which $\omega = 10$ rad/sec $= 5/\pi$ rev/sec. In the other case, the tension must also support the weight of the mass and so $2.0 = (0.050)\ (\omega^2)\ (0.40) + 0.50$ so that $\omega = 1.38$ rev/sec.

10
answers 14-18

17 ☐ 1.88 rad/sec^2

Let us first find its linear acceleration. In the linear problem, $x = 3.0$ m, $t = 4.0$ sec, and $v_0 = 0$. Using $x = v_0 t + \frac{1}{2} at^2$, one finds $a = \frac{3}{8}$ m/sec^2.

But

$$\alpha = \frac{a}{r} = \frac{3/8}{0.20} = 1.88 \text{ rad/sec}^2.$$

Notice that this equation always uses radian measure.

18 ☐ $-4ct^3$; $-12ct^2$

Use the definitions $\omega = d\theta/dt$ and $\alpha = d\omega/dt$.

19 A pendulum of length L is released at an angle θ_0 to the vertical. Find its angular speed as a function of position angle θ. Assume $\theta_0 << \pi/2$.

20 A pendulum of length L is released at an angle θ_0 to the vertical, $\theta_0 << \pi/2$. Find the tension in the string at the bottom of the path if the pendulum ball has a mass m.

19 ☐ $\omega = \sqrt{\frac{g}{L}}\,(\theta_o^2 - \theta^2)$

First find the linear speed of the pendulum ball by energy considerations. Measuring height from its lowest position

$$(U_g + K)_{\text{start}} = U_g + K$$

$$mg\,(L - L\cos\theta_o) + 0 = mg\,(L - L\cos\theta) + \frac{1}{2}mv^2$$

This gives $v = \sqrt{2gL\,(\cos\theta - \cos\theta_o)}$

But this is the tangential velocity and is equal to $L\omega$ from which

$$\omega = \sqrt{\frac{2g\,(\cos\theta - \cos\theta_o)}{L}}$$

This can be simplified by using the expansion $\cos x = 1 - \frac{1}{2}x^2 + \ldots$ and gives

$$\omega = \sqrt{\frac{g}{L}}\,(\theta_o^2 - \theta^2)$$

a

10
answers
19-20

20 ☐ $mg\,(\theta_o^2 + 1)$

From the previous problem, when $\theta = 0$, one has $v = \sqrt{2gL\,(1 - \cos\theta_o)}$ which becomes $v = \theta_o\sqrt{gL}$ for θ small. The string must support the mass *and* furnish the centripetal force so

$$T = \frac{mv^2}{r} + mg = mg\theta_o^2 + mg$$

21 State the law of gravitation in the case of two point masses m_1 and m_2 separated by a distance r.

22 Is the equation given in problem 1 applicable to masses other than point masses?

23 What is the law of superposition as applied to gravitational forces?

24 For the three masses shown, find the value of d such that the gravitational force on the center object is zero.

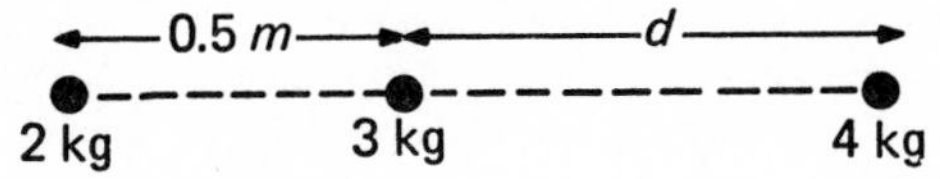

25 Find the gravitational force on the 3-kg mass in the figure below.

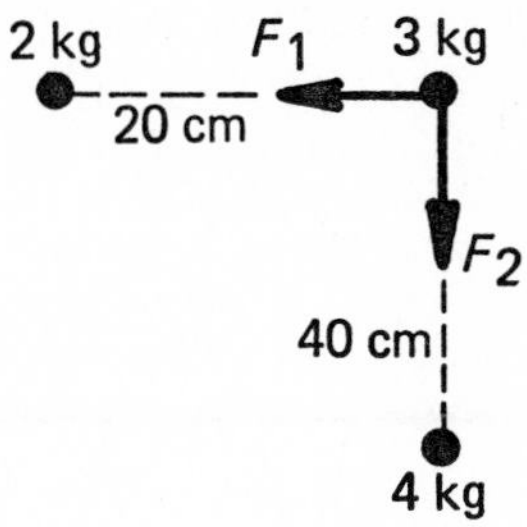

q

10
questions
21-25

21 The two masses exert equal and opposite attractive forces on each other. The direction is along the line connecting the two masses and the magnitude is

$$F = \frac{Gm_1m_2}{r^2}$$

where G is an experimentally determined constant, 6.67×10^{-11} N-m^2/kg^2.

22 In general, no. However, for nontouching uniform spheres, it is correct provided r is the distance between centers.

23 The superposition law says that the resultant gravitational force on an object is the sum of the individual forces given by the two-mass relation of 1. In other words, the gravitational force exerted by one body on a second body is independent of the presence of a third body.

24 ☐ 0.71 m

The forces due to the 4 kg and 2 kg are to right and left, respectively. They must cancel and so

$$G\frac{(2)(3)}{(0.5)^2} = G\frac{(3)(4)}{d^2}$$

from which $d = 0.71$ m.

a

25 ☐ 1.12×10^{-8} N at 207°

The force F_1 due to the 2-kg mass is $F_1 = G(2)(3)/0.04$ while F_2 due to the 4-kg is $F_2 = G(4)(3)/0.16$. As a result, F on the 3-kg mass is given by the triangle

shown and is $\sqrt{F_1^2 + F_2^2}$ with $\tan\theta = F_2/F_1$.

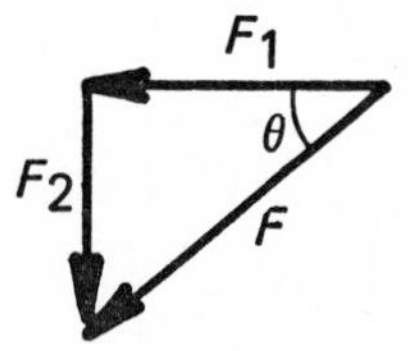

26 Find the gravitational force on the 4-kg mass in the figure below.

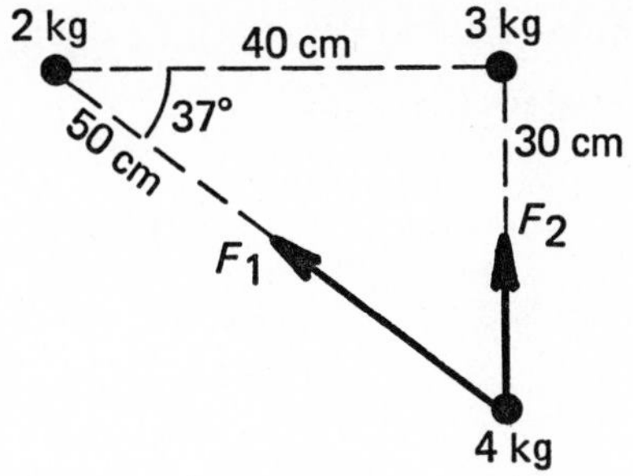

27 Two identical rods are placed as shown. Find the gravitational force on a point mass m placed at point P.

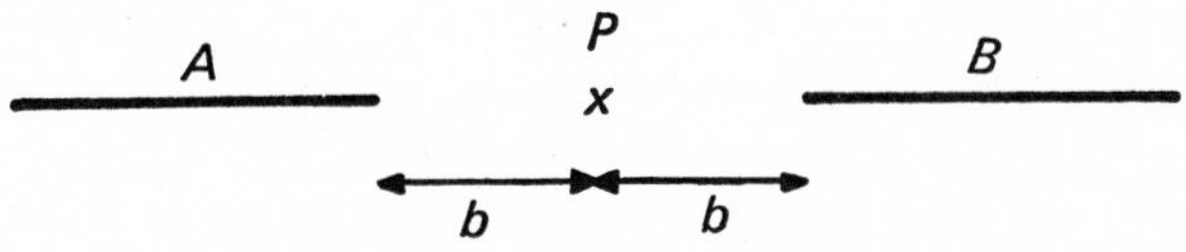

q

10
questions
26-27

26 ☐ 10.3×10^{-9} N

The values of F_1 and F_2 are 2.1×10^{-9} and 8.9×10^{-9} N, respectively. Taking components along horizontal and vertical axes, $F_x = F_{1x} + 0 = 1.7 \times 10^{-9}$ and

$F_y = F_2 + F_{1y} = 10.2 \times 10^{-9}$

Then $F = \sqrt{F_x^2 + F_y^2} = 10.3 \times 10^{-9}$ N.

27 ☐ Zero

I at point P is the gravitational force experienced by unit mass at P. Such a mass would be attracted toward A by a force equal in magnitude to the attraction B would exert on it. Since the two forces are equal and opposite, the total force is zero.

11 rotational dynamics

1 What is the analog to $F = ma$ for the case of a single particle of mass m rotating about an axis at radius r? For a rigid body?

2 What is the meaning of moment of inertia I and radius of gyration k?

3 What is the meaning of the symbolism **A X B**?

4 If **i**, **j**, and **k** are the unit vectors, what are the values of (a) **i X j**, **j X k**, **k X i**, (b) **j X i**, **k X j**, **i X k**, (c) **i X i**, **k X k**, **j X j**?

5 Evaluate (3**i** - 4**j** + 6**k**) X (-2**i** + 4**j** - **k**),

6 For the situations shown below, find the direction of the torque about the axis AB indicated.

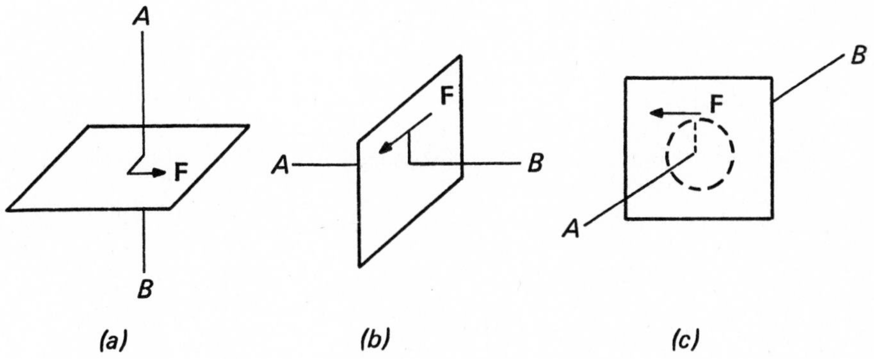

q
11
questions
1-6

1 $\tau = mr^2 \alpha$ where τ is torque and α is angular acceleration. For a rigid body, $\tau = I\alpha$ where I is a moment of inertia.

2 If a body is composed of masses m_i, and if r_i is the distance of each from an axis, then $I \equiv \Sigma m_i r_i^2$. Suppose that one subdivides the body so that all N of the m_i are equal, then

$$I = M\,(\Sigma r_i^2/N) \equiv Mk^2$$

Therefore the radius of gyration k is the square root of the average value of r_i^2.

3 It is a vector defined by

| **A** X **B** | = $AB \sin\,\theta$ and **A** X **B** has a direction perpendicular to the plan of **A** and **B** in a direction given by the right-hand rule. θ is the angle between **A** and **B**.

4 (a) **k, i, j**; (b) **-k, -i, -j**; (c) zero. These follow directly from the definition given in problem 3.

a

11
answers
1-6

5 ☐ -20i - 9j + 4k

This may be written

(3i) X (-2i + 4j -k) - (4j) X (-2i + 4j -k) + (6k) X (-2i + 4j -k)

Using the rules of the previous problem, these terms become:

[0 + 12k + 3j] + [-8k + 0 + 4i] + [-12j - 24i + 0]

6 ☐ $B \rightarrow A$; $A \rightarrow B$; $B \rightarrow A$

These results follow directly from the right-hand rule.

7 Find the moment of inertia of the system shown below about an axis perpendicular to the page through O. Assume the connecting rods to have negligible mass.

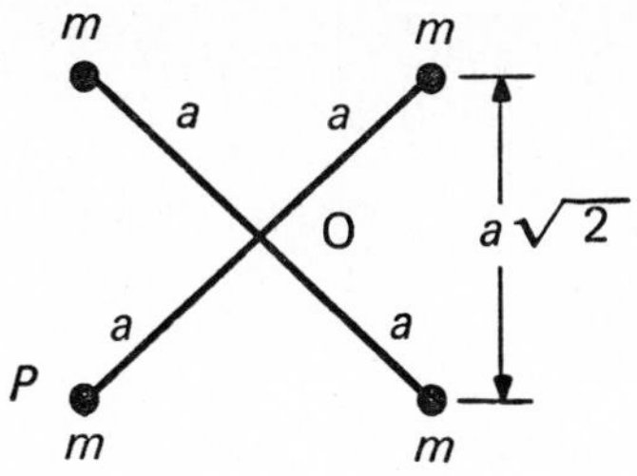

8 Repeat problem 7 for an axis through P.

9 Find I for a uniform thin rod about an axis through its center and perpendicular to the rod.

10 Using the parallel axis theorem, show that the above result can be used to find I about an axis $L/3$ from one end of the rod.

11
questions
7-10

7 ☐ $4ma^2$

By definition

$$I = \Sigma m_i r_i^2 = ma^2 + ma^2 + ma^2 + ma^2 = 4ma^2$$

8 ☐ $8ma^2$

Since

$$I = \Sigma m_i r_i^2 = m\,[2a^2 + 4a^2 + 2a^2] = 8ma^2$$

Notice that the radius of gyration about this axis is larger.

9 ☐ $\frac{\lambda L^3}{12}$

By definition, $I = \Sigma m_i r_i^2$. In the present case, $m_i = \lambda\,\Delta x_i$ where λ is the mass per unit length and Δx_i is the length of m_i. Then $I = \Sigma \lambda x_i^2\,\Delta x_i$. Since λ is constant for all the Δx_i this becomes $\lambda \Sigma x_i^2\,\Delta x_i$. Letting $\Delta x_i \to 0$, this becomes an integral.

$$I = \lambda \int_{-L/2}^{L/2} x^2\,dx$$

where the limits show the range of x_i. This integral gives the above result.

a

11
answers
7-10

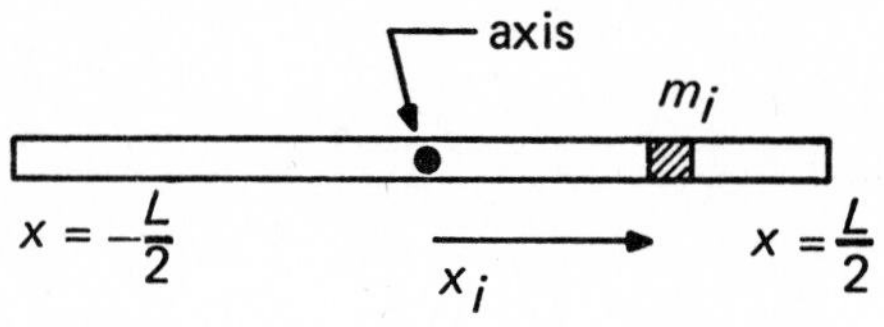

10 ☐ $\frac{\lambda L^3}{9}$

According to the parallel axis theorem

$$I = I_{cm} + Mh^2$$

where I_{cm} is I about the mass center and h is the distance to the parallel axis. In our case, $h = L/2 - L/3 = L/6$ and $M = \lambda L$. Then $I = (\lambda L^3/12) + \lambda L(L^2/36) = \lambda L^3/9$. Is this reasonable? Why?

11 Repeat problem 9 if $\lambda = \beta x^2$ where x is measured from the center of the rod.

12 Find the radius of gyration k for the rod in the previous problem.

13 A meter stick is supported by a nail through a hole in one end so that the stick can swing freely like a pendulum. Find α for the rotation of the stick when it makes an angle θ with the vertical.

11 ☐ $\frac{\beta L^5}{80}$

The problem is the same as problem 9 down to the point where

$$I = \Sigma\lambda x_i^2\, \Delta x_i$$

Since λ is not the same at all x_i, it cannot be factored out. Therefore

$$I = \int_{-L/2}^{L/2} (\beta x^2)x^2\, dx = \beta \int_{-L/2}^{L/2} x^4\, dx = \frac{\beta L^5}{80}$$

12 ☐ $(L/2)\sqrt{3/5}$

By definition of k, $I = Mk^2$. In this case $I = \beta L^5/80$. To find M we make use of the fact that $M = \Sigma m_i = \Sigma\lambda\, \Delta x_i = \Sigma\beta x_i^2\, \Delta x_i$

Passing to the limit so as to replace this by an integral,

$$M = \beta \int_{-L/2}^{L/2} x^2\, dx = \frac{\beta L^3}{12}$$

Substituting this in the first relation gives $I = \frac{\beta L^3}{12} k^2$.

But $I = \frac{\beta L^5}{80}$ and so k^2 must be $\frac{3L^2}{20}$.

a

11

answers

11-13

13 ☐ $3g \sin\theta/L$

The weight of the rod mg supplies the torque which causes the rotation. We write $\tau = I\alpha$. In this case, $\tau = |\mathbf{r} \times \mathbf{F}| = \frac{L}{2}(mg)\sin\theta$. [Notice that this same relation is obtained if we use the lever arm notation with the lever arm being $(L/2)\sin\theta$.] For a uniform rod about one end, $I = mL^2/3$. Therefore,

$$\alpha = \frac{\tau}{I} = 3g \sin\frac{\theta}{2L}.$$

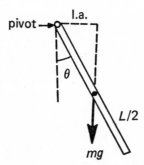

14 How large a torque is needed to accelerate a wheel for which $I = 2$ kg-m^2 from rest to 3.0 rev/sec in 20 sec?

15 After reaching a speed of 3.0 rev/sec, the wheel of the previous problem is allowed to coast to rest and it takes 90 sec. How large is the friction force which restricts rotation on its 2.0-cm-radius axle?

16 The rope shown pulls on the axle of the wheel, accelerating the wheel forward. Suppose the wheel has $m = 2.0$ kg, $I = 0.040$ kg-m^2, and a radius of 30 cm. If it rolls without slipping, how large a force is needed to give its mass center an acceleration of 0.5 m/sec^2?

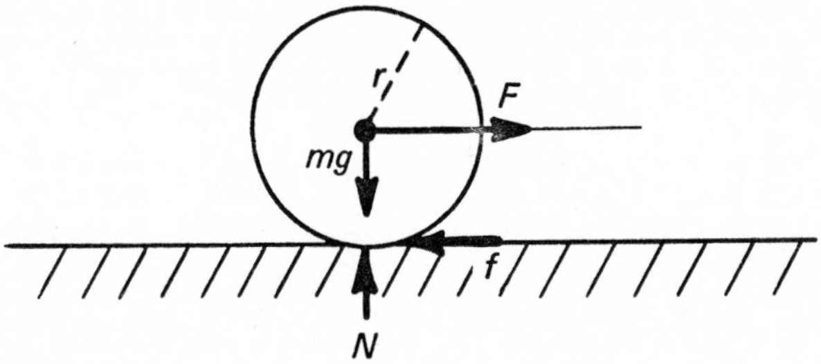

17 Find the acceleration of the sphere shown as it rolls without slipping down the incline.

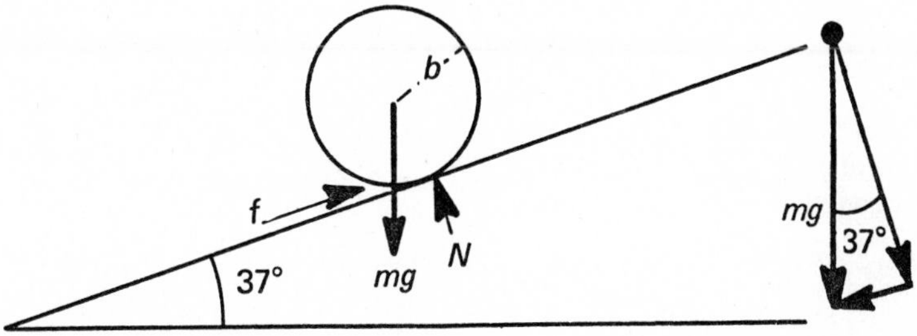

q

11
questions
14-17

14 ☐ $0.60\,\pi$ N·m

First find the acceleration of the wheel from $t = 20$ sec, $\omega_0 = 0$, $\omega = 6\pi$ rad/sec, and $\alpha = (\omega - \omega_0)/t$. We find $\alpha = 0.30\pi$ rad/sec^2. Notice that we changed to radian measure since in $\tau = I\alpha$, one must use radian measure. Placing in the values for I and α gives $\tau = 0.60\pi$ N·m.

15 ☐ 21 N

First find α from a motion problem and then use $\tau = I\alpha$. We use $\omega - \omega_0 = \alpha t$ to give $\alpha = -1/30$ rev/sec^2. For use in $\tau = I\alpha$, this must be changed to $-\pi/15$ rad/sec^2. Then, since $\tau = Fr = I\alpha$ in this case, $F = I\alpha/r$.

16 ☐ 1.22 N

Let us represent the force at the floor by its two components, f and N. The two vertical forces N and mg cancel. Horizontally, $(F - f) = ma$. Taking torques about the center, $fr = I\alpha$. Notice that F causes no torque about the center since its lever arm is zero. Now $\alpha = a/r$ and so we have two equations to solve simultaneously, namely,

$$F - f = ma \quad \text{and} \quad fr^2 = Ia$$

Placing in the values given and solving for F gives 1.22 N.

a

11
answers
14-17

17 ☐ $\frac{3g}{7}$

The forces on the sphere are shown. The normal force $N = mg \cos 37°$ while the component of mg along the plane, $mg \sin 37°$, pulls the sphere down the incline. For motion along the incline

$$mg \sin 37° - f = ma$$

Taking torques about the sphere center

$$fr = I\alpha$$

But for a sphere, $I = \frac{2}{5}mr^2$ and $\alpha = a/r$. Using these values one can solve for a.

One finds $a = 3g/7$.

18 As the rope is pulled upward by the force F, the wheel rotates and is pulled upward. Find its upward acceleration if the mass of the wheel is 2.0 kg, its moment of inertia is 0.040 kg-m^2, b = 30 cm, and F = 50 N.

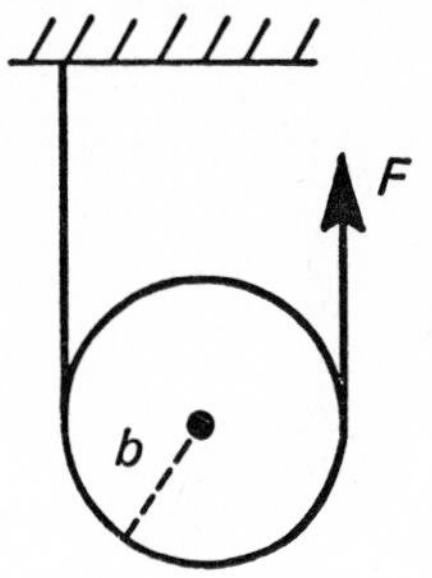

19 For the situation shown in the figure, b = 20 cm and m = 30 g. When m is released, the mass drops 1 m in 2 sec. Find I for the wheel, assuming no friction in the bearing.

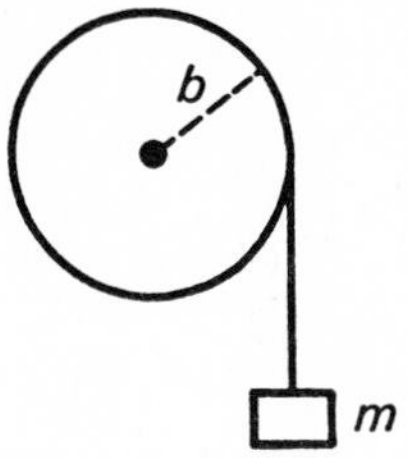

11
questions
18-20

20 If the moment of inertia of the wheel in the previous problem is actually 0.0200 kg-m^2, how large a friction torque resists its motion?

18 ☐ 33 m/sec^2

Calling the tension in the left rope T, $F = ma$ in the y direction gives

$-mg + F + T = ma$ or $-20 + 50 + T = 2a$

Writing $\tau = I\alpha$ for torques about the center of the wheel, one has

$$(0.30)\,(50 - T) = 0.040\,\frac{a}{0.30}$$

Solving simultaneously yields $T = 36$ N and $a = 33$ m/sec^2.

19 ☐ 0.0222 kg-m^2

Let us first find a from a motion problem. Use

$$y = v_0 t + \frac{1}{2}at^2$$

to give $a = 0.50$ m/sec^2. Writing $F = ma$ for m and $\tau = I\alpha$ for the wheel gives

$$(0.030)g - T = (0.030)a$$

$$(0.20)T = I\frac{a}{0.20}$$

from which $I = 0.0222$ kg-m^2.

a

11
answers
18-20

20 ☐ 0.0056 N-m

Everything is the same as before except the torque equation. Calling the friction torque τ_f, one has

$$0.20T - \tau_f = I\frac{a}{0.20}$$

Using $I = 0.0200$ kg-m^2 in these equations yields

$$0.293 - T = 0.015$$

$$0.20T - \tau_f = 0.050$$

from which $\tau_f = 0.0056$ N-m.

12 rotational momentum and energy

1 In what way is the expression $K = \frac{1}{2}I\omega^2$ for a wheel rotating about its axle related to the expression $K = \Sigma(\frac{1}{2}m_i v_i^2)$?

2 Is the angular momentum of a rotating body equal to the sum of the linear momenta of the particles constituting the body?

3 What is the general expression for the kinetic energy of a rigid body which is rotating and translating at the same time?

4 A sphere moving at 40 cm/sec starts to roll up a 37° incline. How high will it go before stopping? How far along the incline does it roll?

5 A hoop of radius b starts from rest and rolls 200 cm down an inclined plane which makes a 30° angle to the horizontal. Find the linear speed of the hoop as it rolls past the 200-cm mark on its way down the incline.

1 The two are identical if the sum extends over all the infinitesimal masses which constitute the wheel. Rotational energy is simply the sum of the translational kinetic energies of the particles constituting the rotating body.

2 No. Unlike the energy situation described in problem 1, linear momentum and angular momentum are not this simply related. For example, the sum of the linear momenta of particles of a wheel rotating on its axis is zero, while the angular momentum of the wheel is not.

3 ☐ $K = \frac{1}{2}mv^2 + \frac{1}{2}I\omega^2$

where v = velocity of the mass center,

I = the moment of inertia about an axis through the mass center, and

ω = the angular velocity about the same axis.

(The angular momentum vector for the rotation is assumed parallel to the axis.)

a

12
answers
1-5

4 ☐ 1.14 cm; 1.90 cm

Its kinetic energy at the bottom will be changed to potential energy at the top. Since the sphere is rotating and translating,

$$\frac{1}{2}mv^2 + \frac{1}{2}I\omega^2 = mgh$$

Since $I = \frac{2}{5}mr^2$ and $\omega = v/r$, we can solve to find h = 0.0114 m = 1.14 cm.

5 ☐ 3.1 m/sec

This is most easily approached using the conservation of energy.

$$(U_g + K_{rot} + K_{tr})_{top} = (U_g + K_{rot} + K_{tr})_{bottom}$$

$$mg\,(2.0 \sin 30^\circ) + 0 + 0 = 0 + (1/2)I\omega^2 + (1/2)mv^2$$

But

$I = mb^2$ and $\omega = v/b$ so this gives v = 3.1 m/sec.

6 If the speed of the hoop in the previous problem was really only 2.0 m/sec, what average friction force retarded its motion?

7 A meter stick is pivoted on a pin at its top end. The stick is pulled aside until it is horizontal. If it is now released, how fast will it be rotating when it reaches the vertical position? The mass of the stick is m.

8 Suppose that the meter stick of the previous problem had a concentrated mass $2m$ attached to its lower end. What then would have been its angular speed as it rotated through the vertical position?

6 ☐ 2.9 N

The basic equation becomes

$$(U_g + K)_{top} + \text{input energy} = (U_g + K_{rot} + K_{tr})_{bottom} + \text{energy output}$$

$$mg\ (2.0 \sin 30°) + 0 = \frac{1}{2} I\omega^2 + \frac{1}{2} mv^2 + f(2.0)$$

Putting in the values for I, ω, and v gives $f = 2.9$ N.

7 ☐ 0.86 rev/sec

Consider the mass of the stick m to be at its center. At the start it possesses $U_g = mgh = mg\ (0.5)$ where we take the zero height to be at the position of the mass center when the stick hangs vertical. When it reaches the bottom of its path, its kinetic energy is $\frac{1}{2} I\omega^2$ where we must use I for an axis at one end. Therefore, the conservation of energy requires

a

$$mg(0.5) = \frac{1}{2} I\omega^2$$

Putting in the value $I = mL^2/3$ with $L = 1.0$ gives

$\omega = 5.43$ rad/sec $= 0.86$ rev/sec.

12
answers
6-8

8 ☐ 0.74 rev/sec

We must now also consider the potential and kinetic energy of this new mass. The basic equation is

$$[U_g\ (\text{stick}) + U_g\ (\text{mass})]_{start} =$$

$$U_g\ (\text{stick}) + U_g\ (\text{mass}) + K_{rot}\ (\text{stick}) + K_{tr}\ (\text{mass})$$

That is

$$mg(0.5) + (2m)g(0.5) = 0 - (2m)g(0.5) + \frac{1}{2}\left(I\omega^2 + 2mv^2\right)$$

Now $I = mL^2/3$ and $v = \omega r = \omega(1)$. Using these values gives

$\omega = 4.63$ rad/sec $= 0.74$ rev/sec.

9 A marble of radius b is placed as shown on the inside of a hemispherical bowl of radius a. When released, it rolls without slipping to the bottom. Find the speed of the marble at the bottom of the bowl.

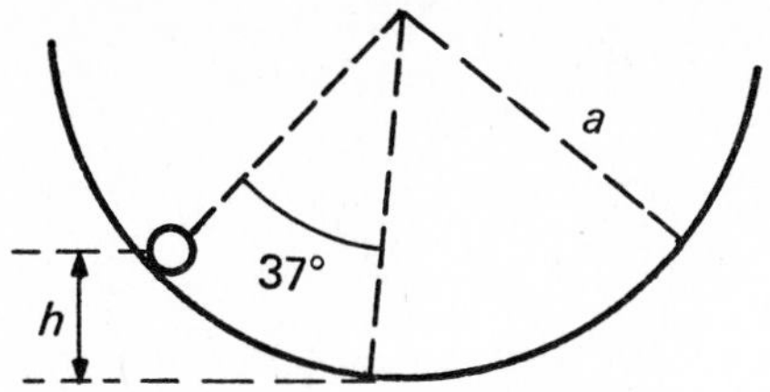

10 The force F accelerates the cylinder (moment of inertia $= I$) from rest. If the cylinder rolls and does not slide, how fast is it moving after it has rolled a distance d?

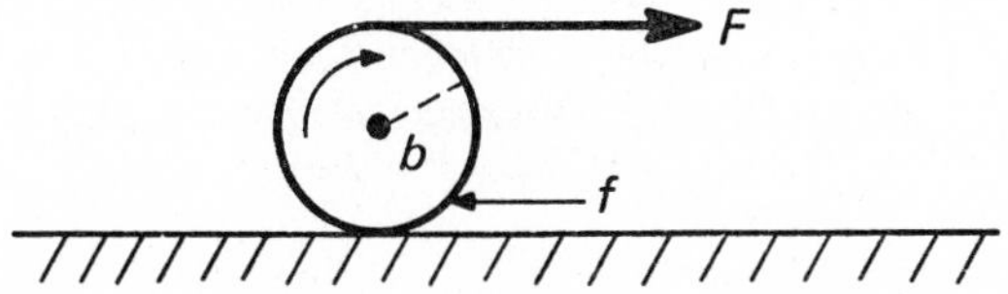

11 Suppose in the previous problem that the cylinder is rolling up a 37° incline. How fast would it be moving after rolling a distance d? (F is directed along the incline.)

12 The two wheels shown each have a radius b and moment of inertia I. If released from rest, how fast will m be moving after it has fallen a distance h?

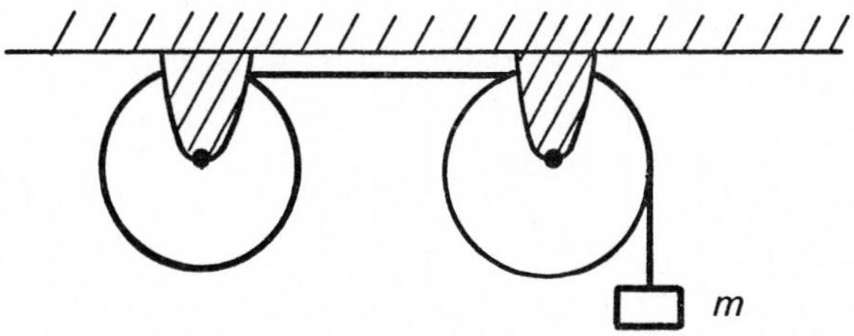

q
12
questions
9-12

9 ☐ 1.67 $\sqrt{a-b}$ m/sec

Using the energy method, we can write

$$(U_g + K_{rot} + K_{tr})_{start} = (U_g + K_{rot} + K_{tr})_{end}$$

$$mg[a-(a-b)\cos 37°] = mgb + \frac{1}{2}I\omega^2 + \frac{1}{2}mv^2$$

Now $I = \frac{2}{5}mb^2$ and $\omega = v/b$. Therefore one finds $v = 1.67\sqrt{a-b}$.

10 ☐ $\sqrt{\dfrac{4Fd}{m + (I/b^2)}}$

First we should note that the friction force does no work if the object rolls. It simply keeps the object from slipping much as the floor keeps it from falling. Therefore all the work done by the force F must appear as kinetic energy. Note that F (pulling out a rope, for instance) moves $2d$ as the wheel moves d.

$$(U_g + K)_{start} + \text{input energy} = (U_g + K)_{end} + \text{output}$$

$$0 + 2Fd = (1/2)\,I\omega^2 + (1/2)\,mv^2 + 0$$

Since $\omega = v/b$, this gives $v^2 = 4Fd/[m + (I/b^2)]$.

a

12
answers
9-12

11 ☐ $\sqrt{\dfrac{4(Fd - 0.6mgd)}{(I/b^2) + m}}$

The basic equation is the same as in problem 10. It now becomes, numerically,

$$0 + 2Fd = \frac{1}{2}I\omega^2 + \frac{1}{2}mv^2 + mg(0.6d)$$

Solving for v gives the answer above.

12 ☐ $\sqrt{\dfrac{mgh}{(I/b^2) + (m/2)}}$

Let us approach this from energy considerations. Basically, the potential energy of the mass is changed to kinetic energy.

$$\left[K_{wheels} + (U_g + K)_{mass}\right]_{start} = \left[K_{wheels} + (U_g + K)_{mass}\right]_{end}$$

$$0 + mgh = \frac{1}{2}I\omega^2 + \frac{1}{2}I\omega^2 + 0 + \frac{1}{2}mv^2$$

Now $\omega = v/b$ and so one can solve for v.

13 The large disk with moment of inertia I_0 is rotating with speed ω_0. The cylinder is dropped onto the disk. Find the final rotation speed as a function of ω_0, I_0, and I_1.

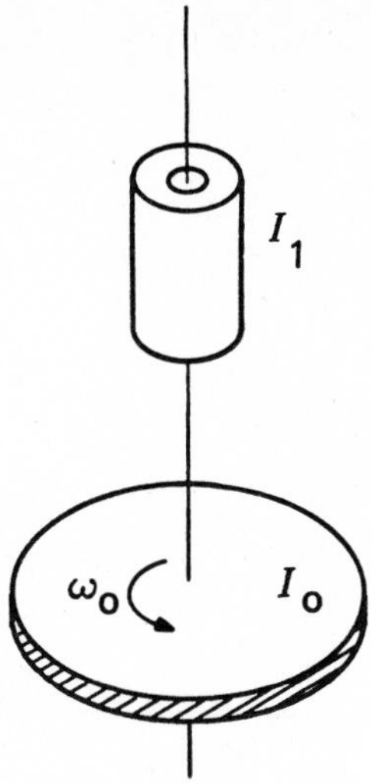

14 Small particles of sand are dropped onto a rotating disk as shown at a radius b and form a ring there. If the moment of inertia of the disk is I and sand is dropping at a rate 20 g/sec, find the deceleration of the rotation.

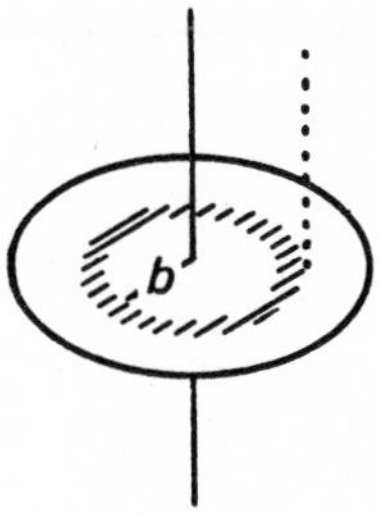

13 ☐ $\dfrac{\omega_0 I_0}{I_0 + I_1}$

Since no external torques act on the system, angular momentum must be conserved during the coupling process. Then

$$I_0\omega_0 = I_0\omega + I_1\omega$$

from which

$$\omega = \frac{\omega_0 I_0}{I_0 + I_1}$$

14 ☐ $\dfrac{0.02b^2 I\omega_0}{(I + 0.02tb^2)^2}$

We will use the law of conservation of angular momentum. When a mass Δm falls onto the plate at a radius b, the mass acquires an angular momentum $(\Delta m)b^2\omega$. The disk must lose this amount in order for momentum to be conserved. After a time t, a mass $\Delta m = 0.02t$ has fallen onto the disk. Therefore,

$$I\omega_0 = I\omega + (\Delta m)b^2\omega$$

$$= I\omega + 0.02tb^2\omega$$

Solving for ω,

$$\omega = \frac{I\omega_0}{I + 0.02tb^2}$$

Using

$$\alpha = \frac{d\omega}{dt}$$

gives

$$\alpha = -\frac{0.02b^2 I\omega_0}{(I + 0.02tb^2)^2}$$

a

12
answers
13-14

15 When a proton is shot at a heavy nucleus, as shown, it is deflected along the dotted path. Find a in terms of b. (The force on the proton is radially out from the nucleus. Assume the mass of the nucleus to be much larger than that of the proton and assume the collision to be perfectly elastic.)

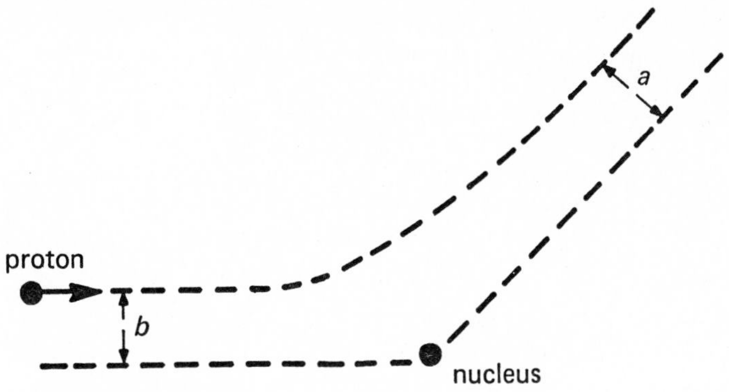

16 Suppose that a meteor of mass m strikes the earth as shown and beds in it. Assuming the meteor's speed to be v, find the increase in speed of rotation of the earth about its axis in terms of the moment of inertia of the earth I. Assume that the orbital motion of the earth is not changed.

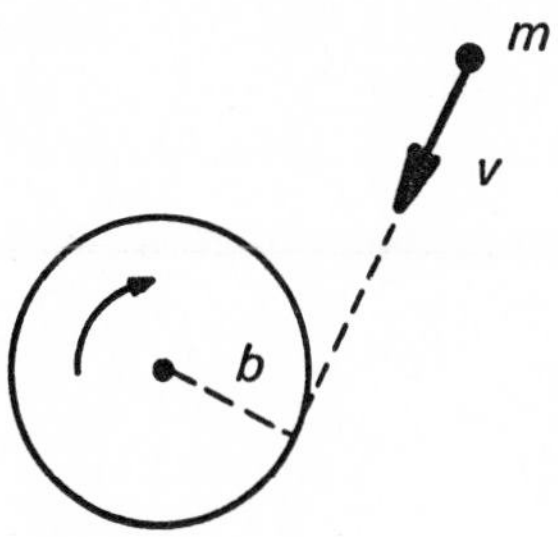

15 ☐ $a = b$

Since the force is radial, no torque is exerted on the system about the nucleus as axis. The angular momentum of the proton about the nucleus must be the same after collision as before. But $\mathbf{J} = \mathbf{r} \times \mathbf{p}$.

From the diagram, the original angular momentum is

$$|J| = |\mathbf{r} \times \mathbf{p}| = rp \sin\theta = rp \sin\phi = bp$$

Similarly, for after collision one finds $|J| = ap'$. Assuming the nucleus to remain nearly motionless, the kinetic energy of the proton should be the same before and after collision. As a result, $p = p'$ and since $J = J'$ one must have $a = b$.

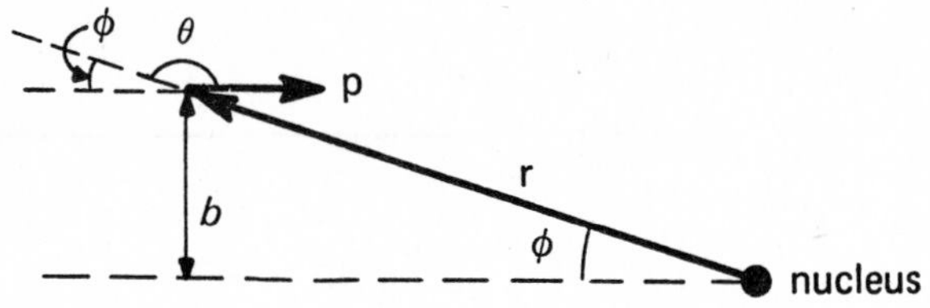

a

12
answers
15-16

16 ☐ $\dfrac{mb\,(v - b\omega_0)}{I + mb^2}$

From the conservation of angular momentum

$$J_{\text{before}} = J_{\text{after}}$$

$$I\omega_0 + mvb = I\omega + mb^2\omega$$

Solving,

$$\omega = \frac{I\omega_0 + mvb}{I + mb^2}$$

We want

$$\omega - \omega_0 = \frac{I\omega_0 + mvb - I\omega_0 - mb^2\omega_0}{(I + mb^2)} = \frac{mb\,(v - b\omega_0)}{I + mb^2}.$$

13 oscillatory motion

1 For the sinusoidal motion shown, give the amplitude, period, frequency, and phase angle.

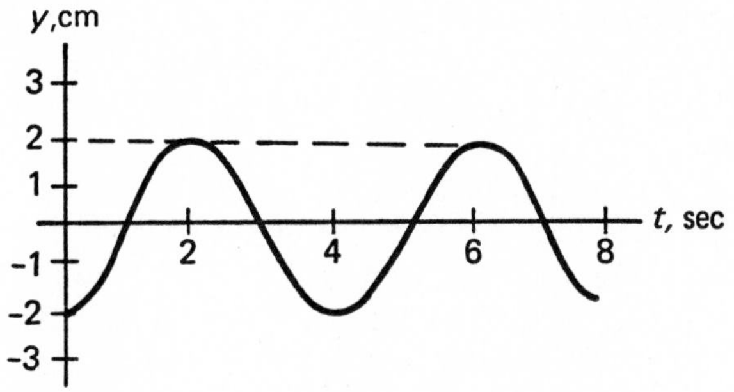

2 Write the equation for the wave shown in the previous problem.

3 What type of force must act on a body if it is to undergo simple harmonic motion?

4 A particular motion is given by the equation $y = 3.6 \cos (0.80t + 0.27)$. Find the amplitude, period, and phase angle for this motion.

5 For the motion of the previous problem, find the speed and acceleration as functions of the time.

6 For the motion of problem 4, find the restoring force constant if the mass of the moving object is 20 g.

7 A long, essentially weightless bar is clamped at one end and extends horizontally. The free end is displaced 2.0 cm when a 1.00-kg mass is attached to it. The end of the bar is lifted until it is again horizontal and is then released. Find (a) the spring constant and (b) the period of vibration.

8 If a 2.0-kg mass vibrates at the end of a spring according to the relation $y = 0.20 \cos (9.42t)$ m, find the following: (a) amplitude of vibration, (b) frequency of vibration, (c) spring constant, and (d) maximum speed of the mass.

1 Amplitude = 2.0 cm; period = 4.0 sec; frequency = 0.25 Hz; phase angle = $-\pi/2$ if the wave is considered to be a sine function.

2 $y = 2.0 \sin (0.50\pi t - \pi/2)$ cm. Notice that when $t = 0$, $y = -2.0$ as it should.

3 A Hooke's law force. That is, $F = -kx$. The force must be a restoring force, hence the minus sign.

4 ☐ $T = 7.9$ sec; $y_o = 3.6$ m; $\phi = 0.27$ rad

We compare the given equation with the standard form $y = y_o \cos(2\pi ft + \phi)$ from which $2\pi f = 0.80$, $y_o = 3.6$ m, and $\phi = 0.27$. The above result for T is found since $T = 1/f$.

5 ☐ $v = -2.9 \sin (0.80t + 0.27)$ m/sec

$a = -2.3 \cos (0.80t + 0.27)$ m/sec^2

These are obtained by recalling that $v = dy/dt$ and $a = dv/dt$.

a

13
answers
1-8

6 ☐ 0.013 N/m

We are asked for k in the Hooke's law equation $F = -kx$. But $F = ma$ and so $-kx = ma$. Using a and x from the previous problem gives $-k[3.6 \cos (0.80t + 0.27)] = m[-2.3 \cos (0.80t + 0.27)]$

from which

$$k = m\left(\frac{2.3}{3.6}\right) = 0.013 \text{ N/m}.$$

7 ☐ 490 N/m; 0.28 sec

From $F = kx$, since a force of 9.8 N displaces the system 0.020 m, $k = 490$ N/m. The period of a Hooke's law system of this type is $2\pi\sqrt{m/k} = 0.28$ sec.

8 ☐ 0.20 m; 1.5 Hz; 180 N/m; 1.88 m/sec

To find the spring constant, use the fact that $2\pi f = \sqrt{k/m}$. Then $k = 180$ N/m. Since $v = dy/dt = -1.88 \sin (9.42t)$, we have $v_{max} = 1.88$ m/sec.

9 For the motion of the previous problem, find the speed of the mass when $y = 10$ cm.

10 Two identical spring-mass systems hang side by side. At $t = 0$, one mass is released from a point 20 cm below its equilibrium position and vibrates with 0.10-sec period. When this mass reaches its highest position, the second mass is released from a point 30 cm below its equilibrium position. Write the equations of motion for each mass.

11 Find the equation of the motion of the second mass in the previous problem if it is released when the first mass is at $y = -10$ cm and going up.

12 A vibration is given by $y = 5 \sin (2\pi ft) - 10 \cos (2\pi ft)$. Find its representation in the form $y = y_0 \sin (2\pi ft + \phi)$.

9 □ -1.63 m/sec

When $y = 10$ cm, one has $0.20 \cos(9.42t) = 0.10$. Then at that time $\cos(9.42t) = 0.5$ so we know $9.42t$ corresponds to 60° or $\pi/3$ rad. From the previous problem, $v = -1.88 \sin(9.42t)$ and so at this instant $v = -1.88 \sin(60°)$ m/sec.

10 □ $y_1 = -20 \cos(62.8t); y_2 = 30 \cos(62.8t)$

These forms are found from the general equation $y = y_0 \sin(2\pi ft + \phi)$. For the first motion, $y_1 = -20$ cm at $t = 0$, and since the amplitude is 20 cm, one can achieve this by letting $\phi = 270°$. Since $\sin(\theta + 270) = -\cos(\theta)$, the result given follows. The second mass is one-half cycle, or 180°, behind the first in phase. Therefore its equation is $y_2 = 30 \sin(2\pi ft + \phi - \pi)$ and this is the same as $y_2 = 30 \cos(2\pi ft)$.

11 □ $y_2 = -30 \cos(62.8t - \frac{\pi}{6})$

a

13
answers
9-12

The first mass is at point A on the graph when the second mass is released. Then $y_1 = -20 \cos(2\pi ft) = -10$ from which $2\pi ft = 60°$. But at that instant $y_2 = -30 = -30 \cos(2\pi ft + \phi)$. Since $2\pi ft = 60°$, ϕ must be $-60° = -\pi/6$ in order to satisfy this equation.

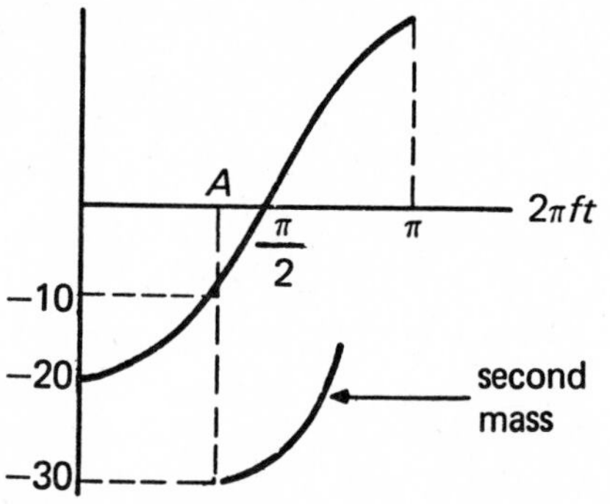

12 □ $y = 11.2 \sin(2\pi ft - 1.10)$

This can be written in the desired fashion by use of the trigonometric identity

$$A \sin\theta + B \cos\theta = \sqrt{A^2 + B^2} \sin(\theta + \phi) \text{ with}$$

$$\sin\phi = \frac{B}{\sqrt{A^2 + B^2}}$$

(See Bueche, Eq. 13.8.)

13 A 20-g mass vibrating at the end of a spring has a speed of 40 cm/sec as it passes through the equilibrium position. Find its speed when it is halfway out to its maximum displacement.

14 A mass on the end of a spring is set in motion with amplitude x_0. What fraction of its original energy remains when its amplitude has damped down to $x_0/3$?

15 A 2-kg mass stretches a spring 5.0 cm. To a force at what frequency will this system resonate?

16 A 2-kg mass oscillates at the end of a spring for which $k = 200$ N/m. The amplitude of oscillation is 15 cm. When the spring is stretched 15 cm, a 1500-g mass is attached to the 2-kg mass. Find the new amplitude of oscillation if the whole system is horizontal.

17 Repeat the previous problem if the spring is vertical.

18 Show that a spring-mass system in a very viscous liquid acts in such a way that the speed of the mass is approximately $(k/\eta)x$.

13 ☐ 35 cm/sec

This is most easily handled by energy methods. Its total energy (=K at the center point) is $\frac{1}{2}$ (0.020)(0.40)^2 or 1.6 X 10^{-3} J. If x_0 is the maximum displacement, then $\frac{1}{2}kx_0^2$ = 1.6 X 10^{-3} J. At the point in question $K + \frac{1}{2}k(x_0/2)^2$ = 1.6 X 10^{-3}. Therefore K = 1.2 X 10^{-3} J = $\frac{1}{2}mv^2$ from which v = 0.35 m/sec.

14 ☐ $\frac{1}{9}$

Original energy $= \left(\frac{1}{2}\right) kx_0^2$

Final energy $= \frac{1}{2}k\,(x_0/3)^2$

Taking the ratio, one finds that the fraction left is $\frac{1}{9}$.

15 ☐ 2.23 Hz

$k = \frac{mg}{x}$ (Hooke's Law)

$$\text{Resonance frequency} = \frac{1}{2\pi}\sqrt{\frac{k}{m}} = \frac{1}{2\pi}\sqrt{\frac{g}{x}} = \frac{1}{2\pi}\sqrt{\frac{9.8}{0.05}} = 2.23 \text{ Hz}$$

a

16 ☐ 15 cm

The energy stored in the system when the new mass is added is still the energy of the spring $\frac{1}{2}k(0.15)^2$. Since the system energy has not changed, the maximum energy stored in the spring must still be the same and so x_0 will not change.

17 ☐ 0.076

At the instant the extra load is added, the energy is completely potential. The masses then fall, stretching the spring further. Eventually they rise and come to a stop at this point once again. Therefore, this point is the top of the new oscillation. Let us compute the equilibrium positions under the two loads at rest. From $F = ky$, they are y_1 = 19.6/200 = 0.098 and y_2 = 34.3/200 = 0.171 m. The new amplitude is therefore y_1 + 0.15 - y_2 = 0.076 m.

18 For such a system the forces acting on the mass are $-kx$ and $-\eta(dx/dt)$. Equating through $F = ma$ gives

$$-kx - \eta\frac{dx}{dt} = ma$$

If the viscosity coefficient η is very large, then ma will be negligible and so

$$-kx = \eta\left(\frac{dx}{dt}\right) = \eta v.$$

19 In the previous problem, show that $x = x_0 \exp\left(-\frac{k}{\eta} t\right)$.

19 This is done by integrating the above relation, namely

$$\frac{dx}{dt} = -\frac{k}{\eta}x$$

Rearranging gives

$$\frac{dx}{x} = -\frac{k}{\eta}t$$

Integrating each side for the limits x_0 to x and 0 to t gives

$$\ell n\, x - \ell n\, x_o = \ell n\, \frac{x}{x_o}$$

Taking antilogs gives the desired result.

a

13
answer
19

14 continuum mechanics

1 Indicate which of the following ordinary substances should be classified in each category—solid, liquid, gas, fluid: ice, water, air, oil, syrup, perfume vapor, an iron bar, mercury.

2 Granulated sugar can, for many purposes, be considered a fluid. Why? If air is blown up uniformly through a layer of granulated sugar, a "fluidized bed" of sugar is obtained. What properties of the fluid are markedly changed by the air flowing through it?

3 The density of uranium is 18.7 g/cm^3. How much would a cube of uranium 10 cm on a side weigh? Express your answer in both newtons and pounds.

4 All humans come very close to being able to float in water. About what is the volume (in m^3) of a 70-kg (155 lb) man?

5 Avogadro's number (6.02×10^{26}) is the number of particles in 1 kg-mole of the substance. One kg-mole is the mass in kilograms equal numerically to the molecular (or particle) weight of the substance. Find the mass of a uranium atom. The atomic mass of uranium is 238.

6 Young's modulus for an aluminum wire is 6×10^{10} N/m^2. How much will a 3-m-long aluminum wire stretch under a load of 5 kg if the diameter of the wire is 1.0 mm?

1 Solids → ice, iron
Liquids → water, oil, syrup, mercury
Gases → air, perfume vapor
Fluids → water, air, oil, syrup, perfume vapor, mercury

2 The fine particles of sugar flow under the action of gravity in such a way as to behave much like water, for example. In a fluidized bed, the viscous forces between the particles are reduced in effectiveness by the motion of the particles caused by the air. Both the viscosity and the density are reduced by the flow.

3 □ 183 N; 41 lb

By definition, density = mass/volume. In the present case, the mass is

mass = (volume)(density) = $(1000\ \text{cm}^3)(18.7\ \text{g/cm}^3) = 18700\ \text{g} = 18.7\ \text{kg}$

Using weight = mg gives the weight to be 183 N. Since 1 N = 0.225 lb, the weight is 41 lb.

a

4 □ $7 \times 10^{-2}\ \text{m}^3$

Since humans nearly float, their densities are close to that of water, $1000\ \text{kg/m}^3$. Using $\rho = m/V$ gives $V = m/\rho = 70 \times 10^{-3}\ \text{m}^3$.

5 □ 3.95×10^{-25} kg

14
questions
1-6

In 238 kg of uranium there are 6.02×10^{26} atoms. Hence

mass per atom = $(238\ \text{kg})/(6.02 \times 10^{26}\ \text{atoms}) = 3.95 \times 10^{-25}\ \text{kg}$.

6 □ 3.1×10^{-3} m

By definition of Y, Young's modulus,

$(F/A)/(\Delta L/L) = Y$ and so $\Delta L = L(F/A)/Y$

Using $F = mg = (5\ \text{kg})(9.8\ \text{m/sec}^2) = 49\ \text{N}$

$A = \pi d^2/4 = \pi(1 \times 10^{-3}\ \text{m})^2/4 = 0.785 \times 10^{-6}\ \text{m}^2$ and $L = 3\text{m}$

gives $\Delta L = 3.1 \times 10^{-3}$ m.

7 How large a pressure is required to compress a cube of rubber to 90 percent of its original volume? Compare this pressure to atmospheric pressure. The compressibility of rubber is $40 \times 10^{-11}\ m^2/N$.

8 Glucose (one form of sugar) has a viscosity at room temperature of about 10^{14} cP. Estimate the time it would take for a 2-cm-diameter sphere of glucose placed on a flat surface to flow flat onto the surface. Express your answer in years. (Assume a 2-cm sphere of water would require about 1 sec to flow flat.)

9 The viscosity of a certain motor oil at room temperature is about 2 P, while at $-40^\circ F$ it is 500 P. Compare the force needed to move a piston lubricated by this oil at the lower temperature to that required at the higher temperature.

10 Find the pressure 1609 m (i.e., 1 mi) deep in the ocean due to the water. Use the specific gravity of sea water to be about 1.02. Express your answer in both N/m^2 and atmospheres.

11 In a particular city in the Rocky Mountains, the normal pressure is about 59 cm of mercury. Express this pressure in N/m^2 and in atm. Make use of the fact that the density of Hg is $13600\ kg/m^3$.

7 ☐ 2.5×10^8 N/m^2; 2500 times greater

By the definition of the compressibility k, $\Delta V/V = Pk$. In our case $\Delta V/V$ is 0.10 or 10 percent. Therefore,

$$P = (0.10)/(40 \times 10^{-11}\ \text{m}^2/\text{N}) = 2.5 \times 10^8\ \text{N/m}^2$$

But atmospheric pressure is 1×10^5 N/m^2, so this pressure is 2500 times greater.

8 ☐ 10^6 years

The viscosity of water is about 1 cP, while that of glucose is 10^{14} cP. It will therefore take glucose about 10^{14} times longer than water. Therefore,

$$\text{Time} = 10^{14}\ \text{sec} = 10^{14}/(3.2 \times 10^7\ \text{sec/yr}) \cong 3.2 \times 10^6\ \text{years}$$

9 ☐ 250 times greater

Assuming the movement to occur at the same speed in the two cases, and since $F \sim \eta v$, we find that the needed force increases in proportion to the viscosity. Hence the force at the lower temperature is 250 times greater.

a

10 ☐ 1.6×10^7 N/m^2; 160 atm

Using the basic equation $P = \rho g h$ we have (since $\rho = 1.02 \times 1.00 \times 10^3$ kg/m^3)

$$P = (1.02 \times 10^3\ \text{kg/m}^3)(9.8\ \text{m/s}^2)(1609\ \text{m}) = 1.6 \times 10^7\ \text{N/m}^2$$

$$= (1.6 \times 10^7\ \text{N/m}^2)/(1 \times 10^5\ \text{N/m}^2/\text{atm}) = 160\ \text{atmospheres}$$

11 ☐ 7.9×10^4 N/m^2; 0.78 atm

This terminology means that the air pressure is equivalent to the pressure due to a height of Hg equal to 59 cm. Then

$$P = \rho g h = (13600\ \text{kg/m}^3)(0.59\ \text{m})(9.8\ \text{m/sec}^2) = 7.86 \times 10^4\ \text{N/m}^2$$

$$= (7.86 \times 10^4\ \text{N/m}^2)/(1.01 \times 10^5\ \text{N/m}^2/\text{atm}) = 0.78\ \text{atmospheres}$$

12 A glass U-tube is partly filled with mercury ($\rho = 13600 \text{ kg/m}^3$). After pouring some oil onto the mercury in one side of the tube, the length of the oil column is 30.0 cm, while the top of the mercury column on one side is 1.80 cm higher than on the other. Find the density of the oil.

13 Consider an air bubble in water. Assuming the bubble to have a volume of 2.0 cm^3 and the density of air within it to be 1.3 kg/m^3, find the buoyant force on the bubble and its upward acceleration if viscous forces can be neglected.

14 A block of metal weighs 26.00 g in air, 18.00 g in water and 17.00 g in an unknown fluid. What is the density of the fluid?

15 Leading from the end of a large water pipe (diameter = 25 cm) is a small pipe with diameter 2.5 cm. If water flows out the small pipe with a speed of 100 cm/sec, how much water flows out each second and how fast is the water moving in the large pipe? Assume both pipes to be completely full.

12 □ 816 kg/m^3

Apparently 30.0 cm of oil is balanced by 1.80 cm of Hg. Hence the pressures due to these heights are equal. Then

$$\rho_{oil} h_{oil} g = \rho_{Hg} h_{Hg} g$$

gives

$$\rho_{oil} = (13600 \text{ kg/m}^3)(1.80/30) = 816 \text{ kg/m}^3$$

13 □ 19.6×10^{-3} N; 7.5×10^3 m/sec^2

The bubble displaces 2×10^{-6} m^3 of water. Since the density of water is 1000 kg/m^3, the mass of water displaced is 2×10^{-3} kg. According to Archimedes, the buoyant force is the weight of this mass, 19.6×10^{-3} N. To find the acceleration, we need to determine the net force on the bubble. The air mass in it is $(1.3 \text{ kg/m}^3)(2 \times 10^{-6} \text{ m}^3) = 2.6 \times 10^{-6}$ kg. Its weight is mg or 25×10^{-6} N. The net upward force on the bubble is $19.6 \times 10^{-3} - 2.5 \times 10^{-5}$. Then from $F = ma$,

$$a = (19.6 \times 10^{-3} \text{ N}/2.6 \times 10^{-6} \text{ kg}) = 7.5 \times 10^3 \text{ m/sec}^2$$

Of course, as soon as the bubble starts to move, viscosity effects will become important.

a

14

questions

12-15

14 □ 1125 kg/m^3

The buoyant force in water is $(26 - 18) \times 10^{-3} \times 9.8$ N. This is the weight of the displaced water, which can also be represented as mg or ρVg where $\rho = 10^3$ kg/m^3 and V is the volume displaced. Equating gives

$$8 \times 10^{-3} \times 9.8 = 10^3 V(9.8) \qquad \text{or} \qquad V = 8 \times 10^{-6} \text{ m}^3$$

The weight of the displaced fluid is $(26 - 17) \times 10^{-3} \times 9.8$ N and this is equal to $\rho_f Vg$. We found V above so equating gives

$$\rho_f (8 \times 10^{-6})(9.8) = (9 \times 10^{-3})(9.8) \qquad \text{or} \qquad \rho_f = 1125 \text{ kg/m}^3$$

15 □ 491 cm^3; 1 cm/sec

A cylinder of water 100 cm long and diameter 2.5 cm flows out each second. Therefore, the volume per second is

$$[\pi(2.5 \text{ cm})^2/4](100 \text{ cm}) = 491 \text{ cm}^3$$

From the equation of continuity, since ρ is constant, $v_1 A_1 = v_2 A_2$ and so $v_2 = (100 \text{ cm/sec})(2.5/25)^2 = 1.0$ cm/sec.

16 Show that, for streamline flow, as a sphere is pulled through a fluid, the work done against viscous forces increases as the square of the flow speed.

17 A long cylindrical drum (radius = 20 cm) spins on its axis at a rate of 5 rev/sec. It is immersed in a large vat of water. Find the pressure difference between a point close to the drum and far from the drum.

18 Oil (ρ = 800 kg/m^3) in a pipe is maintained at a pressure of 3 atm above the water in a surrounding tank. If the oil pipe springs a leak (area of opening = 2.0 mm^2), with what speed will the oil leak into the tank? How much oil will leak out each minute?

16 Call the friction force holding the sphere back f. Now the friction force is, for streamline flow, proportional to ηv. During unit time, the force pulling the sphere pulls it a distance v. Therefore, the work done per unit time by the applied force is fv which is proportional to v^2.

17 ☐ Zero

One must recall that Bernoulli's equation applies to points in a single flow tube. The two points we are concerned with are *not* in the same flow tube. Therefore, Bernoulli's equation does not apply. Note, however, that no motion occurs in the radial direction from the cylinder. Therefore, except for a small centripetal force effect, no unbalanced force occurs in this direction. From this, no appreciable radial variation in pressure occurs.

18 ☐ 866 m/sec; 0.10 m^3

According to Bernoulli's equation,

$$P_o + \rho_o gh + \frac{1}{2}\rho_o v_o^2 = P_w + \rho_o gh + \frac{1}{2}\rho_o v^2$$

Note we are concerned with a stream of oil and so all densities are that of oil. To find the jet velocity v we solve (letting $v_o = 0$)

$$v = \sqrt{2(P_o - P_w)/\rho_o}$$

But $P_o - P_w = 3$ atm $= 3 \times 10^5$ N/m^2. So $v = \sqrt{(2)(3 \times 10^5)/0.80} = 866$ m/sec. To find the flow rate, a volume of cylinder of length 866 m and area 2×10^{-6} m^2 will flow out each second. Therefore, the loss per minute is $(866)(2 \times 10^{-6})(60) = 0.10$ m^3.

a

14
questions
16-18

15 ideal gases

1 What is the physical basis for the fact that gas exerts pressure?

2 In deriving the relation for gas pressure, the impulse due to a molecule hitting a wall in the yz plane is given by $2m_0v_{ix}$. Why does the factor 2 appear?

3 According to the kinetic theory, of what molecular quantity is gas pressure a measure?

4 Change the following temperatures to Fahrenheit temperatures: 30°C and −40°C.

5 Change 100°F and -80°F to centigrade temperatures.

6 An auto tire is filled to a gauge pressure of 30.0 psi on a day when the temperature of the tire is 20°C. Find the gauge pressure in the tire when the tire temperature has risen to 100°C.

1 Gas pressure is the cumulative effect of the collisions of the gas molecules with the container wall.

2 It is assumed that the molecule rebounds elastically so that its x momentum changes from $m_o v_{ix}$ to $-m_o v_{ix}$. The change in momentum, and therefore the impulse, is equal to $2m_o v_{ix}$.

3 Pressure measures the translational kinetic energy of the molecules in unit volume. Specifically, $P = \frac{2}{3}K_{\text{trans}}$.

4 ☐ 86°F; -40°F

Since $\frac{9}{5}$ Fahrenheit degrees are equivalent to 1 centigrade degree, and since 0°C is the freezing point of water, 30°C is 30 X $\frac{9}{5}$ Fahrenheit degrees above freezing. Since the freezing point of water is 32°F, one has 30°C → 32 + 54 = 86°F. Similarly, for -40°C → $32 - 40\left(\frac{9}{5}\right) = -40$°F. At this particular temperature, the two scales have the same numerical value.

a

15
answers
1-6

5 ☐ 37.8°C; -62.2°C

100°F is 100 - 32 = 68 F degrees above freezing. Therefore

100°F → $0 + 68 \cdot \frac{5}{9} = 37.8$°C. Similarly -80°F → $0 - 112 \cdot \frac{5}{9} = 62.2$°C since -80°F is (32 + 80) or 112 F degrees below freezing.

6 ☐ 42.2 psi

First one must note that tire gauges read the difference between atmospheric and tire pressure. Since atmospheric pressure is about 14.7 psi, the original tire pressure was 44.7 psi. Writing the gas law twice, once for the initial and once for the final conditions, gives $P_o V_o = \frac{m}{M} R T_o$ and $P_1 V_1 = \frac{m}{M} R T_1$. Taking the ratio of the two equations and since $V_o = V_1$ and $T_o = 273 + 20$°K and $T_1 = 373$°K, one finds

$P_1 = P_o \frac{373}{293} = 56.9$ psi

Subtracting atmospheric pressure gives the gauge reading.

7 A container of gas has a volume V_0 and pressure P_0. If the gas is compressed to a volume $V_0/10$, what will be its pressure when it returns to its original temperature?

8 A gas at 27°C is heated and compressed in such a way that its volume is halved and its pressure tripled. Find its final temperature.

9 A mixture of 1 mole of chlorine gas and 1 mole of hydrogen gas is originally at pressure P_0 in a closed tank. After complete reaction as follows:

$$H_2 + Cl_2 \rightarrow 2HCl$$

find the final pressure if the original and final temperature are the same and high enough so that the HCl vapor behaves as an ideal gas.

10 Find the rms speed of mercury atoms in mercury vapor at 327°C.

11 If 0.030 g of water is sealed in a 20-cm^3 tube and heated to 427°C, find the water vapor pressure inside the tube. (Assume it to be an ideal gas at this temperature.) Express your answer in atmospheres.

7 ☐ $10P_0$

As before, we write the gas law twice:

$$P_0 V_0 = \frac{m}{M} R T_0 \text{ and } P_1 \frac{V_0}{10} = \frac{m}{M} R T_1$$

Since $T_1 = T_0$, the ratio of these two equations gives $P_1 = 10P$

8 ☐ 177°C

As before,

$$P_0 V_0 = \frac{m}{M} R T_0 \qquad \text{and} \qquad 3P_0 \frac{V_0}{2} = \frac{m}{M} R T_1$$

Taking ratios,

$$T_1 = \frac{3}{2} T_0 = \frac{3}{2}(273 + 27) = 450°\text{K}$$

a

15
answers
7-11

9 ☐ P_0

Since $P = (m/M)RT/V$, the original pressure was $P_0 = RT/V + RT/V$ due to the Cl_2 and H_2, respectively. The final pressure will be $P = (2)RT/V$, since there are now 2 moles of HCl vapor. Combining these two relations gives $P = P_0$.

10 ☐ 273 m/sec

One has $v_{rms} = \sqrt{3RT/M}$. (See Bueche, Eq. 15.6.) In our case, $M = 201$ kg/kg-mole, $R = 8314$ J/(kg-mole)°K, and $T = 600$°K so $v = 273$ m/sec. One usually remembers the relation 15.7 rather than 15.6, namely

$$K_{trans} = \frac{3}{2} kT$$

11 ☐ 4.8 atm

Using the gas law $PV = (m/M)RT$ and since $m = 0.030 \times 10^{-3}$ kg, $M = 18$ kg/kg-mole, and $T = 700$°K, one has $P = 4.8 \times 10^5$ N/m^2. But one atmosphere is 1.01×10^5 N/m^2 and so this is 4.9 atm.

12 A beam of mercury vapor atoms is shot at a small disk. If the speed of the atoms is 400 m/sec and if they stick to the disk when they hit, what force does the beam exert on the disk? (A mass of 2×10^{-6} g strikes the disk each second.)

13 At what temperature would the rms speed of hydrogen *atoms* in hydrogen gas be 0.10 the speed of light?

14 In a gas, what is the ratio of the number of gas molecules with the rms speed to those having 10 times this speed?

15 The probability distributions for sand particles in a can half filled with sand is shown on the graph. The coordinate y is measured from the bottom of the can. Discuss the meaning of $P(y)$ and find $\langle y \rangle$.

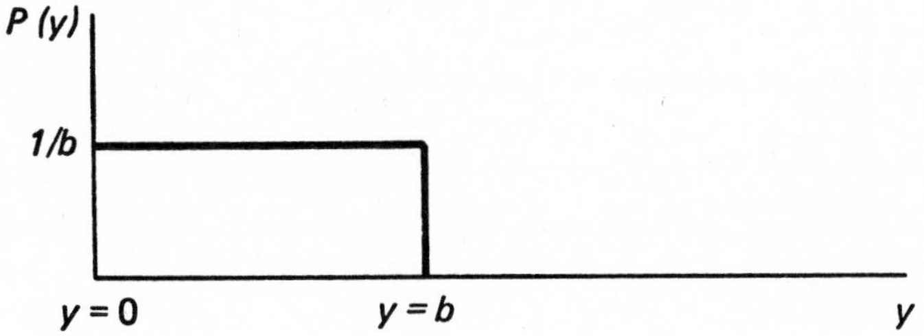

q

15
questions
12-15

12 □ 8×10^{-7} N

The atoms exert an impulse as they strike and stick to the disk. Since the final speed of the atoms is zero, the change in momentum of a mass m of atoms is mv_0. From the definition of impulse, $Ft = mv_0$ or $F = v_0 \frac{m}{t}$. But $\frac{m}{t}$ is the mass striking the disk each second, 2×10^{-9} kg and $v_0 = 400$ m/sec and so the force is 8×10^{-7} N.

13 □ 3.6×10^{10} °K

We know that $K_{trans} = \frac{3}{2} kT$ and that $K_{trans} = \frac{1}{2} m_0 v^2$, where m_0 is the mass of a hydrogen atom. Since the atomic mass of hydrogen is unity, $m_0 = 1/(6 \times 10^{26})$ kg. (Recall that one atomic mass in kilograms contains 6×10^{26} atoms.) Using $k = 1.38 \times 10^{-23}$ J/°K and $v = 0.10 \times 3 \times 10^8$ m/sec gives $T = 3.6 \times 10^{10}$ °K.

14 □ 8.4×10^{62}

a

According to the Maxwell distribution,

$$P(v) = Av^2 \exp \frac{-m_0 v^2}{2kT}$$

where A is a constant. We are interested in the cases $v = v_{rms}$ and $10v_{rms}$ with $\frac{3}{2}kT = \frac{1}{2}m_0 v^2_{rms}$. Putting in these values to give two values for P, namely $P(v_{rms})$ and $P(10v_{rms})$, and taking the ratio gives $\left(\frac{1}{100}\right) e^{149.5}$ which is 8.4×10^{62}. In other words, only 1.2×10^{-63} as many molecules have a speed $10v_{rms}$ compared to those with speeds v_{rms}.

15
answers
12-15

15 □ $\frac{b}{2}$

$P(y)$ shows that the sand is of uniform density from $y = 0$ to $y = b$. Above $y = b$ the can is empty and so $P(y)$ drops to zero. To find $\langle y \rangle$, we use the defining equation for the average in terms of a distribution function, $P(y)$, recalling that $P(y) = 0$ for $y > b$. Then

$$\langle y \rangle = \int_0^{\infty} yP(y)\, dy = \int_0^b yP(y)\, dy = \int_0^b y(1/b)\, dy$$

$$= \frac{1}{b}\int_0^b y\, dy = \frac{1}{b}\frac{b^2}{2} = \frac{b}{2}$$

We find the average height of the sand particles to be in the middle, as we would expect.

16 Prove that $P(y)$ given in the previous example is normalized.

17 Show that the distribution function (or probability distribution) for particles as a function of height can be written as

$$P(y) = \frac{m_0 g}{kT} \exp \frac{-m_0 g y}{kT}$$

where m_0 is the mass of a particle.

18 If the law of atmospheres were exact, how high above the earth would one have to go in order to find the pressure reduced to $\frac{1}{2}$ atm?

15
questions
16-18

16 To be normalized, the following must be true: $\int_0^{\infty} P(y)\,dy = 1$. Placing in the value

$$\int_0^{\infty} P(y)\,dy = \int_0^{b} \frac{1}{b}\,dy = \frac{1}{b}\int_0^{b} dy = 1$$

and so the normalization condition is fulfilled.

17 The Maxwell-Boltzmann distribution gave the relation

$$n = n_0 \exp \frac{-(m_0 g y)}{kT}$$

where n_0 is the number of particles at $y = 0$. Since the probability of a particle being at a height y is proportional to n, we have

$$P(y) \sim n \sim \exp \frac{-(m_0 g y)}{kT}$$

Or, using a proportionality constant A

$$P(y) = A \exp \frac{-(m_0 g y)}{kT}$$

To find A we make use of the normalizing condition $\int_0^{\infty} P(y)\,dy = 1$ to find

$$1 = A\int_0^{\infty} \exp \frac{-(m_0 g)y}{kT}\,dy = A\,\frac{kT}{m_0 g}$$

a

15

answers

16-18

from which $A = m_0 g/kT$ and the proof is complete.

18 ☐ 6300 m

According to the law of atmospheres,

$$P/P_0 = \exp \frac{-mgy}{kT}$$

Assuming the air to be mostly nitrogen, $m = 28/(6 \times 10^{26})$ kg. Setting $P/P_0 = 0.50$, $g = 9.8\ \text{m/sec}^2$, $k = 1.38 \times 10^{-23}$ J/°K, and $T = 300$°K, one finds $0.50 = e^{-0.00011y}$ from which $y = 6300$ m

19 Estimate the linear size of a water molecule (assumed cubical) from the fact that the density of water is 1 g/cm^3.

q

15
question
19

19 □ 3×10^{-8} cm

One gram of water contains $(6 \times 10^{23}/18) = \frac{1}{3} \times 10^{23}$ molecules of water. Since 1 g occupies 1 cm^3, the total volume of these molecules must be 1 cm^3. Then $\frac{1}{3} \times 10^{23} \times V = 1\ cm^3$, where V is the volume of a molecule. If b is the cube edge, then $V = 3 \times 10^{-23}\ cm^3 = b^3$. Solving for b, one finds $b = 3.1 \times 10^{-8}$ cm and this is a measure of the diameter of the molecule.

a

15
answer
19

16 thermal properties of matter

1 When heat flows from one object to another, what is happening on a molecular scale?

2 What physical quantity does the calorie measure? How is it related to mechanical units?

3 Define specific heat capacity c.

4 How many calories of heat are required to raise the temperature of 200 g of iron by 30°C?

5 How much ice at 0°C would the iron of the previous problem melt as it cools?

6 A room $5 \times 5 \times 4\ m^3$ is filled with N_2 at STP. How much heat is needed to change the temperature of this gas by 10°C?

q

16 questions 1-8

7 Estimate the heat required to change the temperature of a 220-lb man by 1°C and compare with the result of problem 6.

8 (a) Under constant-volume conditions, heat added to a monatomic gas appears as the __________ of the molecules.

(b) The temperature of a gas in terms of the molecular kinetic energy (KE) is given by T = __________, where m is the mass of each of the molecules.

(c) Since the average kinetic energy of a molecule is __________, an increase of 1°C in the temperature will cause an increase of __________ J in the average molecular energy.

(d) Since k, Boltzmann's constant, is $(1.38)(10^{-23})$ J/°K, the energy per molecule needed to raise the temperature of a monatomic gas 1°C is _____ J or __________ cal.

(e) There are $(6.0)(10^{23})$ molecules in 1 gram-atomic weight of a substance, and so the heat energy needed to raise the temperature of 1 gram-atomic weight of monatomic gas molecules by 1°C is __________ cal.

1 Kinetic energy due to the random thermal motion of the molecules is being taken from the hot body and given to the cooler body.

2 The calorie is an energy unit and it measures thermal kinetic energy. One calorie = 4.184 J.

3 $c = \Delta Q/m\Delta T$ where ΔQ is the heat energy required to change the temperature of a mass m of a substance by an amount ΔT. Its units are, commonly, cal/g°C.

4 ☐ 660 cal

We make use of $\Delta Q = cm\Delta T$, the defining equation for c. The value found for iron in tables of specific heats is $c = 0.11$ cal/g°C and so $\Delta Q = (0.11)(200)(30)$ cal.

5 ☐ 8.25 g

Each gram of ice requires 80 cal to melt it. Therefore $m = 660$ cal/80 cal/g.

a

6 ☐ 2.21×10^5 cal

The volume of the room is 100 m^3. We know that at STP one mole (28 g) of nitrogen occupies 22.4 liters = 0.0224 m^3. Therefore the room has (28 g) X (100/0.0224) = 1.25×10^5 g of N_2. Since for nitrogen $c = 0.177$ cal/g°C $\Delta Q = cm\,\Delta T = (0.177)(1.25 \times 10^5)(10)$ cal.

16
answers
1-8

7 ☐ 10^4 cal; $\sim\frac{1}{3}$

A 220-lb man has a mass of about 100 kg. He is composed mainly of water and organic material. Assuming reasonable values, his combined c must be in the range 0.5 to 1 cal/g°C. Taking it to be 0.8 cal/g°C, we have $Q = (0.8$ cal/g°C$) \times (1 \times 10^5$ g$)(1°$C$) = 8 \times 10^4$ cal, which is about one-third of the previous result.

8 (a) Translational KE;

(b) $\left(\frac{2}{3k}\right)\left(\frac{1}{2}mv^2\right)$;

(c) $\frac{3}{2}kT$, $\frac{3}{2}k\,(T+1) - \frac{3}{2}kT = \frac{3}{2}k$;

(d) 2.07×10^{-23}, 4.94×10^{-24}, (e) 3.0.

9 A 20-g copper calorimeter contains 100 g of water, all at 30.0°C. Into this is poured 40 g of glass beads which have been heated to a temperature of 100.0°C. If the final temperature of the mixture is 34.0°C, what is the specific heat capacity for the glass?

10 A copper calorimeter (water equivalent = 5.0 g) contains 40 g of oil at 50.0°C. When 100 g of lead at 30.0°C is added to this, the final temperature is 48.0°C. What is the specific heat capacity of the oil?

11 How much water at 20°C is needed to just melt 500 g of mercury at -39°C?

12 How much heat is required to heat a mass m of monatomic ideal gas from 27°C to 227°C at constant volume?

13 Suppose in the case of the gas of the previous problem that P is maintained at 1 atm. Find the heat required in that case.

14 Compute the external work done in the previous example. Do it in two different ways.

9 ☐ **0.154 cal/g°C**

From the law of conservation of energy

heat lost by beads = heat gained by water + can

$c\,(40)\,(100 - 34) = (1)\,(100)\,(34 - 30) + (0.093)\,(20)\,(34 - 30)$

where appropriate c values are used. Solving gives $c = 0.154$ cal/g°C.

10 ☐ 0.57 cal/g°C)

Heat lost by can and oil = heat gained by lead. $(1)\,(5)\,(50 - 48) + c\,(40)\,(50 - 48) = (0.031)\,(100)\,(48 - 30)$. Notice, the can is equivalent to 5 g of water.

11 ☐ 11.7 g

The water loses heat in three ways: cooling to 0°C, changing to ice, cooling as ice from 0° to -39°C. This must equal heat needed to melt 500 g of mercury (500 g X 2.8 cal/g, where 2.8 cal/g is the heat of fusion for Hg).

$(1)\,(m)\,(20) + (80)\,(m) + (0.50)\,(m)\,(39) = (500)\,(2.8)$

a

16
answers
9-14

12 ☐ $300R \dfrac{m}{M_0}$

The heat required is $cm\Delta T$ which is $\Delta Q = (cM_0)\,(m/M_0)\,(200^\circ K)$ where M_0 is the atomic weight of the gas. Since $cM_0 = C$ and since $C = C_v$, in this case one has $\Delta Q = 200 C_v\,(m/M_0)$. For a monatomic gas $C_v = \frac{3}{2}R$ and so $\Delta Q = 300R\,\dfrac{m}{M_0}$.

13 ☐ $500R \dfrac{m}{M_0}$

We are now interested in C_P for a monatomic gas. In this case $C_P = C_v + R$ and so $\Delta Q = (200)\,(\frac{5}{2})\,R\,(m/M_0)$. Notice that P is not needed as long as it is constant.

14 ☐ $200R \dfrac{m}{M_0}$

The simplest way is to subtract the result of problem 12 from the answer to 13. This gives W since the difference in ΔQ in the two cases represents the external work. We can also compute W directly from the fact that $dW = P\,dV$. In our case, since P is constant,

$$W = \int dW = \int P\,dV = P \int dV = P(V - V_0)$$

Now, from the gas law, $V_0 = (m/M_0)\,RT_0/P$
and $V = (m/M_0)\,RT/P$ from which

$$W = P(V - V_0) = \frac{m}{M_0}\,R\,(T - T_0) = 200\;R\frac{m}{M_0}$$

15 One mole of O_2 gas and two moles of H_2 gas are confined to a fixed volume. They are reacted to obtain two moles of H_2O gas. Compare the specific heat capacities of the gases before and after combustion. (For H_2 at 15°C, C_P = 6.78 cal/g atom and γ = 1.410.)

16 A block of iron has the following dimensions at 0°C: 20.000 X 5.000 X 3.000 cm^3. Find its length and volume at 100°C.

17 Correct α for the difference between 0°C and 20°C in the previous problem and find L at 100°C.

18 An asbestos sheet 0.20 cm thick is used as a spacer between two brass plates, one at 100°C and the other at 20°C. How much heat flows through 1 m^2 of area from one plate to the other in 1 hr?

15 ☐ $\frac{C}{C_0} = 0.89$

Before combustion one has

$$\Delta Q = C_{vO_2}\,\Delta T + 2C_{vH_2}\,\Delta T$$

and after combustion

$$\Delta Q = 2C_{vH_2O}\,\Delta T$$

The ratio of the specific heat capacities will be

$$\frac{\Delta Q}{\Delta T}\bigg/\frac{\Delta Q_0}{\Delta T} = \frac{2C_{vH_2O}}{(C_{vO_2} + 2C_{vH_2})}$$

Using values from table 16.3 of Bueche, this is 0.89.

16 ☐ 20.024 cm; 301.1 cm^3

We make use of $\Delta L/L = \alpha\,\Delta T$ and $\Delta V/V = \gamma\Delta T$. Since the difference in α and γ at 0°C and 20°C will be negligible, we use the values from table 16.6 of Bueche or any similar table for α and γ: Then

$$\Delta L = (20)\,(100)\,(12 \times 10^{-6}) = 2.4 \times 10^{-2}\ \text{cm}$$

Similarly for ΔV.

a

16

answers

15-18

17 ☐ 20.024 cm

First find L_{20} by use of $\Delta L/L_{20} = \alpha_{20}\Delta T$.

$$L_{20} - L_0 = L_{20}\,\alpha_{20}\,\Delta T$$

from which

$$L_{20} - 20.000 = L_{20}\,(12 \times 10^{-6})\,(20)$$

and therefore $L_{20} = 20.0048$. Then using $L_{100} - L_{20} = L_{20}\,\alpha_{20}\,\Delta T$ one finds $L_{100} = 20.024$ cm within the allowed number of significant figures.

18 ☐ 7.2 $\times$ 10^6 cal

The heat flow equation for a parallel plate device is given by $\Delta Q = (\Delta t)\,\frac{\lambda A}{L}\,\Delta T$. Since λ in this case is 5×10^{-4} (cal/sec) /°C/cm, one has, using the proper units,

$$\Delta Q = (60 \times 60)\,\frac{5 \times 10^{-4} \times 10^{+4}}{0.20}\,(80)\ \text{cal}$$

19 A glass rod 30 cm long is sealed to a brass rod 10 cm long. Both rods have cross-sectional areas of 4.0 cm^2. If the end of the brass rod is maintained at 0°C and the distant end of the glass rod is at 100°C, find the heat flow along the rod and find the temperature at the junction. (Ignore heat loss from the sides of the rods.)

q

16
question
19

19 ☐ 0.027 cal/sec; 0.33° C

$\Delta Q/\Delta t$ must be the same for both the brass and glass rods once equilibrium is achieved since heat energy cannot build up further along the rods. Then

$$\frac{\lambda_B A}{L_B}(T_j - 0) = \frac{\lambda_G A}{L_G}(100 - T_j)$$

where T_j is the junction temperature. Since table 16.7 of Bueche or any similar table gives the λ's, one can solve for T_j to find $T_j = 0.33°\text{C}$. Notice that nearly all the temperature drop occurs along the glass rod. We can now find $\Delta Q/\Delta t = (\lambda_B A/L_B) \times (T_j - 0)$ and it is 0.027 cal/sec.

a

16
answer
19

17 thermo-dynamics

1 Write an equation which expresses the first law of thermodynamics. Define each quantity in it.

2 Two liters of ideal gas confined to a cylinder by a piston expands to three liters when heat is added. If the pressure on the piston is atmospheric, how much work was done by the gas?

3 By how much does the internal energy of a gas change as 200 cal of heat is added to it if the gas is maintained at constant volume? Where does the energy go if the gas is ideal and monatomic? Diatomic?

4 By how much does the internal energy of n moles of a gas change as it expands isothermally from V_0 to V against a piston which originally confined the gas at pressure P_0?

5 In the previous problem, how much work did the gas do and how much heat was added to the gas? Assume the process to be reversible.

6 The pressure and volume of an ideal gas behave as shown during an expansion from A to B. How much work was done by the gas in the process?

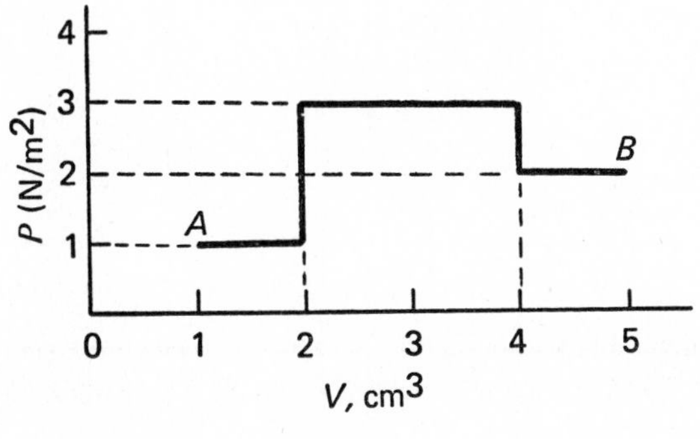

q

17
questions
1-6

1 $\Delta U = đQ - \Delta W$

ΔU = increase in internal energy of system

ΔW = work done *by* the system

$đQ$ = heat which flowed *into* the system.

2 ☐ 101 J

We have $dW = P\,dV$ and so $W = \int P\,dV = P(V - V_0)$, since P is constant. But $V_0 = 2 \times 10^3\ \text{cm}^3 = 2 \times 10^{-3}\ \text{m}^3$ and $V = 3 \times 10^{-3}\ \text{m}^3$ while $P = 1.01 \times 10^5\ \text{N/m}^2$. $W = 101$ J.

3 ☐ 837 J

From the first law, $\Delta U = đQ - \Delta W$. Since $\Delta W = 0$ in this case, $\Delta U = đQ = 200$ cal = 837 J. For a monatomic gas, the energy goes to increased translational kinetic energy. In the case of a diatomic gas, it goes to translational and rotational and vibrational energy.

a

4 ☐ Zero

Since the gas is assumed ideal, its internal energy could change only if the kinetic energies of its molecules changed. Since T is constant, the molecular kinetic energy is constant and so $\Delta U = 0$.

17
answers
1-6

5 ☐ $P_0 V_0 \ln \frac{V}{V_0}$

Since $W = \int P\,dV$, we can substitute for P from the ideal gas law to find

$$W = \int_{V_0}^{V} \frac{nRT}{V}\,dV = nRT \int_{V_0}^{V} \frac{dV}{V} = nRT \ln \frac{V}{V_0}$$

Since $P_0 V_0 = nRT$, this can be rewritten as above. We find $\Delta W = đQ$ in this case since $\Delta U = 0$.

6 ☐ 9×10^{-6} J

The work done is equal to the area under the curve. It was $W = 1 \cdot 1 + 3 \cdot 2 + 2 \cdot 1\ (\text{N/m}^2)(\text{cm}^3)$. Or $W = 9\ \text{N-cm}^3/\text{m}^2 = 9 \times 10^{-6}\ \text{N-m} = 9 \times 10^{-6}$ J.

7 An ideal gas originally at pressure P_0 is adiabatically compressed to one-third its original volume. Find the ratio T/T_0 of its final to its original temperature. (γ = 1.40 for this gas.) Also find P/P_0.

8 It is desired to ignite a gas at 1000°C by compressing it adiabatically from 27°C. By what ratio must its volume be changed? Use γ = 1.40.

7 □ 1.56; 4.7

In an adiabatic change, $P_1V_1^\gamma = P_2V_2^\gamma$ and $T_1V_1^{\gamma-1} = T_2V_2^{\gamma-1}$. Using the latter relation, one finds $T/T_0 = (3)^{\gamma-1} = (3)^{0.40}$. To evaluate this we note that log $(T/T_0) = 0.40 \log (3) = 0.192$. Thus $T/T_0 = \text{antilog } (0.192) = 1.56$. To find P/P_0 we use the gas law (since $P = nRT/V$) to give $\frac{P}{P_0} = \frac{T}{T_0}\frac{V_0}{V} = (1.56)(3) = 4.7$.

8 □ $\frac{V}{V_0} = 0.027$

We have, for an adiabatic change, $T_1V_1^{\gamma-1} = T_2V_2^{\gamma-1}$. Since $T_1 = 300°K$ and $T_2 = 1273°K$, we find

$$\left(\frac{V_2}{V_1}\right)^{\gamma-1} = \frac{300}{1273} = 2.36 \times 10^{-1}$$

Taking logs gives

$$(\gamma - 1) \log \frac{V_2}{V_1} = \log (2.36) - 1$$

from which

$$\log \frac{V_2}{V_1} = \frac{[0.373 - 1]}{0.40} = -1.57$$

Taking antilogs,

$$\frac{V_2}{V_1} = 10^{-1.57} = 10^{-2+0.43} = 10^{0.43} \times 10^{-2} = 2.7 \times 10^{-2}$$

9 How much work would be done on the gas in problem 8? Assume that $P_0 = 10^5\ N/m^2$ and $V_0 = 100\ cm^3$.

10 Find the work done by the gas confined to a cylinder as it is carried around the P-V cycle shown.

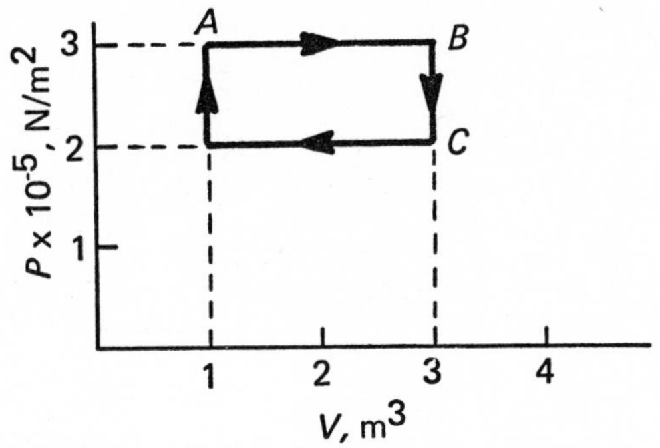

11 For the cycle of the previous problem, what was the temperature of the gas at points B and C if the temperature at A was 27°C? Assume an ideal gas.

17
questions
9-11

9 ☐ 3225 J

Since $W = \int P\,dV$ we must find P as a function of V before integrating. In an adiabatic process,

$$P_0V_0^{\gamma} = PV^{\gamma} \text{ and so } W = \int \frac{P_0V_0^{\gamma}}{V^{\gamma}}\,dV = P_0V_0^{\gamma}\int \frac{dV}{V^{\gamma}}$$

Now

$$\int dx/x^n = -\frac{1}{(n-1)x^{n-1}} \text{ so } W = \frac{P_0V_0}{\gamma - 1}\left[\frac{1}{V_0{}^{\gamma-1}} - \frac{1}{V^{\gamma-1}}\right]$$

From the previous problem, $V = 0.027V_0$ and so

$$W = \frac{10^5 \cdot 10^{-4}}{0.40}\left[\frac{1}{(10^{-4})^{0.4}} - \frac{1}{(2.7 \times 10^{-6})^{0.4}}\right] = -3225\text{ J}$$

a

10 ☐ 2×10^5 J

The work done is equal to the area enclosed by the cycle, namely, 2×10^5 N-m, which is 2×10^5 J.

11 ☐ 627°C; 327°C

17 answers 9-11

We can use the gas law to write $P_AV_A = \frac{m}{M}RT_A$ and $P_BV_B = \frac{m}{M}RT_B$

which give

$$T_B = T_A\,\frac{P_BV_B}{P_AV_A} = (300°\text{K})\,(3) = 900°\text{K}$$

Similarly,

$T_C = 600°$K

12 One gram of water at 100°C is heated in a piston-cylinder arrangement until it is all changed to steam at 100°C. The piston is pushed out by the steam so as to preserve a pressure of 10^5 N/m^2 during the process. Find the work done by the steam and compare it to the heat energy required to vaporize the water.

13 Mercury has a boiling point of 357°C. About what maximum efficiency could one expect for a "steam" engine using mercury rather than water as the working fluid?

14 A 20-g piece of ice at 0°C is thrown into a large beaker of water at 100°C. Assuming the final temperature of the system to still be close to 100°C, find the entropy change of the material which was originally ice.

15 For the previous problem, find the change in entropy of the universe because of this process.

12 ☐ 172 J; 41 versus 540 cal

The work done by the steam is $\int P\,d\,V$ and since $P = 10^5$ N/m², this becomes $10^5 \times (V - V_o)$. Now $V_o = 1$ cm³. Considered as an ideal gas, 1 g of steam at 100° will occupy a volume

$$V = \frac{m}{M}\frac{(RT)}{P} = \frac{10^{-3}}{18}\frac{(8314 \cdot 373)}{10^5} = 1.72 \times 10^{-3}\ \text{m}^3$$

Therefore the work is 172 J. This is equivalent to 41 cal, which is to be compared with the approximately 540 cal needed to vaporize water. Clearly, the major portion of the energy is used in tearing the molecules apart.

13 ☐ 48 percent

The engine efficiency cannot exceed that for a Carnot cycle, $1 - (T_2/T_1)$. In a practical case, T_1 would not much exceed the boiling temperature 357 + 273 = 630°K and T_2 would be about 300°K. Therefore eff. ≅ 1 - (300/630).

a

14 ☐ 12.2 cal/°K

By its definition, $dS = đQ/T$. In this case

$$S - S_o = \int_{\text{ice}}^{\text{water}} đQ/T + \int_{273}^{373} đQ/T = \frac{1600}{273} + \int_{273}^{373} \frac{20\,dt}{T}$$

17 answers 12-15

since $đQ = 20\,dT$ in the second phase. Therefore,

$$S - S_o = 5.9 + 20\,ln\,\frac{373}{273} = 12.2\ \text{cal/°K}$$

15 ☐ 2.5 cal/°K

The ice gained 12.2 cal/°K in entropy while the beaker of hot water lost

$$\int \frac{đQ}{T} = \frac{1}{373}\int đQ = \frac{1}{373}\ (1600 + 2000)\ \text{cal/°K}$$

in entropy. Thus the universe gained entropy in the amount 12.2 - (3600/373) = 2.5 cal/°K.

16 A certain ideal gas is carried around the cycle shown starting at A. During the portion AB of the cycle, 70 J of heat was added. Find:

(a) Work done in going from A to B;

(b) Change in internal energy in going from A to B;

(c) Work done by the gas during the cycle;

(d) Net heat added to the system during the cycle.

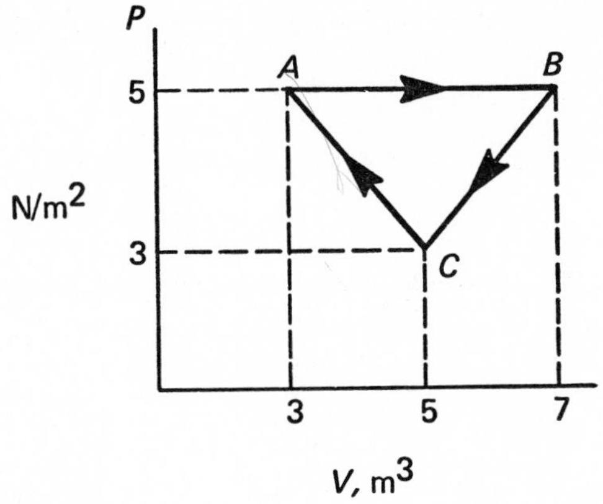

17 Two kg-moles of argon gas (monatomic, $C_V = 3$ cal/mole°K) starts at point A at a pressure of 10^5 N/m^2 and 273°K. Its original volume is 4.9×10^{-2} m^3. It is isothermally compressed to one-fourth its original volume and thereby taken to point B. It is then adiabatically expanded to its original volume and reaches point C. Then it is allowed to return to its original state, point A.

(a) Draw the PV diagram for the cycle.

(b) Find ΔU for part AB of the cycle.

(c) Find ΔQ for part AB of the cycle.

(d) Find ΔU for part BC of the cycle in terms of γ.

16 ☐ 20 J; 50 J; 4 J; 4 J

(a) $\Delta W = \int P\,dV = (5\ \text{N/m}^2)\,(4\ \text{m}^3) = 20\ \text{J};$

(b) $dU = đQ - \Delta W$ from which $\Delta U = 70 - 20 = 50\ \text{J};$

(c) $W = (\text{area enclosed}) = 4\ \text{J};$

(d) $dU = đQ - dW$ gives, since $dU = 0, đQ = dW = 4\ \text{J}.$

17 ☐ Zero; $-4.5 \times 10^6 \ln 4$ J; $\dfrac{4900}{\gamma - 1}(4^{\gamma-1} - 1)$ J

(a)

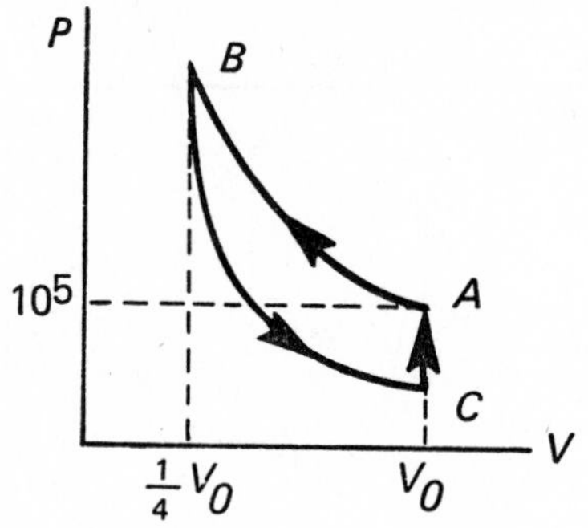

(b) $\Delta U = 0$ since T is constant.

(c) Since $\Delta U = 0$, $\Delta Q = \Delta W$ and $\Delta W = \int P\,dV$. Substituting for P from $PV = (m/M)RT$ and since $(m/M) = 2$, we have $\Delta W = 4.5 \times 10^6$

$$\int_{V_0}^{V_0/4} dV/V = 4.5 \times 10^6 \ln \frac{1}{4} \quad \therefore \Delta Q = -4.5 \times 10^6 \ln 4\ \text{J}.$$

(d) Since $\Delta Q = 0$, $\Delta W = \Delta U$.

$\Delta W = \int P\,dV$. But $PV^\gamma = \text{const} = P_0 V_0^{\gamma}$.

Therefore

$$\Delta W = P_0 V_0^{\gamma} \int_{V_0/4}^{V_0} \frac{dV}{V^\gamma} = + \frac{P_0 V_0^{\gamma}}{\gamma - 1}\left[\left(\frac{4}{V_0}\right)^{\gamma-1} - \left(\frac{1}{V_0}\right)^{\gamma-1}\right]$$

Therefore

$$\Delta U = \frac{(10^5)\,(4.9 \times 10^{-2})}{\gamma - 1}\left[(4)^{\gamma-1} - 1\right]\ \text{J}$$

18 the electrostatic field

1 What is meant by the statement "charge is quantized"?

2 What is the charge on the hydrogen nucleus? The carbon nucleus?

3 What is the force law for the interaction between two point charges q_1 and q_2?

4 The electron in the hydrogen atom is about 1 Å (10^{-10} m) from the center of the nucleus. Find the force the nucleus exerts on it.

5 Find the number of electrons in a 1.0-g copper coin. Copper has an atomic number of 29 and an atomic mass of 63.5.

6 Consider the case of two copper coins such as those in problem 5, separated by 2 m. Find the force on and the acceleration of one of the coins if 1 percent of its electrons were to be transferred to the other coin. You may approximate them to be point charges.

1 All charges are made up of integer multiples of the basic charge unit $\pm e$ where

$$e = 1.6021 \times 10^{-19}\ \text{C}$$

2 □ $+1.6 \times 10^{-19}$ C; $+9.6 \times 10^{-19}$ C

Nuclear charges are equal to e multiplied by the atomic number of the element in question.

3 □ Coulomb's law $F = \dfrac{1}{4\pi\epsilon_o} \dfrac{q_1 q_2}{r^2}$

The force is along the radius between the two charges. Like charges repel each other while unlike charges attract. In the mks system

$$\frac{1}{4\pi\epsilon_o} \quad 9 \times 10^9\ \text{N-m}^2/\text{C}^2$$

4 □ 2.3×10^{-8} N

The nucleus has a charge e while the electron has a charge $-e$. Using Coulomb's law for these essentially point charges gives

$$F = 9 \times 10^9 \frac{e^2}{10^{-20}} = 2.3 \times 10^{-8}\ \text{N}$$

a

18

answers

1-6

5 □ 2.74×10^{23}

63.5 g of Cu contains 6×10^{23} atoms and so 1 g contains 9.5×10^{21} atoms or $29 \times 9.5 \times 10^{21}$ electrons.

6 □ 4.4×10^{14} N; 4.4×10^{17} m/sec^2

From problem 5, the charge on each will be $\pm 2.74 \times 10^{21} \times 1.6 \times 10^{-19}$ C. Using Coulomb's law to find the force on one,

$$F = 9 \times 10^9 \frac{(4.4 \times 10^2)^2}{4} = 4.4 \times 10^{14}\ \text{N}$$

Notice that this force is tremendously large and so the situation is probably quite unrealizable. To find the coin's acceleration, we use $F = ma$ to give

$$a = \frac{4.4 \times 10^{14}}{1 \times 10^{-3}} = 4.4 \times 10^{17}\ \text{m/sec}^2$$

7 A point charge of q is to be placed on a line between two charges ($+4 \times 10^{-6}$ and $+3 \times 10^{-6}$ C) which are separated by a distance of 50 cm. Where should the charge be placed so that the force on it will be zero?

8 Find the force on the 3 μC charge in the diagram below.

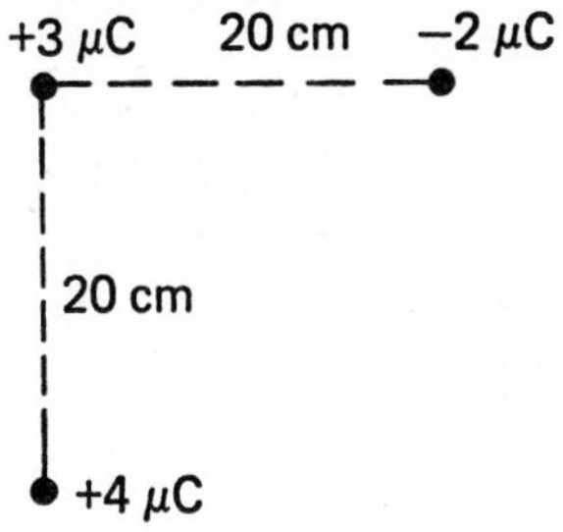

q

18
questions
7-8

7 ☐0.27 m

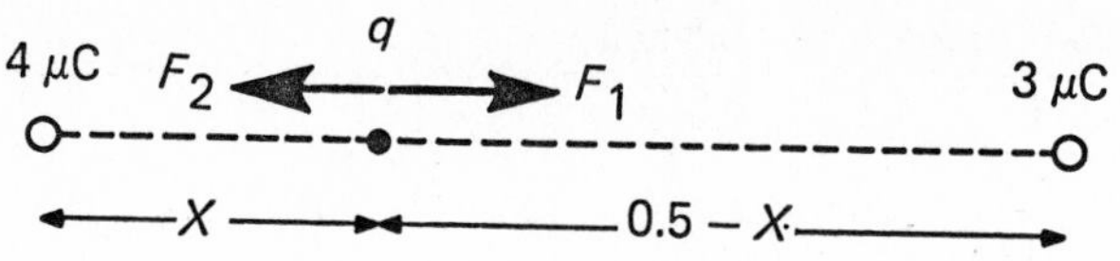

We wish F_1 to equal F_2 so that $\mathbf{F}_1 + \mathbf{F}_2 = 0$.

Therefore

$$\frac{1}{4\pi\epsilon_0}\frac{(4 \times 10^{-6})q}{x^2} = \frac{1}{4\pi\epsilon_0}\frac{(3 \times 10^{-6})q}{(0.5 - x)^2}$$

from which one finds $x = 3.732$ and 0.268 m. One must discard the larger value since for that value of x, F_1 and F_2 would be in the same direction and would not cancel.

8 ☐3.0 N

The forces on the 3 μC charge are as shown and have magnitudes

$$F_1 = 9 \times 10^9 \, (3 \times 10^{-6}) \frac{2 \times 10^{-6}}{0.040}$$

$$= 1.35 \text{ N and } F_2 = 2.70 \text{ N}$$

Therefore

$$F = \sqrt{(1.35)^2 + (2.7)^2} = 3.0 \text{ N}$$

with $\tan\theta = F_1/F_2$, so $\theta = 27°$.

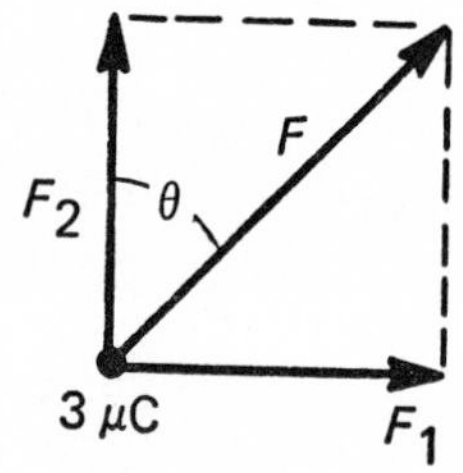

9 Find the force on the -2 μC charge in the previous problem.

10 A charge Q is placed near the end of a uniformly charged rod as shown. Find the force on the rod because of this charge. Call the charge per unit length of rod λ.

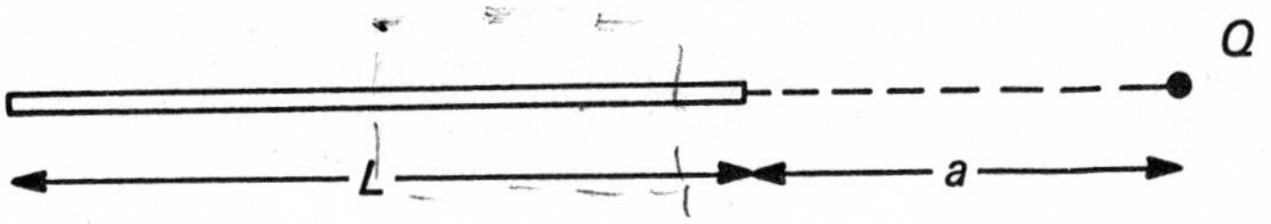

q

18
questions
9-10

9

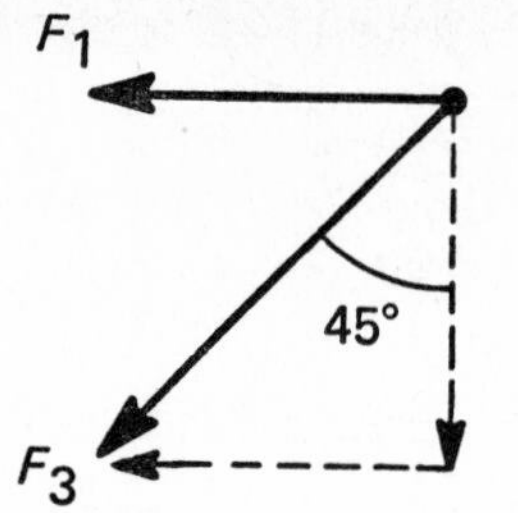

The vector forces on the -2 μC are shown. We have F_1 = 1.35 N and F_3 = 0.90 N. To find the resultant force we add components

$$F_x = F_1 + F_3 \sin 45^0 = 2.0 \text{ N}$$

$$F_y = F_3 \cos 45^0 = 0.64 \text{ N}$$

from which

$$F = \sqrt{F_x^2 + F_y^2} = 2.1 \text{ N}$$

10 ☐ $\dfrac{\lambda Q}{4\pi\epsilon_0}\left[\dfrac{1}{a} - \dfrac{1}{(L+a)}\right]$

Since Coulomb's law only applies to point charges, we section the rod into small lengths Δx, each carrying a charge $\lambda\, \Delta x$. Let us find the force on Q and then the force on the rod is equal and opposite. The force on Q due to the charge $\lambda\, \Delta x$ shown is

$$\Delta F = \frac{1}{4\pi\epsilon_0}(\lambda\, \Delta x)\frac{Q}{x^2}$$

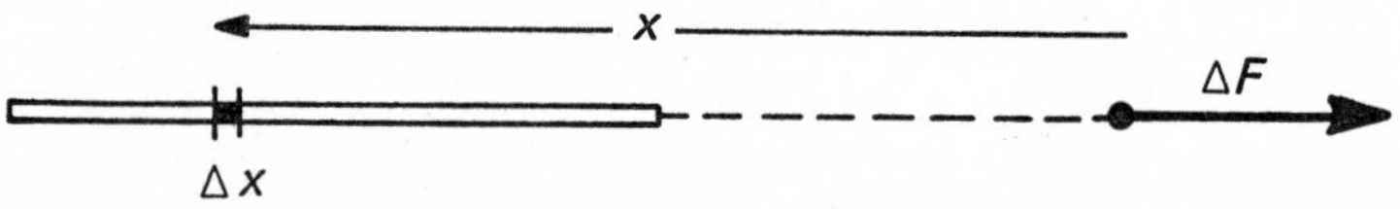

Since all the ΔF vectors are in the same direction, they can be added directly to give

$$F = \Sigma\, \Delta F_i = \frac{Q}{4\pi\epsilon_0}\Sigma\frac{\lambda\, \Delta x}{x_i^2}$$

In the limit $\Delta x \to 0$, this becomes an integral and since λ is constant we have

$$F = \frac{\lambda Q}{4\pi\epsilon_0}\int_{x=a}^{L+a}\left(\frac{dx}{x^2}\right)$$

Notice in particular the limits on the integral. Since $\int dx/x^2 = -1/x$ we find the answer given.

11 Two charges lie on the x axis, q_2 at $x = 0$ and q_1 at $x = 50$ cm. If q_1 and q_2 are both positive, where will the electric field due to these charges be zero? Let $q_1 = \frac{1}{4} q_2$.

12 An oil droplet of mass 10^{-11} g is found to stay motionless, neither falling nor rising, when placed in a uniform electric field of 10^5 N/C directed vertically downward. What is the charge on the droplet?

11 □ 33 cm

For the field to be zero, the force on a positive test charge due to these charges must be zero. In part (*a*) we see that F_1 and F_2 could not cancel each other and so no point off axis has zero field. Only in the situation illustrated in (*b*) will F_1 and F_2 cancel. Thus the point we seek is between q_1 and q_2. Equating F_1 to F_2 gives

$$\frac{q_1}{(0.5 - x)^2} = \frac{q_2}{x^2}$$

from which $x = 1$ or $\frac{1}{3}$ m. Why must the first answer be discarded?

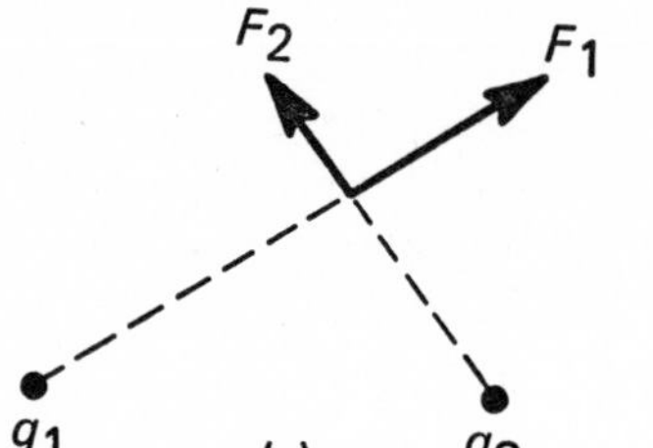

(*a*)

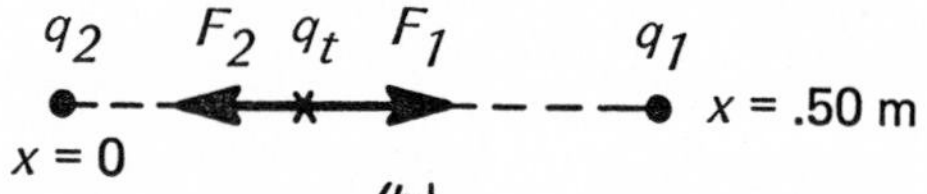

(*b*)

18
answers
11-12

12 □ -9.8×10^{-19} C

For the drop to remain motionless, the gravitational force mg must be balanced by the electrical force on the charge qE. (Recall that E is the force on unit charge so qE is the force on charge q.) Taking down positive and equating $-qE = mg$ and using $m = 10^{-14}$ kg and $g = 9.8$ m/sec^2 gives $q = -9.8 \times 10^{-19}$ C, indicating that the droplet has six excess electrons on it.

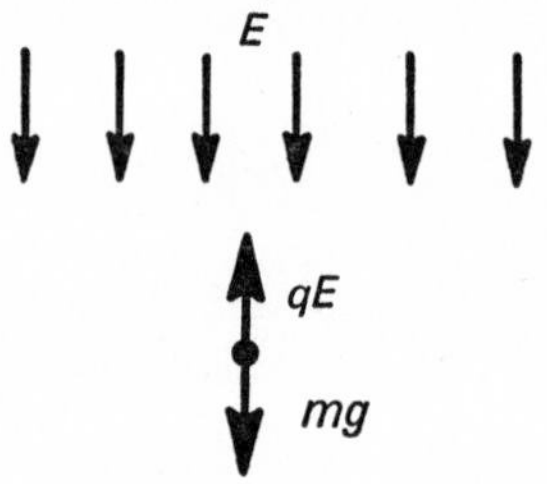

13 A proton ($m = 1.67 \times 10^{-27}$ kg) enters a region of space with velocity $10^6\mathbf{j}$ m/sec. In this region an electric field $-10^5\mathbf{j}$ N/C exists. Find the distance the proton goes before stopping.

14 Consider a positively charged flat plate about 10 cm X 10 cm X 0.5 cm. Sketch the electric field as seen (a) by a microbe on the central portion of the top surface and (b) by a bird flying high above it.

15 Find the electric field at point P for the situation depicted below.

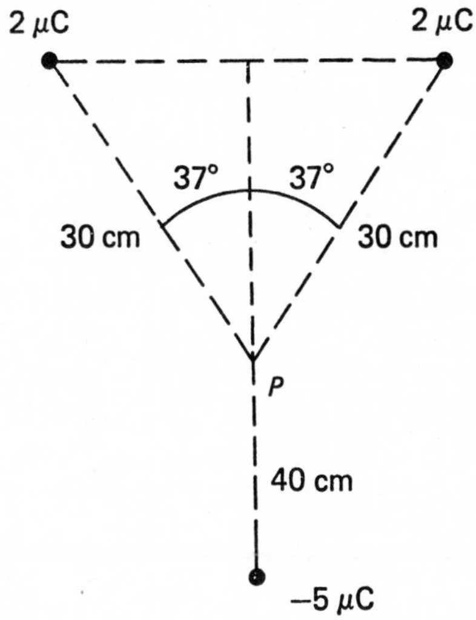

q
18
questions
13-15

13 □5.2 cm

Since the force on the proton is qE, it is in the $-y$ direction and opposes the proton's motion. Using $F = ma$, one has $a = (qE)/m$ from which $a = -9.6 \times 10^{12}$ m/sec^2.
Using $v^2 - v_0^2 = 2ay$ and since $v_0 = 10^6$ m/sec and $v = 0$, one finds $y = 5.2$ cm.

14

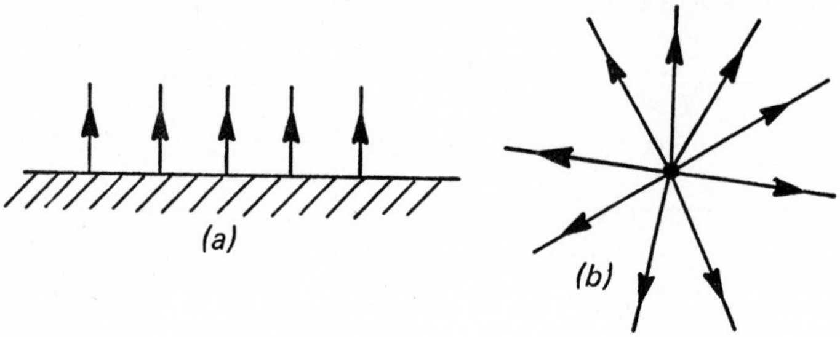

a

18
answers
13-15

15 □ 6 X 10^5 N/C

The field vectors at P due to the individual charges are as shown. Their magnitudes are

$$E_1 = E_2 = 9 \times 10^9 \, \frac{2 \times 10^{-6}}{(0.30)^2} = 2 \times 10^5 \text{ N/C}$$

$$E_3 = 9 \times 10^9 \, \frac{5 \times 10^{-6}}{(0.40)^2} = 2.8 \times 10^5 \text{ N/C}$$

Splitting the vectors into components and adding gives

$$E_x = E_2 \cos 53^\circ - E_1 \cos 53^\circ = 0$$

and

$$E_y = -E_3 - 2E_1 \sin 53^\circ = -6.0 \times 10^5 \text{ N/C}$$

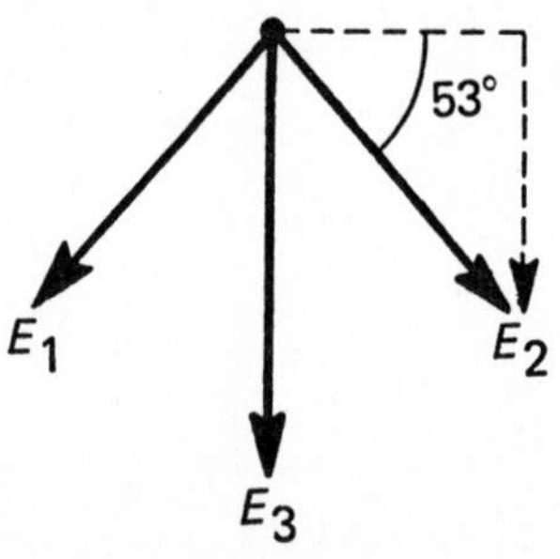

16 The two thin rods shown carry uniform charge λ per unit length. Find E at point P due to them.

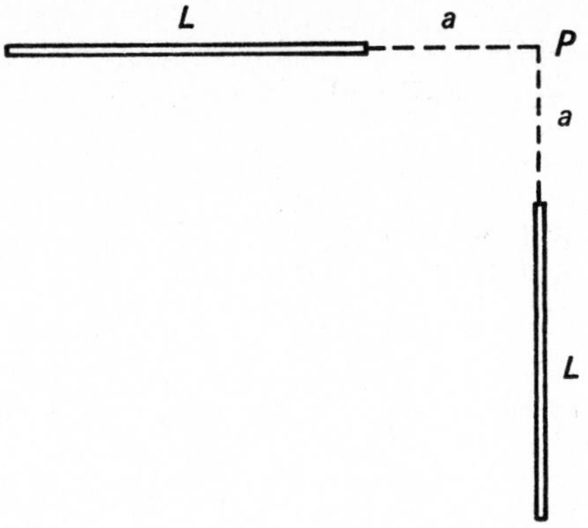

17 The portion of arc shown carries a uniform charge λ per unit length. Find E at its center.

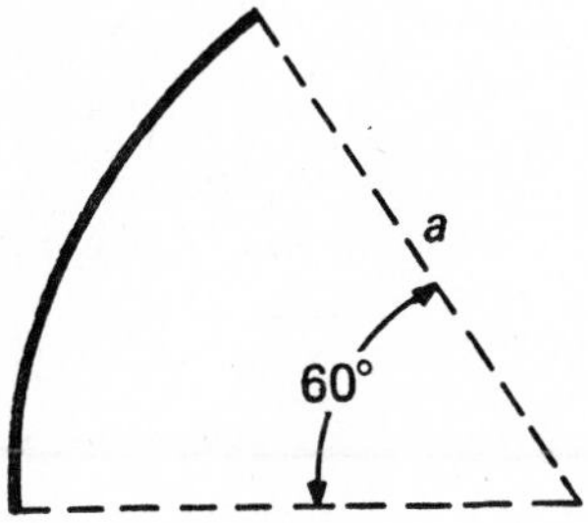

q

18
questions
16-17

16 $\frac{\lambda\sqrt{2}}{4\pi\epsilon_0}\left[\frac{1}{a}-\frac{1}{L+a}\right]$

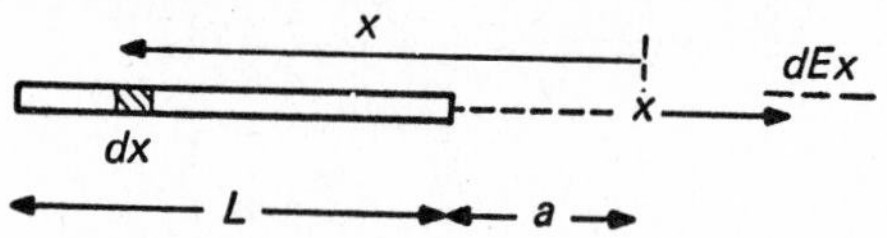

We first find the field at the end of a rod. The field due to length dx which has a charge $\lambda\, dx$ will be

$$dE_x = \frac{\lambda\, dx}{4\pi\epsilon_0 x^2}$$

Since each incremental length dx of the rod gives a dE_x in the same direction, the total E_x due to the rod is

$$E_x = \int dE_x = \frac{\lambda}{4\pi\epsilon_0}\int_a^{L+a}\frac{dx}{x^2} = \frac{\lambda}{4\pi\epsilon_0}\left[\frac{1}{a}-\frac{1}{L+a}\right]$$

Now in the present problem, both E_x and E_y will be the same and so $E = \sqrt{2}\,E_x$ directed 45° above the horizontal.

a

18
answers
16-17

17 □ $\frac{\lambda}{4\pi\epsilon_0 a}$

One can simplify the calculation by taking x and y axes so as to split the 60° angle as shown. In this case $E_y = 0$. We have

$$dE = \frac{1}{4\pi\epsilon_0}\,\frac{\lambda ds}{a^2}$$

and

$$dE_x = \frac{\lambda}{4\pi\epsilon_0 a^2}\,(ds)\cos\theta$$

But $ds = a\,d\theta$ and so, upon adding the dEs, one has

$$E_x = \frac{\lambda}{4\pi\epsilon_0 a}\int_{-30°}^{30°}\cos\theta\, d\theta$$

Notice the limits on the integral. Since $\int \cos\theta\, d\theta = +\sin\theta$, the answer is found to be $\lambda/4\pi\epsilon_0 a$.

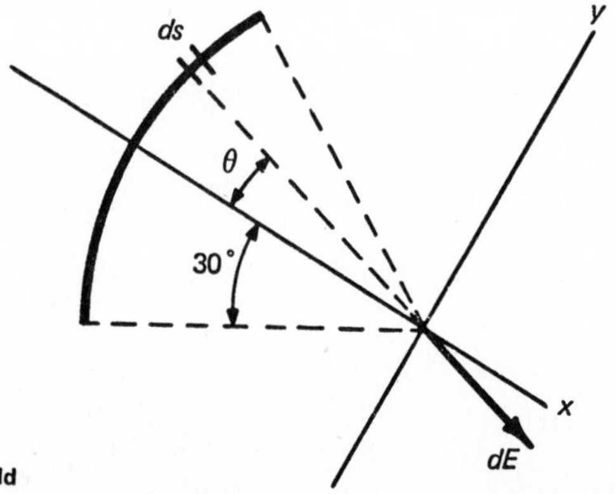

18 The electric field shown in the region between two parallel plates is 10^5 N/C. A proton with speed 10^6 m/sec is shot in as shown. Find its speed as it emerges on the other side.

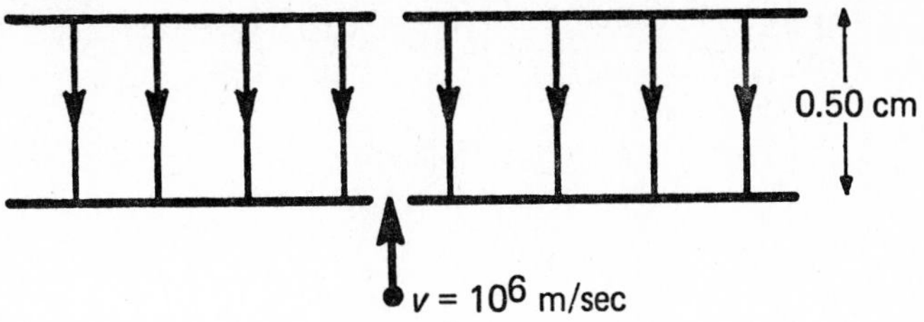

q

18
question
18

18 ☐ 9.5×10^5 m/sec

The proton will be slowed by the downward electric field. From $F = ma$ we find $a = -Eq/m = -9.6 \times 10^{12}$ m/sec^2. Then using $v^2 - v_o^2 = 2ax$ gives
$v^2 = 10^{12} - 9.6 \times 10^{10} \cong 90 \times 10^{10}$
from which $v = 9.5 \times 10^5$ m/sec.

a

18
answer
18

19 Gauss' law

1 How many flux lines pass through an area **dA** in a region where the electric field is **E**?

2 The loop of area A rotates in the uniform field E in such a way that the angle ψ is given by ωt. Find the flux through the area as a function of time.

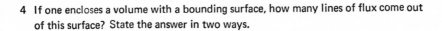

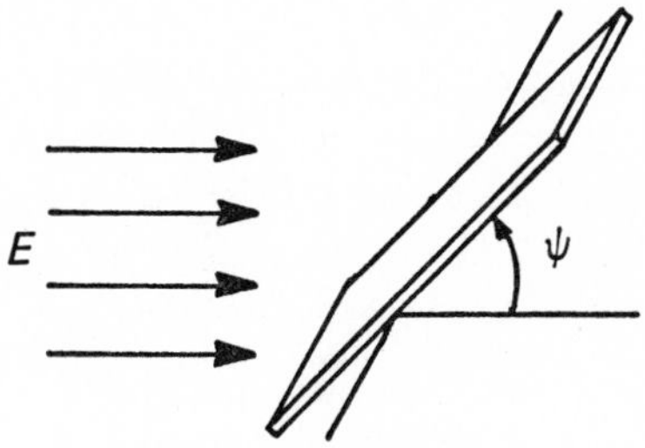

3 What can one say about the number of lines of flux coming into or emanating from a charge Q?

4 If one encloses a volume with a bounding surface, how many lines of flux come out of this surface? State the answer in two ways.

5 What is Gauss' law?

6 Why don't charges outside the enclosed volume enter into Gauss' law?

7 Starting from the fact that E is zero in the body of a metal, prove that no excess charge can exist there under electrostatic conditions.

q
19
questions
1-7

1 ☐ $d\phi = \mathbf{E}\cdot d\mathbf{A} = E\,dA\cos\theta$

where θ is the angle between the area vector and **E**. The area vector is perpendicular to the plane of the area.

2 ☐ $+EA\sin(\omega t)$

Since $d\phi = \mathbf{E}\cdot d\mathbf{A} = E\,dA\cos(90^\circ - \psi)$

$$\phi = \int E\,dA\cos(90^\circ - \psi) = E\cos(90^\circ - \psi)\int dA$$

$$= EA\cos(\omega t - 90^\circ) = +EA\sin(\omega t)$$

3 The number of lines is Q/ϵ_0. They go into negative charges and come out of positive charges.

4 ☐ Q_{inside}/ϵ_0 ; $\int \mathbf{E}\cdot d\mathbf{A}$ over the surface

Since q/ϵ_0 lines originate on each charge, if the charge inside the surface is Q_{inside}, the given number of lines must come out. Notice that Q is the algebraic sum of the qs. The latter representation is obtained directly from the number of lines through area dA.

a

19
answers
1-7

5 Gauss' law simply equates the two equal expressions for the flux coming from a closed surface as given in the previous question. It is

$$\epsilon_0\int \mathbf{E}\cdot d\mathbf{A} = Q_{inside} = \Sigma q_i$$

6 Lines of flux coming from such charges pass through the entire volume and are counted as negative when they enter and positive when they leave, thereby giving an additive value of zero.

7 Apply Gauss' law to the surface shown which encloses a small piece of the interior of the metal. Then $\epsilon_0\int \mathbf{E}\cdot d\mathbf{A} = Q_{inside}$.

But since E is zero on this surface, the left side of the equation is zero. Therefore, $Q_{inside} = 0$.

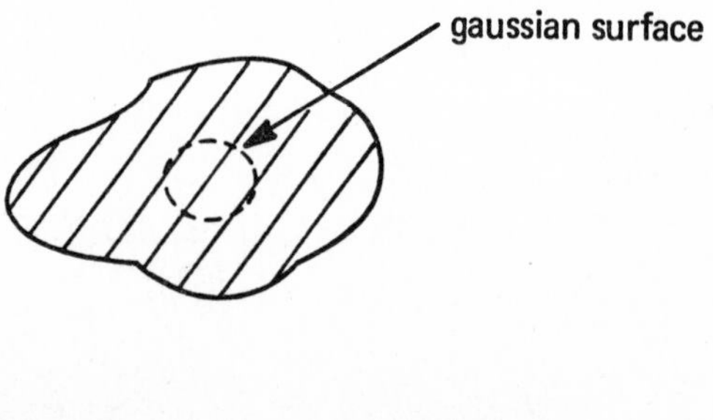

8 Show that in a region of space where $\mathbf{E}$ = (const) $\mathbf{i}$, no net charge exists.

9 A metal spherical shell has inner radius a and outer radius b. It carries a net positive charge Q. At the center of the spherical cavity is placed a charge $-q$, with $Q > q$. Show on a diagram the charge and flux distribution and find E outside and inside the shell.

8 The field looks as shown. Take the rectangular box shown as the gaussian surface. Then $Q_{inside} = \epsilon_o \int \mathbf{E} \cdot d\mathbf{A}$. Since **E** is parallel to all four small sides, no flux goes through them and $\mathbf{E} \cdot d\mathbf{A}$ is zero there. For the left side, $\int \mathbf{E} \cdot d\mathbf{A} = -E_x A$ since the flux lines go in. On the right side, $\int \mathbf{E} \cdot d\mathbf{A} = E_x A$. Therefore the total integral is zero and no charge exists inside.

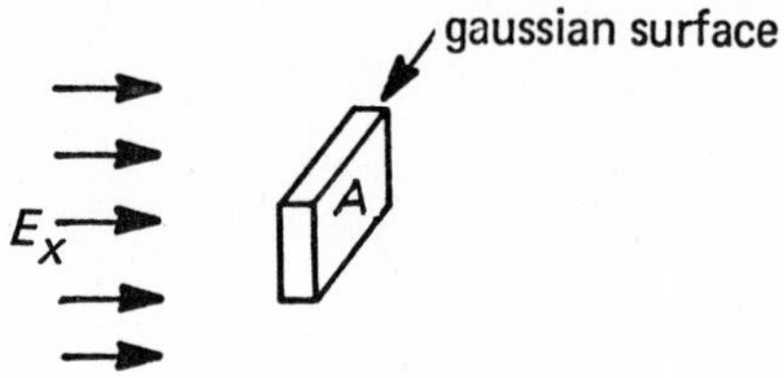

9 Inside the shell, only the charge $-q$ has influence and so $E = -q/4\pi\epsilon_o r^2$. Outside, all of the charge appears localized at the center and so $E = (Q - q)/4\pi\epsilon_o r^2$.

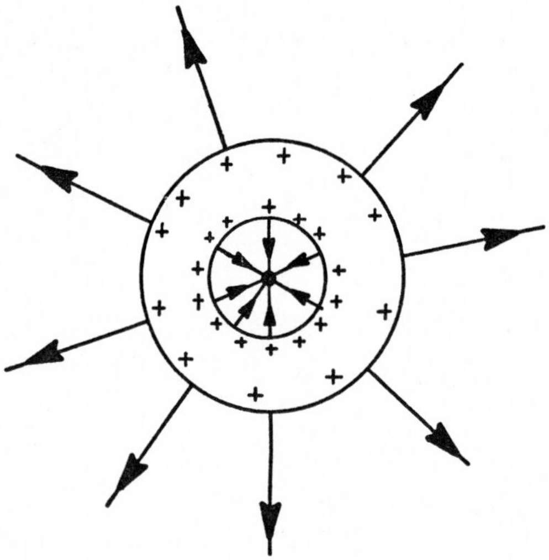

a

19
answers
8-9

10 A student claims it is possible to have two parallel, infinite metal plates with positive charge on each as shown. Prove that this would violate Gauss' law as well as being impossible from a flux diagram approach.

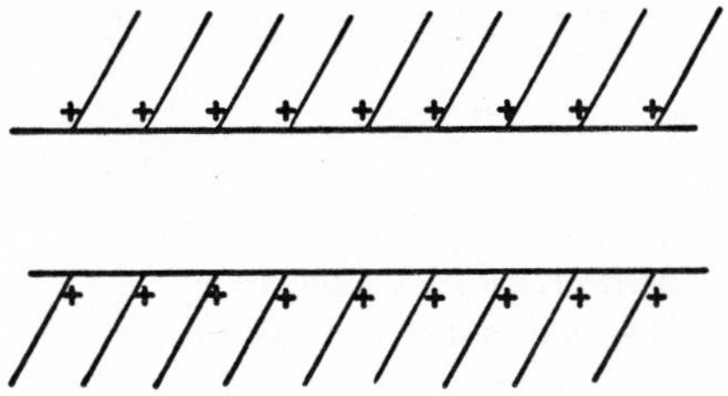

11 A uniformly charged metal sphere of radius a carries a charge Q. Surrounding it is a volume charge $-\rho$ per meter cubed. Find the electric field outside the sphere.

10 Take a gaussian surface in the form of a box. No flux goes through the four vertical sides since the flux lines must be vertical. (The plates are parallel and infinite so no preferential side exists.) No flux goes through the top or bottom since they are in the metal and $E = 0$ there.

Therefore

$$Q_{\text{inside}} = \int \mathbf{E} \cdot d\mathbf{A} = 0$$

Hence no net charge can exist on the two plates and so the supposition of both with positive charge must be wrong. In addition, since lines of flux come out of + charges and do not penetrate into the metal, it is impossible to draw flux lines for the case supposed.

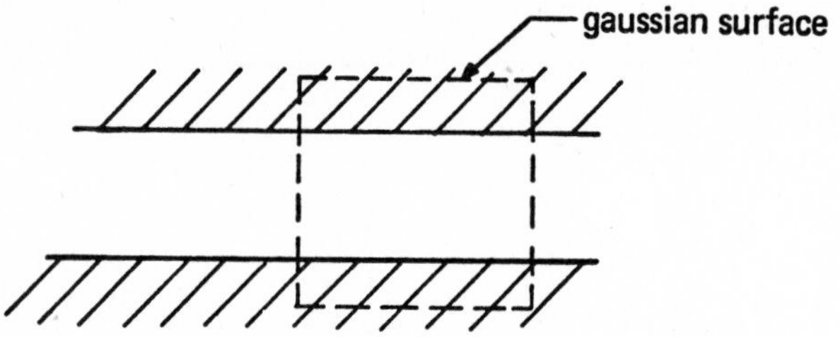

11 □ $\dfrac{Q}{4\pi\epsilon_0 r^2} - \dfrac{\rho}{3\epsilon_0}\left(r - \dfrac{b^3}{r^2}\right)$

The charge inside the gaussian surface shown is

$$Q - \rho \frac{4\pi}{3}\left(r^3 - b^3\right)$$

Therefore Gauss' law gives

$$\epsilon_0 \int \mathbf{E} \cdot d\mathbf{A} = Q - \rho \frac{4\pi}{3}\left(r^3 - b^3\right)$$

Because of the spherical symmetry, **E** will be radial and constant on the surface and so

$$\epsilon_0 \int \mathbf{E} \cdot d\mathbf{A} = \epsilon_0 E \int dA = \epsilon_0 E\,(4\pi r^2)$$

Using this in the above gives E.

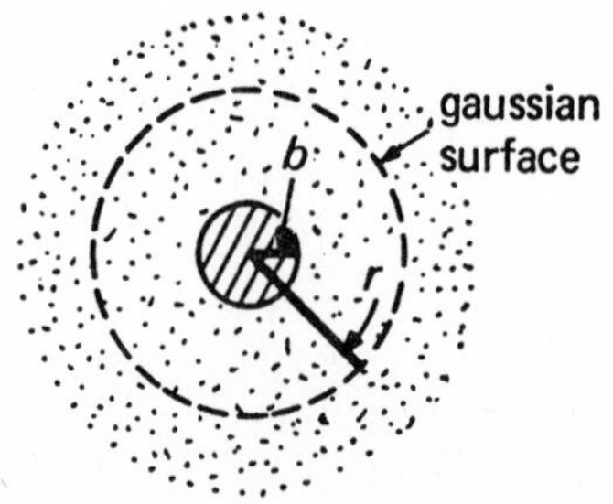

12 Repeat the previous problem if the sphere is replaced by an infinite cylinder of radius a which has a uniform surface charge σ per unit area.

q
19
question
12

12 □ $\frac{\sigma a}{r\epsilon_0} - \frac{\rho}{2r\epsilon_0}\left(r^2 - a^2\right)$

The diagram of the previous problem now becomes the end view of a cylinder. Take the gaussian cylinder to have length L. Then the charge enclosed is

$$2\pi a L\sigma - \pi\rho(r^2 - a^2)\,L$$

Using this in Gauss' law and since no flux goes through the ends of the gaussian surface (the cylinder is infinite so the flux must be radial), one has

$$2\pi r L\epsilon_0 E = 2\pi a L\sigma - \pi\rho(r^2 - a^2)\,L$$

a

19
answer
12

20
potential

1 What does it mean to say that the potential difference between two points A and B is V volts with B being at the higher potential?

2 What is the origin and meaning of the relation $V = Ed$?

3 If the potential difference between two points A and B is 20 V with A being at the higher potential, how much work is done in moving a proton from A to B? An electron?

4 Two electrodes A and B (metal plates) are in a glass vacuum chamber as shown. What would happen to an electron released at point P? A proton? Assume P to be quite close to plate A.

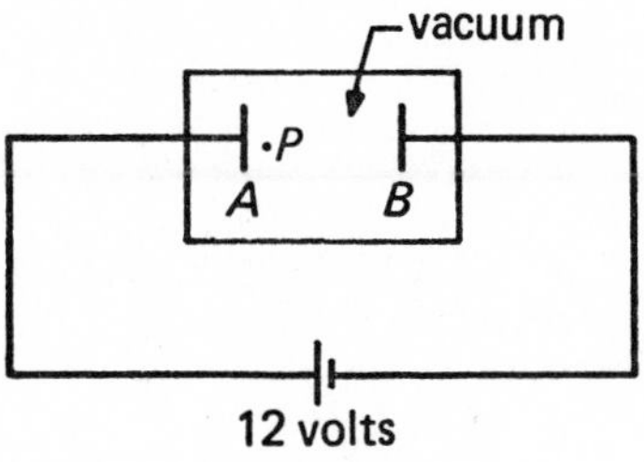

5 In a TV tube, electrons are accelerated between a hot negative filament and a positive metal plate, the potential difference between the two being perhaps 20,000 V. Find the speed of the electron as it reaches the plate.

1 It means that V joules of work are needed to carry a 1 C negative charge from A to B or a 1 C negative charge from B to A. Notice a rise in potential for a positive charge is a decrease in potential energy for a negative charge.

2 The work done in moving a charge $+q$ through a distance d against a constant electric field E is simply $W = \int \mathbf{F} \cdot \mathbf{ds} = (Eq)\,d$ since $Eq = F$ and is constant. But the work done in moving unit charge W/q through a displacement d is the potential difference between the start and end points V. Therefore $V = Ed$. Notice that this is correct only if E is constant.

3 ☐ -3.2×10^{-18} J; 3.2×10^{-18} J

By definition of potential difference, 20 J of work is done in moving a +1 C charge from B to A. Or -20 J in going from A to B since the + charge is "going downhill" in this case. In general, $W = q\,(V_B - V_A) = -20q$ J. But $q = 1.6 \times 10^{-19}$ C for the proton and so $W = -3.2 \times 10^{-18}$ J. Since the electron is negative, the work done is reversed in sign.

a

4 Plate A is attached to the positive side of the battery and is therefore positively charged while B is negative. An electron at point P would be attracted to the plate A and would neutralize one of the positive charges on it. A proton would be attracted to B, the negative plate, and would fall through about 12 V in reaching it. Its speed would be found from $Vq = \frac{1}{2} mv^2$ to be 4.8×10^4 m/sec.

5 ☐ 8.1×10^7 m/sec

20
answers
1-5

The speed will probably be relativistic. Therefore the energy acquired by the electron in falling through the potential V, namely Vq, will be equal to the kinetic energy of the electron, $mc^2 - m_0c^2$ in this relativistic case.

$$2 \times 10^4\,(1.6 \times 10^{-19}) = (9.1 \times 10^{-31})\,(9 \times 10^{16}) \cdot \left[\frac{1}{\sqrt{1 - (v/c)^2}} - 1\right]$$

which gives $\frac{v}{c} = 0.27$.

6 A proton with speed 10^5m/sec is shot as shown. What must be the potential of the battery if the proton is to stop just before it strikes the plate on the right?

10^5 m/sec

$V = Ed$

$\frac{1}{2}mv^2 = $ potential eV

$J = $ energy

$V = J/q$

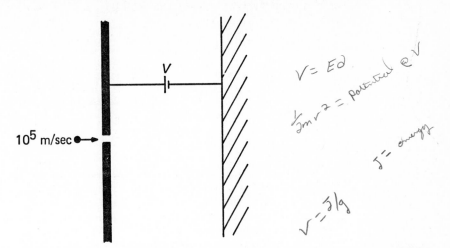

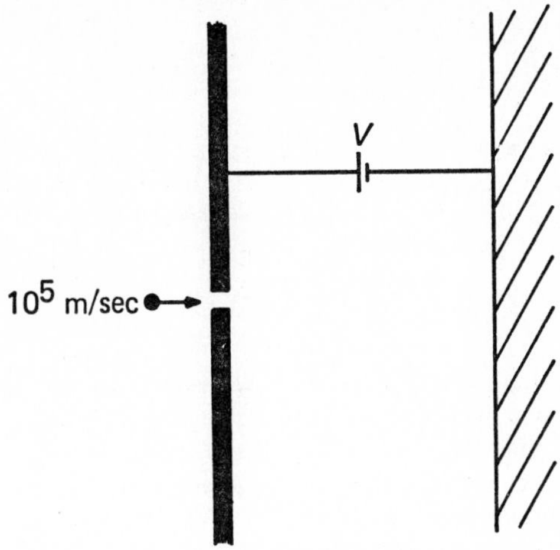

7 It is desired to obtain an electric field of 10^5 N/C between two parallel metal plates which are 1 mm apart. What voltage difference must be impressed across the plates?

8 In a certain region of space, $\mathbf{E}$ = 2000 $\mathbf{i}$ – 1000 $\mathbf{j}$ V/m. Find the potential difference between point A whose coordinates are (0, 0, 0) and point B at (0, 3, 0) meters.

9 Repeat the previous problem if the second point, point B, has coordinates (4, 3, 0) meters.

20
questions
6-10

10 The electric field along the x axis is $\mathbf{E}$ = (2 X $10^4/x^2$)$\mathbf{i}$ V/m. Find the potential difference between x = 2 m and x = 7 m. Which point is at the lower potential?

6 □ 52 V

First, the battery must be reversed or the proton would be accelerated rather than decelerated. If that is done, then Vq, the work done by the proton, must equal the original KE. In this nonrelativistic case $Vq = \frac{1}{2}mv^2$ and $V\,(1.6 \times 10^{-19}) = \frac{1}{2}\,(1.67 \times 10^{-27})\,(10^{10})$, from which $V = 52$ V.

7 □ 100 V

Since $E = 10^5$ N/C $= 10^5$ V/m and since in this case E is constant, one can write $E = \frac{V}{d}$. (Notice how natural the units are here.) Then $V = (10^5)\,(10^{-3}) = 100$ V.

8 □ $V_B - V_A = 3000$ V

Back to the definition of potential difference. We need the work done in carrying a +1 C charge from A to B. We are moving the charge along the y axis and so work will only be done against the y component of E. Since $E_y = -1000$ V/m, the force $E_y q$ will be such as to push the charge back to A. Hence B will be at the higher potential. Since the force is constant, and since $q = 1$ C, we find $V_B - V_A = \text{work/C} = (1000)\,(3) = 3000$ V. Did we use the relation

$$-\int_A^B \mathbf{E}\cdot d\mathbf{s} = V_B - V_A\,?$$

a

9 □ $V_B - V_A = -5000$ V

We get from A to B in two steps. First take the +1 C charge to (0,3,0) during which 3000 J of work is done as found above. Now go along the x direction to $x = 4$. We are now moving in the direction of the field and so the charge is going downhill (the field is pushing it). Since E is constant, the work done is $(-2000)\,(4) = -8000$ J/C. Therefore the total work done is 3000 − 8000 J/C.

20
answers
6-10

10 □ −7140 V; $x = 7$ m

Since E is not constant we cannot use $V = Ed$. Instead, we use the original work equation before integration.

$$V_B - V_A = -\int_A^B \mathbf{E}\cdot d\mathbf{s}.$$ In our case

$$V_B - V_A = -\int_2^7 \frac{2 \times 10^4}{x^2}\,dx = \frac{2 \times 10^4}{x}\Big|_2^7 = -7140 \text{ V}$$

Notice that the answer is negative, indicating that $x = 7$ m is at the lower potential. This should have been immediately obvious since the field was pushing $+q$ to larger x values.

11 What does a person mean when he says "the absolute potential at point P is -30 V"?

12 In a certain region in space, the absolute potential is given by $V = -30x^2 + 7y + 3z^3$ V. Find the components of the electric field in this region.

13 For the situation shown, find the absolute potential at point P.

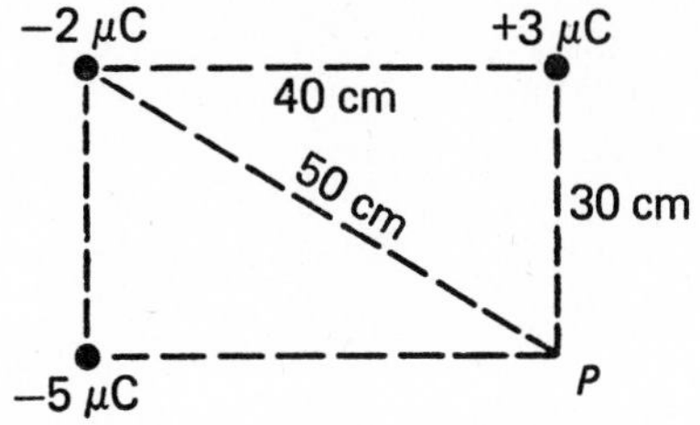

14 A charge q_1 is placed on the x axis at $x = 0$ while a charge q_2 is placed at $x = 4$ m. If the total charge is $5\,\mu$C, what must be the values of q_1 and q_2 for V to be zero at $x = 3$ m?

$E = \dfrac{koq}{r^2}$

$V = \dfrac{koq}{r}$

$\dfrac{koq}{r}$

$\dfrac{koq}{r^2}$

$\dfrac{koq}{r}$

$V = \dfrac{koq}{r}$

$E =$

$\dfrac{koq}{r}$

$En \ 9 \quad V = E = \dfrac{koq}{r^2}$

$\dfrac{koq}{r^2} \ r$

$V = ER$

11 He means that -30 J of work are done in moving a +1 C charge from infinity to point P. Point P is at a lower potential or downhill from infinity. Since the electrostatic field is conservative, this work is independent of path.

12 ☐ $E = 60\,x\mathbf{i} - 7\mathbf{j} - 9z^2\mathbf{k}$ volts/m

E is related to V by $E_x = -\partial V/\partial x$, etc. We thus have

$$E_x = 60x \text{ volts/m}$$

$$E_y = -7 \text{ volts/m}$$

$$E_z = -9z^2 \text{ volts/m}$$

13 ☐ 42,750 volts

We recall that potential is not a vector and so we do not add vectorially as we would for E. The potential due to a point charge is $\frac{1}{4\pi\epsilon_o} \times \frac{q}{r}$ and so

$$V_P = \frac{1}{4\pi\epsilon_o} \Sigma \frac{q_i}{r_i} = 9 \times 10^9 \left[\frac{-2 \times 10^{-6}}{0.5} + \frac{3 \times 10^{-6}}{0.3} + \frac{-5 \times 10^{-6}}{0.4}\right]$$

$$= 42{,}750 \text{ volts}$$

20

answers

11-14

14 ☐ 7.5 and -2.5 μC

We have $q_2 = 5 \times 10^{-6} - q_1$ and we wish $0 = 9 \times 10^9 \left[\frac{q_1}{3} + \frac{5 \times 10^{-6} - q_1}{1}\right]$

From this we find $q_1 = 7.5 \times 10^{-6}$ C and $q_2 = -2.5 \times 10^{-6}$ C.

15 Find V at point P if the rod is uniformly charged, λ per unit length.

16 A circular loop of radius a carries a charge λ per unit length. Find V and E at the center of the loop.

17 Repeat problem 16 to find V if λ varies as $\lambda = \lambda_0 \sin\theta$.

18 An electron is shot into a region between two infinite parallel metal plates, as shown. Find the components of its velocity just before it hits one plate.

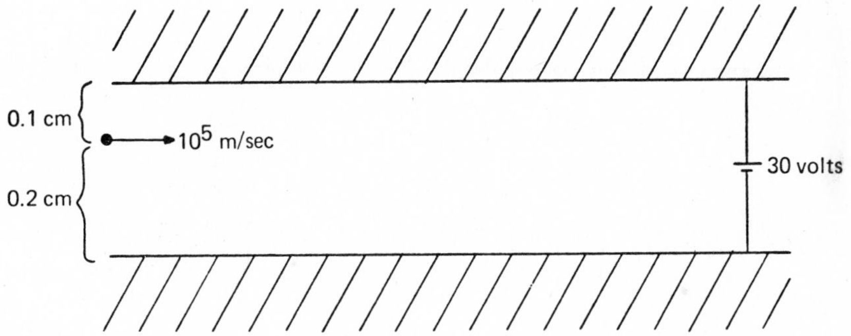

20
questions
15-18

15 ☐ $\frac{\lambda}{4\pi\epsilon_0} \ln \left[\frac{L+b}{b}\right]$

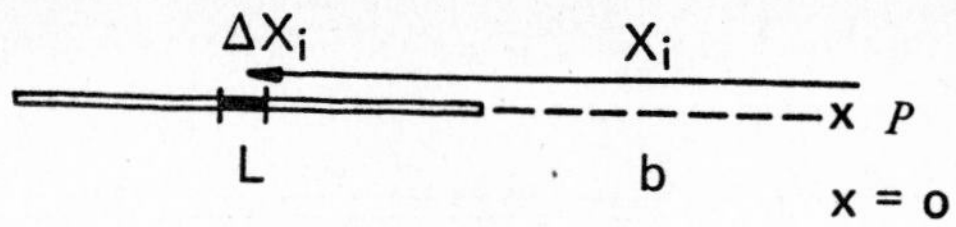

Section the rod into point charges $\lambda\,\Delta x_i$. Then $V = \frac{1}{4\pi\epsilon_0} \Sigma \frac{q_i}{x_i}$

Or, since $q_i = \lambda\Delta x_i$ and since $\Delta x_i \to 0$, $V = \frac{1}{4\pi\epsilon_0} \int_b^{L+b} \frac{\lambda\,dx}{x} = \frac{\lambda}{4\pi\epsilon_0} \ln\left(\frac{L+b}{b}\right)$

As a check, we note that V is positive, as it should be.

16 ☐ $\frac{\lambda}{2\epsilon_0}$

E is of course zero since the fields from opposite segments of the loop cancel each other. (Remember, **E** is a vector.) However,

$V = \frac{1}{4\pi\epsilon_0} \Sigma \frac{\lambda\,\Delta s_i}{a}$ since V is not a vector. Then

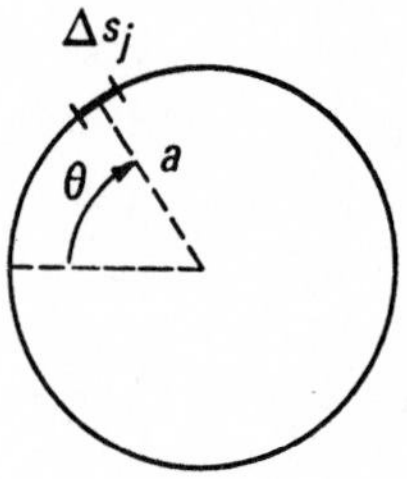

$V = \frac{\lambda}{4\pi\epsilon_0 a} \Sigma\,\Delta s_i = \frac{\lambda}{4\pi\epsilon_0 a}(2\pi a) = \frac{\lambda}{2\epsilon_o}$

a

20
answers
15-18

17 ☐ Zero

In this case $V = \frac{1}{4\pi\epsilon_0 a} \Sigma\,\lambda_0 \sin\theta\,(\Delta s_i)$ Now $\Delta s = a\,\Delta\theta$ and so after passing to the limit,

$$V = \frac{\lambda_0}{4\pi\epsilon_0} \int_0^{2\pi} \sin\theta\,d\theta = \frac{\lambda_0}{4\pi\epsilon_0} (-\cos\theta)\Big|_0^{2\pi} = 0$$

Could you have guessed this answer at the outset?

18 ☐ 10^5 m/sec and 1.9 X 10^6 m/sec

The electron will hit the upper (positive) plate. Since the field is uniform between the plates, the potential will vary uniformly and so the electron falls through (0.1/0.3) (30) = 10 V. Therefore $Vq = \frac{1}{2}mv_y^2$ gives v_y = 1.9 X 10^6 m/sec. Of course, v_x remains unchanged since the field is vertical.

21 circuit elements

1 What is the basic purpose of batteries or other electromotive force sources in a circuit?

2 What is the definition of electric current in a wire? Of current density?

3 In a certain TV tube a beam of electrons shoots down the tube and causes a current of 1 mA. How many electrons hit the TV screen each second?

4 In the previous problem, if the speed of the electrons is nearly the speed of light, 3×10^8 m/sec, how many electrons exist in each centimeter length of the beam?

5 A certain piece of radioactive material emits β particles (electrons) and has a strength of 1 microcurie. (That is to say, 3.7×10^4 disintegrations occur in the material each second and there are this many β particles emitted each second.) How much current must flow from the material to keep it electrically neutral?

6 Find the resistance of 1000 m of 2-mm-diameter copper wire.

7 Two wires of equal length, one of copper and the other of tungsten, are to carry the same current when connected across the same battery. What must be the ratio of their diameters?

1 They supply the energy needed to produce currents in the circuit.

2 The current I in a wire is the quantity of charge (coulombs) passing a given point in the wire in unit time (seconds) and has the units coulombs per second or amperes. Current density J is the current per unit area, I/A, where A is the cross-section area of the wire.

3 ☐ 6.3×10^{15}

Since $I = \Delta Q/\Delta t$ and since $I = 10^{-3}$ A, in 1 sec 10^{-3} C strike the screen. But each electron carries a charge 1.6×10^{-19} C and so the number per second is $10^{-3}/1.6 \times 10^{-19} = 6.3 \times 10^{15}$.

4 ☐ 2.1×10^5

All the electrons in a beam 3×10^8 m long would strike the screen in 1 sec and, in the previous problem, we found this number to be $6.3 \times 10^{+15}$. Therefore in a 1-cm length of beam there will be $(0.01/3 \times 10^8) \cdot (6.3 \times 10^{15})$ electrons.

a

5 ☐ 5.9×10^{-15} A

The charge being emitted is negative and constitutes a current of $(3.7 \times 10^4) \times (1.6 \times 10^{-19})$ C/sec. Therefore an equal flow of electrons into the sample is needed to keep it neutral, namely 5.9×10^{-15} A. Since current is the flow of positive, not negative charge, the current flows from the sample.

21
answers
1-7

6 ☐ $5.4\ \Omega$

Since $R = \rho L/A$ and since $\rho = 1.7 \times 10^{-8}\ \Omega$m,

$$R = \frac{(1.7 \times 10^{-8})(1000)}{(\pi \cdot 10^{-6})} = 5.4\ \Omega$$

7 ☐ $d_{Cu}/d_W = 1.81$

We wish $R_{Cu} = R_W$ from which $\rho_{Cu}/r^2_{Cu} = \rho_W/r^2_W$. Therefore

$$\frac{r_{Cu}}{r_W} = \sqrt{\frac{\rho_W}{\rho_{Cu}}} = \sqrt{\frac{5.6}{1.7}} = 1.81$$

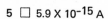

8 Estimate the room-temperature resistance of a tungsten-filament light bulb which has a resistance of 400 Ω at 1820°C.

9 Show that the capacitance of a small metal sphere of radius b suspended in the center of a room is approximately $4\pi\epsilon_0 b$.

10 A parallel-plate air capacitor which has a plate separation of 10^{-4} cm and a capacitance of 10^{-3} μF carries a charge of 0.10 μC. Find the electric field between the plates.

11 If the charge on a capacitor is changing in the following way

$$Q = Q_0 + At + Bt^2$$

what is the current in the wires leading to the capacitor?

12 A particular capacitor-resistance circuit has a time constant of 1 μsec. What fraction of the total final charge is on the capacitor 0.10 μsec after starting charging?

13 How long must one wait, in units of the time constant, for a capacitor to lose 99 percent of its charge? What is the current at that time, as a fraction of the original current?

8 ☐ 44 Ω

The constants in tables such as Bueche, table 21.1 are not strictly correct over such a large range. However, to first approximation, $\alpha = \alpha_{20} = 4.5 \times 10^{-3}/°C$ and $R_{1820} = R_{20}(1 + \alpha_{20} \times 1800)$

$400 = R_{20}(1 + 8.1)$ from which $R_{20} \cong 44\ \Omega$.

9 The metal sphere constitutes one plate of the capacitor and the earth or room walls constitute the other. We approximate the situation by saying the outer plate is effectively at infinity. Then the potential of the sphere relative to the walls (infinity) is $V = \left(\frac{1}{4\pi\epsilon_0}\right)\frac{Q}{b}$. Since by definition $C = \frac{Q}{V}$, one has $C = 4\pi\epsilon_0 b$.

10 ☐ 10^8 volts/m

For a parallel-plate capacitor, since E is constant between the plates, $V = Ed$. Since $C = 10^{-9}$ F and $Q = 10^{-7}$ C, $V = Q/C = 100$ volts. Therefore $E = V/d = 10^8$ volts/m.

a

11 ☐ $A + 2Bt$

By the definition of current as the charge per second passing a given point in the wire, $I = dQ/dt$.

12 ☐ 0.095

The charging equation for a capacitor is (Bueche, Eq. 21.17) $Q = CV_0 (1 - e^{-t/\tau})$ where τ is the time constant and CV_0 is the final charge. Therefore, in our case

$$\frac{Q}{Q_0} = 1 - e^{-0.10}$$

$$= 1 - \left[1 - 0.10 + \frac{(0.10)^2}{2!} - \ldots\right]$$

$$\cong 0.095$$

13 ☐ 4.60; 0.01

The discharge of a capacitor follows the relation (Bueche, Eq. 21.20) $Q = Q_0 e^{-t/\tau}$, and so $0.01 = e^{-t/\tau}$ from which $t/\tau = 4.60$. But $I = dQ/dt = I_0 e^{-t/\tau}$ and so $I/I_0 = 0.01$.

14 A capacitor–resistor circuit charges to a maximum charge Q_0. (a) How much energy is stored in the capacitor at the end? (b) How much energy was lost in the resistor? (c) How much energy did the battery supply? (d) Show that the sum of (a) and (b) is (c).

15 Show that at any instant when a capacitor is being charged through a resistor R by a battery V_0, the power output of the battery is equal to the sum of the power expended in resistor and capacitor.

16 Reduce the capacitor scheme below to a single equivalent capacitor. (All capacitances are in microfarads.)

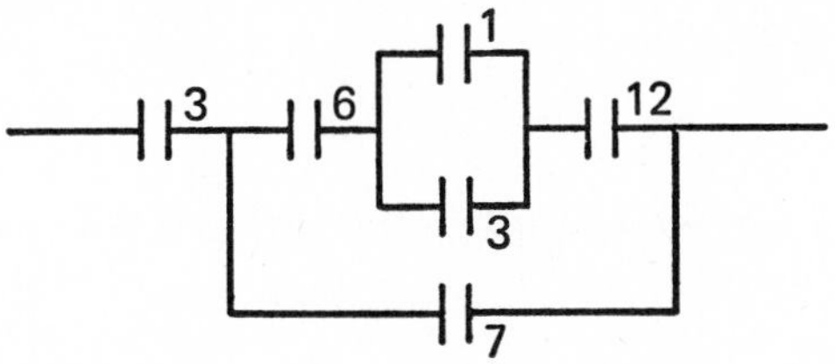

14 (a) Final energy $= \frac{1}{2}CV_0^2 = \frac{1}{2}Q_0V_0 = \frac{Q_0^2}{2C}$

(b) Work $= \int_0^\infty (\text{Power})\ dt = \int_0^\infty i^2R\ dt = \frac{V_0^2}{R}\int_0^\infty e^{-2t/RC}\ dt = \frac{1}{2}CV_0^2$

(c) Energy $= \int_0^\infty (\text{Power})\ dt = \int_0^\infty V_0 i\ dt = \frac{V_0^2}{R}\int_0^\infty e^{-t/RC}\ dt = CV_0^2$

(d) $\frac{1}{2}CV_0^2 + \frac{1}{2}CV_0^2 = CV_0^2$

15 Since power $= VI$, one has, for the battery, $P_B = V_0I$. For the resistor one has $P_R = I^2R$ and for the capacitor $P_C = V_CI = (Q/C)I$. Now

$$I = (V_0/R)e^{-t/RC} \quad \text{and} \quad Q = CV_0\,(1 - e^{-t/RC})$$

$$P_R = IV_0\,e^{-t/RC} \quad \text{and} \quad P_C = IV_0\,(1 - e^{-t/RC})$$

Clearly, $P_R + P_C = P_B$.

16 ☐ 2.25 μF

Since capacitors in parallel add directly, the system is equivalent to

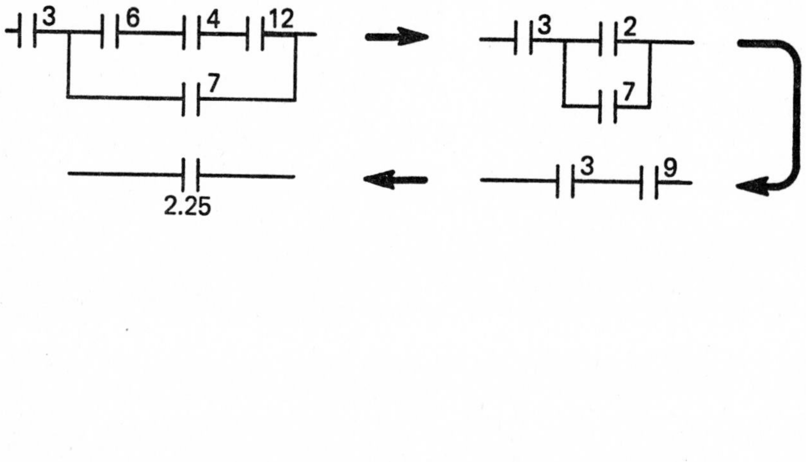

17 For the capacitor system of the previous problem, find the charge on the 6-μF capacitor if the combination is connected across an 8-V battery.

18 In the circuit shown, the voltmeter reads 12V. Find the capacitance of C_X.

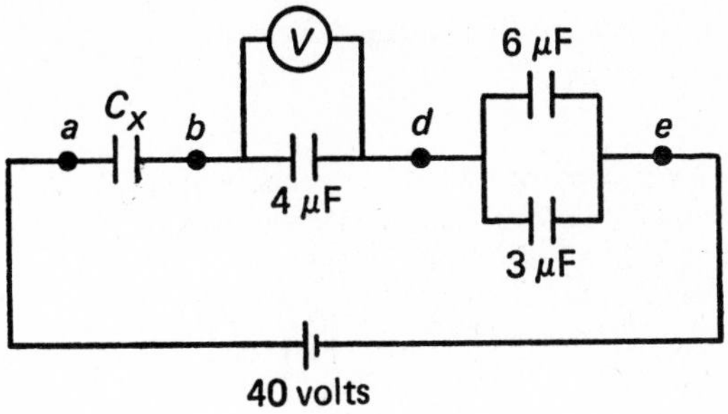

19 A 5-μF capacitor is fully charged across a 12-V battery. It is then disconnected and connected across an unknown, uncharged capacitor C_X. The voltage is now 3 V. How large is C_X?

17 ☐ 4 μC

We work backward through the diagram as follows, recalling that capacitors in series must have the same charge.

The potential difference across the 9-μF capacitor is $V = Q/C = 2$ volts. Thus the potential across the 2-μF is 2 volts and so its charge is 4 μC. But the 2-μF is equivalent to a 6-, 4-, and 12-μF capacitor in series

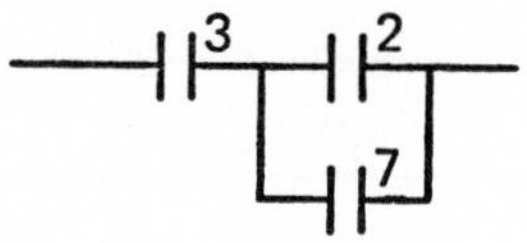

and each of these must also have 4μC.

18 ☐ 2.1 μF

The charge on the 4-μF capacitor is $Q = CV = 48$ μC. But C_x and the 9-μF equivalent of the 6- and 3-μF combination must also each have 48 μC charges. Therefore, the voltage drops are as follows: $V_{bd} = 12$ volts; $V_{de} = 5.3$ volts. Using Kirchhoff's loop equation one has $- V_{ab} - 12 - 5.3 + 40 = 0$ from which $V_{ab} = 22.7$ volts. Then, using $C_x = Q/V =$ 48μC/22.7 volts gives $C_x = 2.1$ μF.

19 ☐ 15 μF

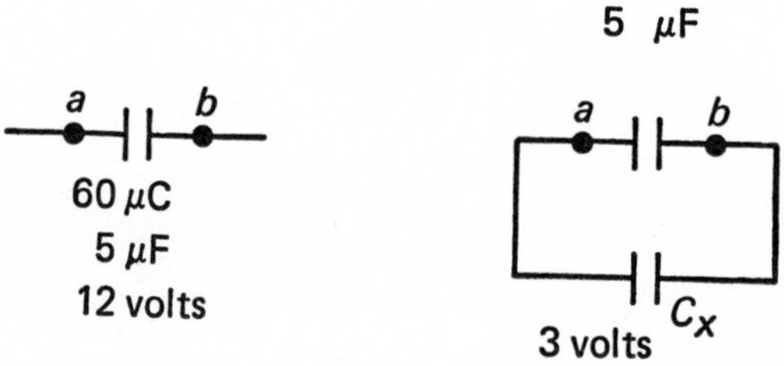

The situation is shown. Originally the capacitor had 60 μC charge. After, it had only 15 μC. Therefore, C_x must have 45 μC. Since the voltage across it is 3 volts, one has $C_x = Q/V =$ 45 μC/3 volts.

20 Repeat the previous problem if C_x was originally charged to a potential of 12 V also.

q
21
question
20

20 □ 3 μF

In order for the voltage to drop when they are connected, the + side of 5 μF must be connected to - side of C_x, otherwise V would still be 12 volts. Denoting the original and final charge on C_x by Q_{xo} and Q_x, one has

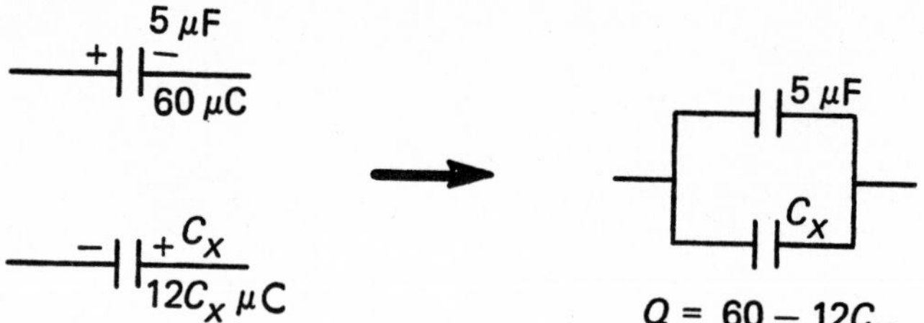

$Q = 60 - 12C_x$

$V = 3$ volts

$C = 5 + C_x$ μF

For the final situation, $Q = CV$ gives

$$60 - 12C_x = (5 + C_x)3$$

from which

$$15C_x = 45$$

and $C_x = 3\,\mu F$

a

21
answer
20

22 dc circuits

1 (a) The algebraic sum of all the currents coming into a given point in a circuit is ________ .

(b) In addition, the sum of all the voltage rises and drops around a closed circuit (rises being taken as positive, drops as negative) is________.

(c) In moving across a resistor in the direction in which the current is assumed to flow, there is a voltage drop given by Ohm's law as ________.

(d) Similarly, going through a battery from its ________ to ________ terminal is equivalent to a voltage drop denoted by the symbol $-\mathcal{E}$.

2 (a) When a current I is being drawn from the + side of a battery, the terminal voltage of the battery, in terms of the emf $\mathcal{E}$ and the internal resistance r, is equal to ________.

(b) Under these conditions the terminal voltage is always ________ than $\mathcal{E}$.

(c) The terminal voltage can be greater than $\mathcal{E}$ when ________ .

(d) In that case, the terminal voltage is ________ .

3 (a) When a current I is flowing through a circuit element from its + to - end and the element has a voltage difference V across it, the power being furnished to the element is ________.

(b) If the element is a resistor, V will be equal to ________ so the power dissipated in a resistor is ________.

(c) If the current is charging a battery, the terminal voltage is ________; where r is the internal resistance of the battery, ________ is the power furnished to the battery.

(d) That part of the power represented in (c) by the term ________ is the energy per second being stored inside the battery, and the term I^2r represents ________.

1 (a) Zero

(b) Zero

(c) $-IR$

(d) + to -

2 (a) $\mathcal{E} - Ir$

(b) Less

(c) The battery is being charged.

(d) $\mathcal{E} + Ir$

3 (a) VI

(b) $IR; I^2R$

(c) $\mathcal{E} + Ir; \mathcal{E}I + I^2r$

(d) $\mathcal{E} I$; power dissipated by the internal resistance.

a

22
answers
1-3

4 State Kirchhoff's two laws.

5 (a) In the circuit below, the current in wires *ef, fa,* and *ab* is _________ while in *bc, cd,* and *de* it is _________.

(b) Traversing loop *abefa* in that order gives the loop equation _________.

(c) The term -4 carries a negative sign because _________, while the term $-8I$ is negative because _________.

(d) Traversing the loop *bcdeb* gives the equation _________.

(e) From these two equations we find I_1 = _________ ampere and I_3 = _________ ampere.

(f) To find I_2, we consider the point rule applied to point b, which yields the equation _________, where currents into the point are positive and those out are negative.

(g) Substituting in (f) the values found for I_1 and I_3 in (e) yields I_2 = _________ ampere.

(h) The negative sign tells us _________.

(i) The power furnished by the 6–, 4–, and 2–volt batteries is _________ watt, _________ watt, and _________ watt, respectively, while the total power consumed in the resistors is _________ watts. We note that the power furnished by the batteries equals the power consumed by the resistors.

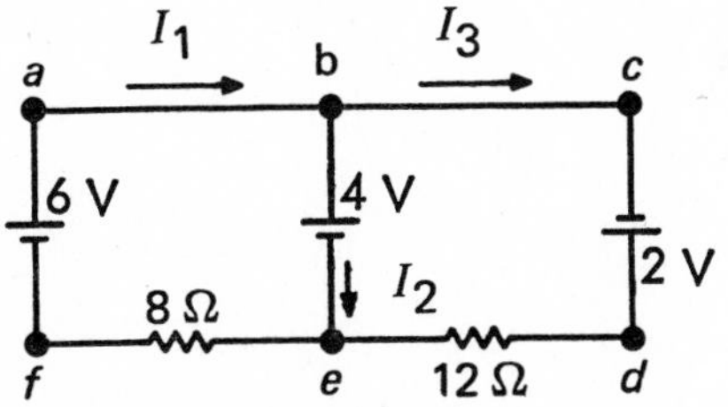

4 Loop law: The algebraic sum of the potential rises and drops around a closed loop in a circuit is zero. Point law: The algebraic sum of the currents coming into any point in a dc circuit is zero.

5 (a) $I_1; I_3$

(b) $-4 - 8I_1 + 6 = 0$

(c) Moving from the + to the - terminal of a battery corresponds to a voltage drop; moving through a resistor in the direction in which the current is flowing corresponds to a voltage drop.

(d) $+2 - 12I_3 + 4 = 0$

(e) $\frac{1}{4}; \frac{1}{2}$

(f) $I_1, -I_2 - I_3 = 0$

(g) $-\frac{1}{4}$

(h) That I_2 really flows opposite to the direction indicated.

(i) 1.5; 1.0; 1.0; 3.5.

a

22
answers
4-5

6 For the circuit shown, find.

(a) Equivalent resistance.

(b) Voltage drop across the 5 Ω.

(c) Current through the 2 Ω.

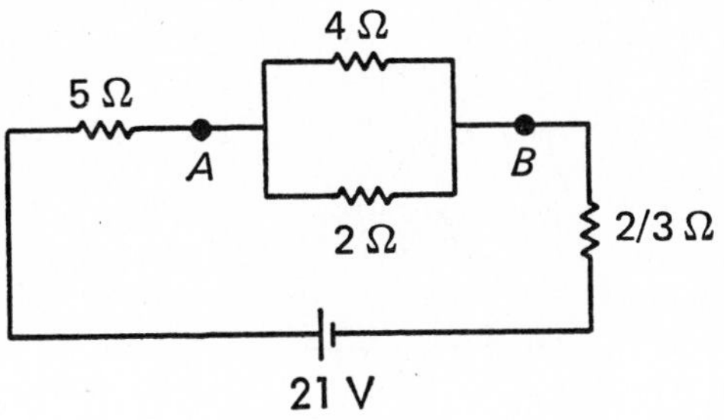

7 When the battery shown in the previous problem is replaced by another battery with unknown voltage, the current through the 4Ω resistor is 3.0 A. Find the voltage of the new battery.

6 ☐ 7 Ω; 15 volts; 2 A

Reduce the parallel portion to yield

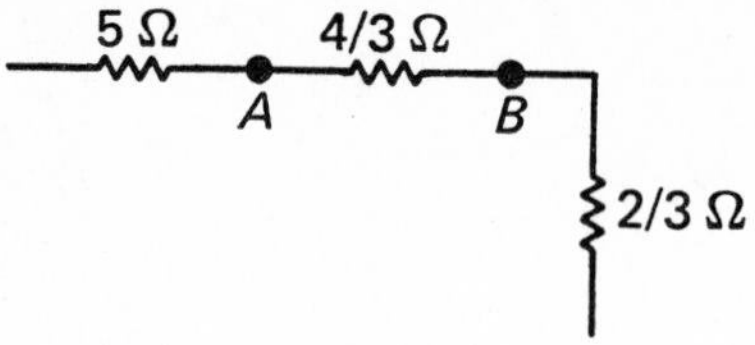

These added in series yield the circuit

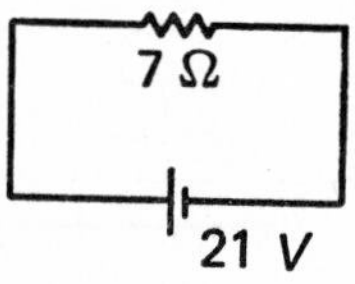

The current through this is $I = V/R = 3$ A. Therefore the drop across the 5 Ω is $V = (3)(5) = 15$ volts. The drop across the $\frac{4}{3}$ Ω is 4 volts and is also the drop across the 2 Ω resistor (since both are the drop from A to B). Therefore I in 2 Ω is $\frac{4}{2}$ A.

7 ☐ 63 volts

The potential drop from A to B will be 3 X 4 = 12 volts. This must also be the drop across the 4/3 Ω equivalent resistor between A and B. Therefore the current through the main circuit is $I = V/R = 12/(4/3) = 9$ A. Since the main circuit has a total equivalent resistance of 7 Ω and a current of 9 A, the battery must have a voltage of (7) (9) = 63 volts.

8 Find the equivalent resistance.

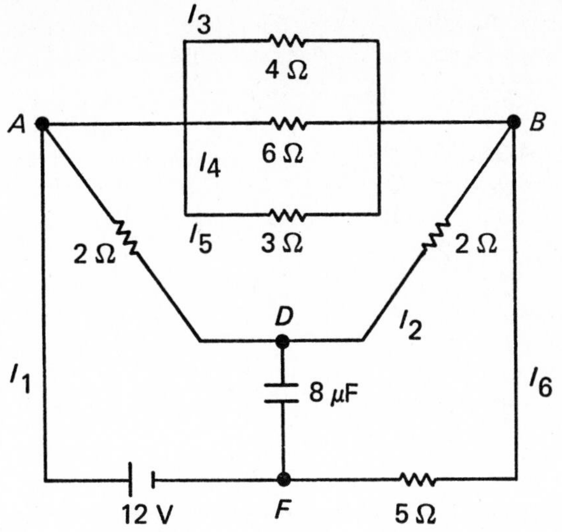

9 For the circuit in problem 8 find $I_1, I_2,$ and I_3; the charge on the capacitor; and the energy stored in the capacitor.

10 For the circuit shown, find $I_1, I_2,$ and I_3.

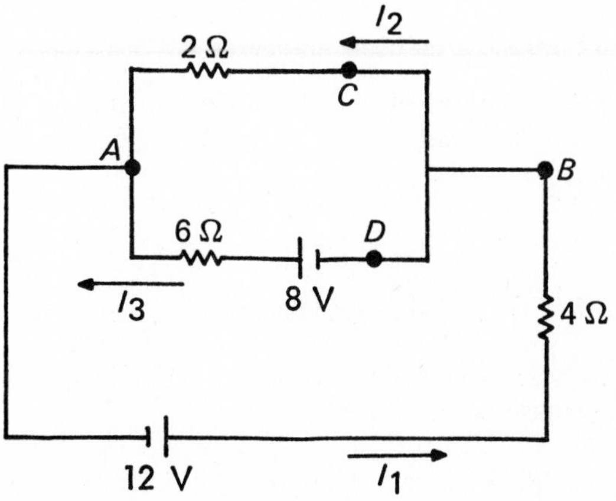

8 ☐ 6 Ω

Since no current flows through a capacitor in a dc circuit, the resistance between D and F through the capacitor is infinite and so the wire can be removed. The circuit is shown below and so $R_{eq} = 6\ \Omega$.

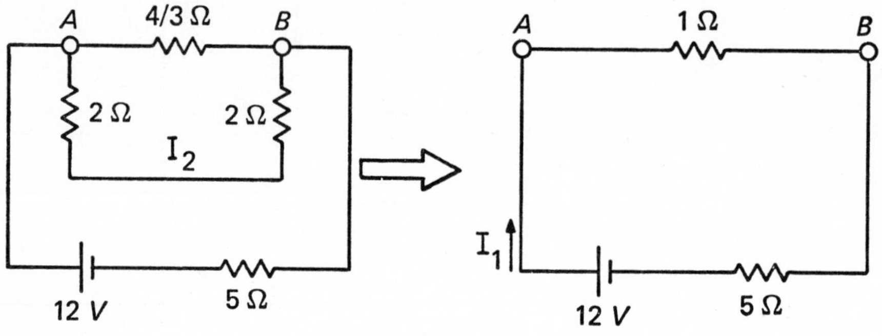

a

9 ☐ 2 ampere; 0.5 ampere; 0.5 ampere; 88 μC; 4.8 X 10^{-4} J

From the equivalent resistance found in problem 8, $I_1 = \frac{12}{6} = 2$ ampere. The potential drop from A to B is $I_1 R_{AB} = 2$ volts. To find I_2 notice that, from the simplified diagram, $I_2 = V_{AB}/4 = \frac{1}{2}$ ampere. Similarly, since the full 2-volt drop from A to B exists across the upper resistor, $I_3 = \frac{2}{4} = \frac{1}{2}$ ampere. We need V_{DF} to find Q. Writing the loop equation for $DFAD$ gives $V_{DF} + 12 - 2(1/2) = 0$ so $V_{DF} = 11$ volts. Therefore $Q = CV = 88\ \mu C$. The stored energy is $\frac{1}{2}QV = 4.8 \times 10^{-4}$ J.

22
answers
8-10

10 ☐ 28/11 ampere; 10/11 ampere; 18/11 ampere

The upper two wires *cannot* be reduced as a parallel-resistance system because of the battery. We write the loop equations:

Loop $ABDA$: $+12 - 4I_1 + 8 - 6I_3 = 0$

Loop $ADCA$: $+6I_3 - 8 - 2I_2 = 0$

and the point equation for point A:

$I_2 + I_3 = I_1$

Solving simultaneously for $I_1, I_2,$ and I_3 gives the answers listed above.

11 Find I_1, I_2, I_3, and I_4.

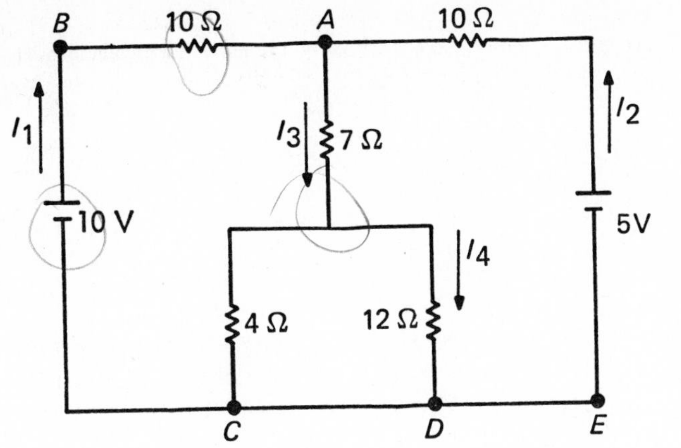

12 The voltmeter reads 5 volts and the ammeter reads 2 ampere with I in the direction shown. Find R and $\mathcal{E}$.

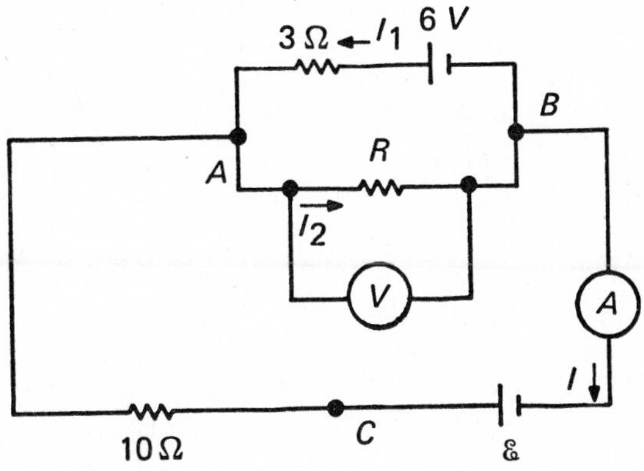

13 Find I_1 and I_2 and the charge on the capacitor when K is open.

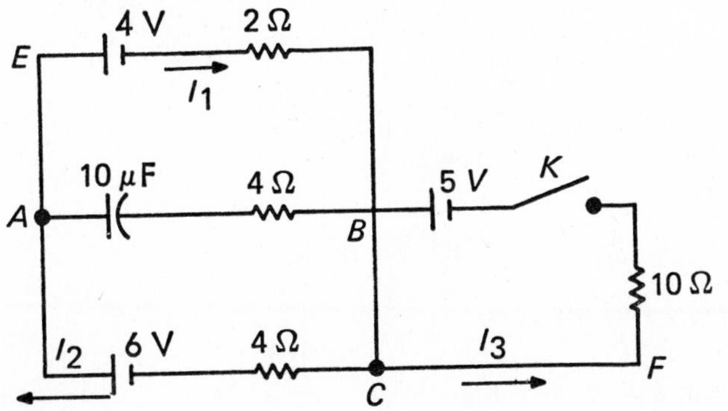

14 Repeat the previous problem if K is closed. Also find I_3.

22
questions
11-14

11 □ $\frac{1}{2}$; 0; $\frac{1}{2}$; $\frac{1}{8}$ ampere

First replace the 4-, 12-ohm combination by a single 3 Ω equivalent resistor thereby giving the central wire 10 Ω resistance.

Loop $ABCA$: $+10I_1 - 10 + 10I_3 = 0$

Loop $AEBA$: $+10I_2 - 5 + 10I_3 = 0$

At point A: $I_1 + I_2 - I_3 = 0$

Solving simultaneously yields the given values. To find I_4 we note that the voltage drop across the 12-Ω resistor is the same as that across the 3-Ω equivalent, $3I_3$.

Then $12I_4 = 3\left(\frac{1}{2}\right)$ gives $I_4 = \frac{1}{8}$ ampere.

12 □ 25 volts; 2.1 Ω

Notice that $V_{AB} = 5$ volts and so for Loop $ABCA$: $-5 + \mathcal{E} - (10)(2) = 0$ from which $\mathcal{E} = 25$ volts.

Through the 6-volt battery from A to B, one has $-5 = +3I_1 - 6$ so $I_1 = \frac{1}{3}$ ampere.

Applying the point rule at A gives $I_2 = 2.33$ ampere. Then $I_2R = 5$ gives $R = 2.14$ Ω.

a

22

answers

11-14

13 □ $\frac{1}{3}$; $\frac{1}{3}$ ampere; $\frac{140}{3}$ μC

Since the capacitor and open switch pass no current, $I_1 = I_2$. Writing the loop equation: $-4 - 2I_1 - 4I_1 + 6 = 0$; $I_1 = \frac{1}{3}$ ampere. Calling V_C the voltage drop across the capacitor

Loop $ABCA$: $-V_C + (0)(4) - \left(\frac{1}{3}\right)(4) + 6 = 0$ so $V_C = \frac{14}{3}$ volts. But $Q = CV_C =$ 140/3 μC.

14 □ $\frac{1}{3}$; $\frac{1}{3}$ ampere; $\frac{140}{3}$ μC; $\frac{1}{2}$ ampere

Loop $EBCAE$: $-4 - 2I_1 - 4I_2 + 6 = 0$

Loop $BFCB$: $-5 + 10I_3 = 0$

and at point A: $I_1 - I_2 = 0$

Solving gives $I_1 = I_2 = \frac{1}{3}$, $I_3 = \frac{1}{2}$ ampere. Q is found in the same way as before to be 140/3 μC.

23
magnetic fields

1 (a) When a small magnet is placed in a magnetic field, it lines up ________ to the field, with its ________ pole pointing in the direction of the field.

(b) The strength of the magnetic field is measured in the mks system in ________ or ________.

(c) The magnetic field caused by a current in a wire ________ the wire, while the magnetic field of a magnet points out of the ________ pole and into the ________ pole.

2 (a) If a positive charge q moves with velocity **v** through a magnetic field **B**, it experiences a force given by the relation ________.

(b) The direction of the force is perpendicular to the plane determined by ________ and ________.

(c) If the particle is negative rather than positive, the direction of the force is ________ to the force direction a positive charge would experience.

(d) When the particle is moving ________ to the field, the particle experiences no force.

(e) When the particle is moving ________ to the field, it is deflected into a circular path.

(f) The radius of the path may be found by equating the ________ force, given by the relation ________, to the required centripetal force, given by the relation ________.

3 (a) A straight wire of length **dL** carrying a current I through a magnetic field **B** experiences a force given by the relation ________.

(b) The direction of the force is perpendicular to the plane determined by ________ and ________.

(c) The appropriate direction can be found from the ________ rule.

1 (a) parallel; north

(b) webers/m^2 or tesla

(c) circles; north; south

2 (a) $\mathbf{F} = q\mathbf{v} \times \mathbf{B}$

(b) **v** and **B**

(c) opposite

(d) parallel

(e) perpendicular

(f) magnetic, qvB; mv^2/r

3 (a) $d\mathbf{F} = I\, d\mathbf{L} \times \mathbf{B}$

(b) **dL** and **B**

(c) right-hand

a

23
answers
1-3

4 Find the direction and magnitude of the force on the positive charges shown.

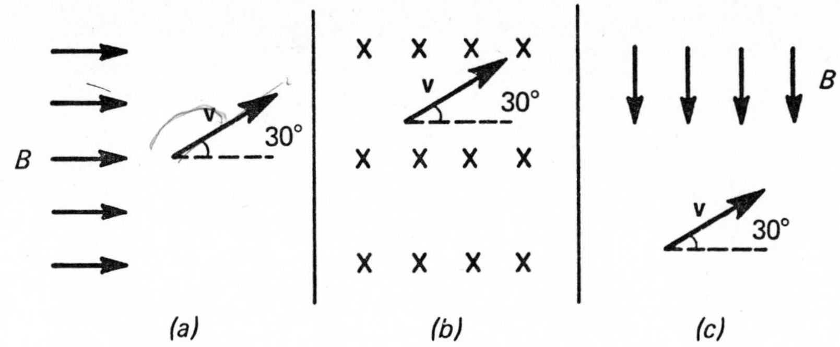

5 Repeat the previous problem with the vector **v** replaced by a current element I **dL**.

6 Repeat problem 4 with q being a negative charge.

7 A charge q falls through a potential difference V and enters a region where a magnetic field B exists directed perpendicular to its motion. Find the radius of the circular path which it will describe, assuming nonrelativistic speeds.

8 An electron with speed 10^6 m/sec enters a region perpendicular to a magnetic field of 200 G. How long will it take for the electron to reverse its direction? (G stands for gauss.)

9 Find the force per unit length of wire shown in a magnetic field of 300 G.

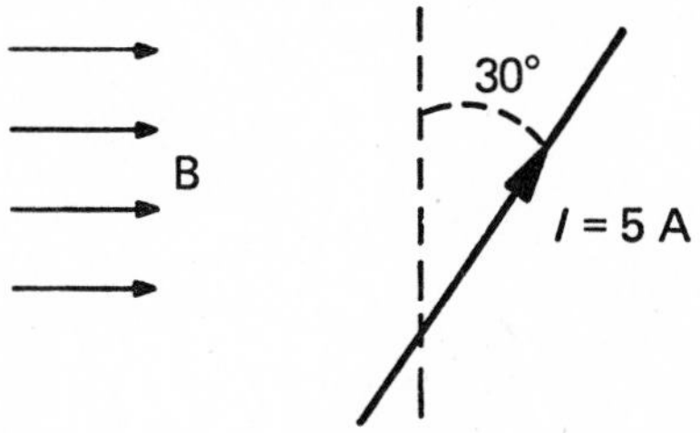

4 (a) Into page and of magnitude = $qvB \sin 30°$.

(b) Taking the usual x and y axes in the plane of the page, at 120° to the $+x$ axis, $F = qvB$.

(c) $qvB \cos 30°$ into the page.

5 All answers are the same with qv replaced by $I\,dL$.

6 All answers are the same except the forces are in the opposite direction.

7 □ $\sqrt{2Vm/qB^2}$

Equating centripetal and magnetic force gives $mv^2/r = qvB$, from which $r = mv/qB$. However, in falling through the potential V, it acquires a kinetic energy Vq so that $Vq = \frac{1}{2}mv^2$ gives $v = \sqrt{2qV/m}$. Substitution in the relation for r gives the desired result.

a

23
answers
4-9

8 □ 8.8×10^{-10} sec

First find the radius of the circular path in which it will move from $mv^2/r = qvB$. We use $B = 2 \times 10^{-2}$ T and find $r = 2.8 \times 10^{-4}$ m. The time taken to move halfway around such a circle (i.e., to reverse its direction) is $t = \pi r/v = 8.8 \times 10^{-10}$ sec.

9 □ 0.13 N/m

The force is

$$|d\mathbf{F}| = |I\,d\mathbf{L} \times \mathbf{B}| = IB\,dL \sin 60°$$

Therefore

$$\frac{dF}{dL} = IB \sin 60° = (5)(0.030)(0.87) = 0.13 \text{ N/m}$$

10 For the situation shown below, show that the force on the wire is simply IyB.

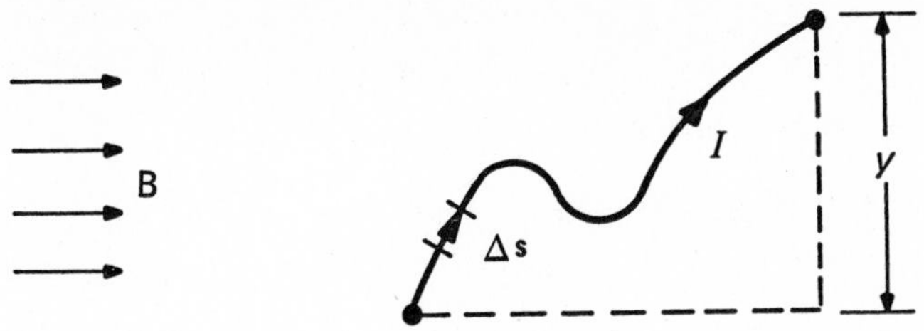

11 The Hall coefficient for bismuth is about -10^{-8}(V • m)/(A • T). What is the corresponding value of n, the density of free elections? Compare this value with the number of Bi atoms per unit volume (ρ_{Bi} = 9.8 g/cm^3).

12

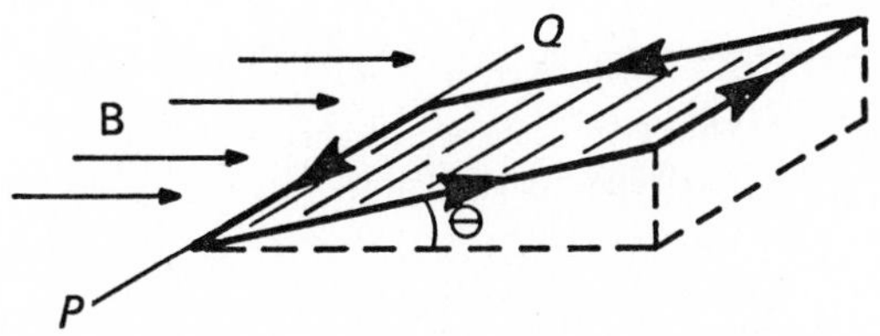

The current loop shown has an area A and a current I around it. Find the magnitude and direction of the torque on it.

13 It is desired to use a meter which carries a maximum of 1 ma as a voltmeter designed to register full scale for 10,000 V. How large a resistance must be placed in series with it? What power must the resistor be capable of dissipating?

10 Notice that the y component of the vector length Δs is $\Delta s \sin\theta$ where θ is the angle between **B** and Δs.

But

$$|\Delta \mathbf{F}| = |I\,\Delta \mathbf{s} \times \mathbf{B}| = IB\,\Delta s \sin\theta = IB\,\Delta y$$

As a result $F = IB\Sigma\,\Delta y = IBy$ and the point is proven.

11 ☐ 6.3×10^{26} electrons/m^3; 45 atoms/electron

The Hall constant is $1/nq$ and so the charge carriers are negative. Equating

$$10^{-8} = \frac{1}{n(1.6 \times 10^{-19})}$$

gives $n = 6.3 \times 10^{26}$ electrons/m^3. The density of Bi is 9.8×10^3 kg/m^3 and its atomic weight is 209 so in 1 m^3 there are $6 \times 10^{26}\,(9.8 \times 10^3/209)$ $= 2.8 \times 10^{28}$ atoms/m^3. This large discrepancy indicates that the electrical properties of Bi cannot be described simply in terms of its valence electrons.

a

23
answers
10-13

12 ☐ $AIB \sin(90° + \theta)$ directed from P to Q

In general the torque on a current loop is $\tau = AI\mathbf{n} \times \mathbf{B}$ or, in magnitude alone, $\tau = AIB \sin(90° + \theta)$ since **n** is perpendicular to the area and upward. Turning **n** into line with **B**, we see that a right-handed screw would advance along PQ toward Q so the torque is a vector from P to Q. This means the loop will rotate so as to decrease θ, as one may easily verify by examining the forces on the wires of the loop. In equilibrium, $\theta = -90°$.

13 ☐ $10^7\ \Omega$; 10 W

When 10^4 volts is placed across the meter, we want a current of 10^{-3} A to flow through it. Therefore $V = IR$ gives $R = 10^7\ \Omega$. Since the resistance of the milliampere meter will be negligible in comparison, we must add a series resistance of $10^7\ \Omega$. The power loss in the resistor will be I^2R which will be $(10^{-3})^2(10^7) = 10$ W. Ordinary 10-MΩ resistors would not be capable of dissipating this power without burning out.

14 A 20-μA meter (full-scale deflection) having resistance of 50 Ω is to be made into a 1.0-A meter. How large a shunt resistance must be placed in parallel with it?

15 How long a piece of copper wire of diameter 0.50 mm must be used for the shunt in the previous problem?

$\rho_{Cu} = 1.7 \times 10^{-8}\ \Omega \cdot m.$

16 An electron accelerated through 10^6 V will describe how large a circle when moving perpendicular to a 500-G field?

q

23
questions
14-16

14 □ $10^{-3}\,\Omega$

The current going through the shunt will be $1.0 - 20 \times 10^{-6} \cong 1.0$ A. Since the same potential drop must exist across both the shunt and meter, $(1.0)R_s = (20 \times 10^{-6})(50)$ from which the shunt resistance

$$R_s = 10^{-3}\,\Omega$$

15 □ 11.6 cm

We have $R = \dfrac{\rho L}{A}$ and $A = \pi r^2 = 1.97 \times 10^{-7}$ m^2. Therefore $L = 1.16$ cm.

16 □ 1.16 cm

A relativistic particle such as this will satisfy the equation

$$\frac{mv^2}{r} = qvB$$

provided the relativistic mass is used. Now $(10^6)(1.6 \times 10^{-19}) = mc^2 - m_oc^2$ so that $m = 27.0 \times 10^{-31}$ kg $\cong 3m_o$. To find v we note $(m_o/m)^2 = 1 - (v/c)^2$ so that $v/c = 0.94$ giving $v = 2.8 \times 10^8$ m/sec. Solving for r, we find 9.4 cm.

a

23
answers
14-16

24 sources of magnetic fields

1 The two fundamental relations for computing magnetic fields are__________.

2 Ampere's circuital law is most useful when the physical situation possesses__________. In that case__________.

3 For the current element $d\mathbf{L}$ shown at the origin of coordinates, find the direction of **B** at points P, Q, R, S, and T.

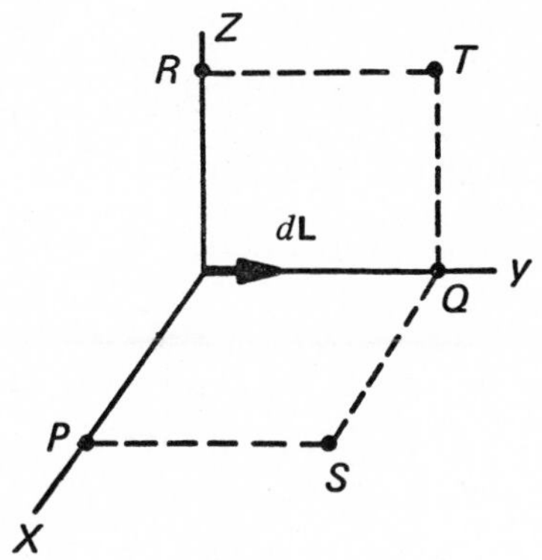

4 Two long parallel wires a distance b apart carry currents I_1 and I_2 in opposite directions. Are there any points near the wires where B will be zero?

q

24 questions 1-4

1 Ampere's circuital law:

$$\int \mathbf{B} \cdot d\mathbf{s} = \mu_0 \int \mathbf{J} \cdot d\mathbf{A}$$

Biot-Savart law:

$$dB = \frac{\mu_0 I}{4\pi} \frac{d\mathbf{L} \times \hat{\mathbf{r}}}{r^2}$$

2 A large amount of symmetry. B can be removed as a constant from the integral.

3 Using the right-hand rule and recalling that **B** is perpendicular to the plane of $d\ell$ and **r**, the field directions are: at P, $-Z$ direction; at Q, no field; at R, $+x$ direction; at S, $-Z$ direction; at T, $+x$ direction.

4 ☐ Yes; if $I_1 > I_2$, $r = \dfrac{I_2 b}{I_1 - I_2}$

a

24
answers
1-4

In the region between the wires, **B** is into the page from both currents so the fields cannot cancel there.

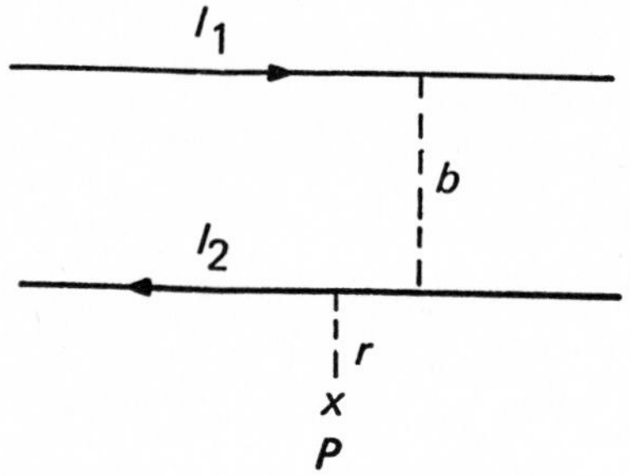

If $I_1 > I_2$, then there is a possibility that the fields will cancel at points such as P. The condition would be

$$B_1 = B_2 = \frac{\mu_0 I_1}{2\pi(r+b)} = \frac{\mu_0 I_2}{2\pi(r)}$$

from which

$$r = \frac{I_2 b}{I_1 - I_2}$$

If $I_2 > I_1$, the point P would be on the other side of I_1.

5 Two long wires carry equal currents I out along the $+x$ and $+y$ axes. Find the magnetic field at the point (0, 0,5).

6 Prove that the magnetic field is zero inside a wire which is actually a cylindrical shell.

7 For the wire of the previous problem, show that B outside the wire does not depend upon whether or not the wire is hollow.

5 ☐ $\frac{\mu_0 I}{5\pi\sqrt{2}}$

The fields due to the two wires are as shown. Since

$$B_1 = B_2 = \frac{\mu_0 I}{2\pi(5)}$$

and since the two fields are mutually perpendicular,

$$B = \sqrt{B_1^2 + B_2^2} = \frac{\mu_0 I}{5\pi\sqrt{2}}$$

directed at an angle of 45° below the $+x$ axis.

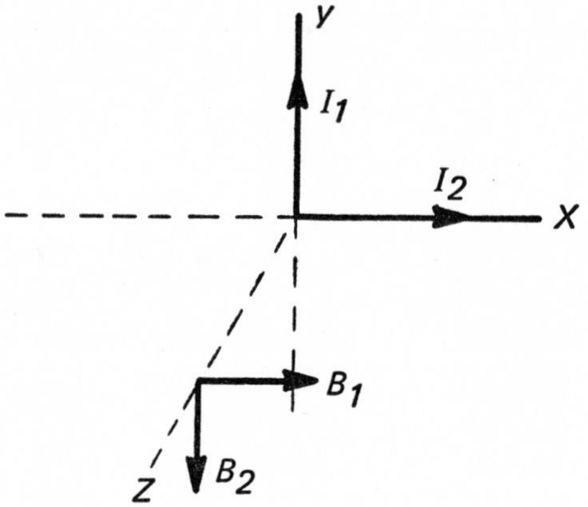

a

24
answers
5-7

6 Take a circular path as shown for use of Ampere's law: $\oint \mathbf{B} \cdot d\mathbf{s} = \mu_0 I$ enclosed. Since I is zero inside this path, B must be zero along it.

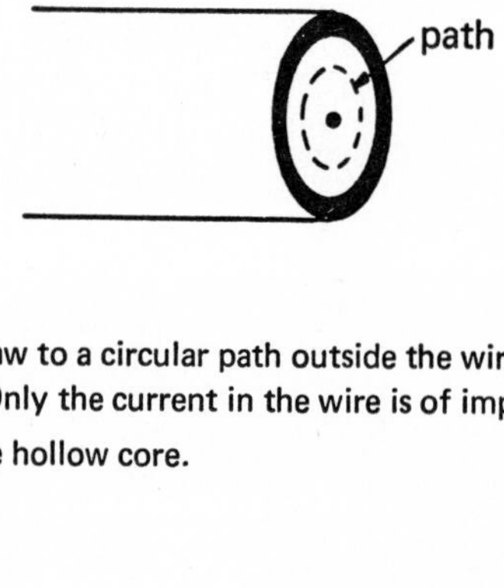

7 If we apply Ampere's law to a circular path outside the wire and concentric to it, we obtain $B = \mu_0 I/2\pi r$. Only the current in the wire is of importance and no effect is observed because of the hollow core.

8 A uniformly charged sphere spins about an axis as shown. What can one conclude from an application of Ampere's law to the dotted path?

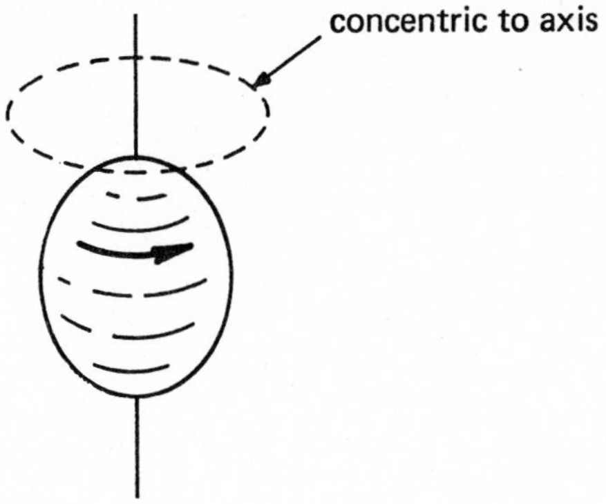

9 Repeat the previous problem using a circular path concentric to the sphere but having the rotation axis as a diameter.

10 Find the magnetic field at point P, the center of curvature of the arc shown.

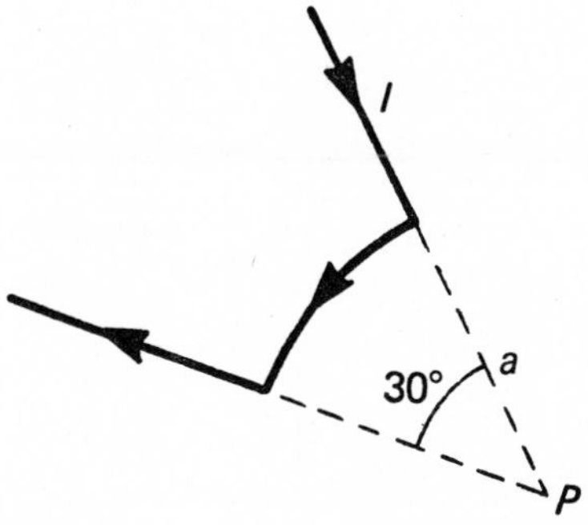

q

24
questions
8-10

8 First one notices that no current flows through the area defined by this path. Therefore $\oint \mathbf{B} \cdot ds = 0$. From symmetry, B is constant on the path and so the component of B tangential to the dotted circle is zero. Therefore, if a field exists, it must be radial or axial or both, but not tangential.

9 As the sphere spins, charge passes out of one-half the circular area and into the other half, thereby making $I = 0$. However, nothing very definite can be said about B because all points on such a path are not equivalent.

10 ☐ $\frac{\mu_0 I}{24a}$

Because the lead-in and lead-out wires have no effect (why?), we could find this by simply taking 30/360 of the field due to a circular loop. Or, we could use Biot-Savart:

$$dB = \frac{\mu_0 I}{4\pi} \frac{d\ell \sin 90°}{a^2}$$

Since all the dBs are in the same direction $B = \frac{\mu_0 I}{4\pi a^2} \int_0^{2\pi a/12} d\ell = \frac{\mu_0 I}{24a}$

a

24

answers

8-10

11 The loop of inner radius a and outer radius b carries a current I_1. At P a long straight wire carries a current I_2 out of the page. Find the total force on the loop because of the field of I_2.

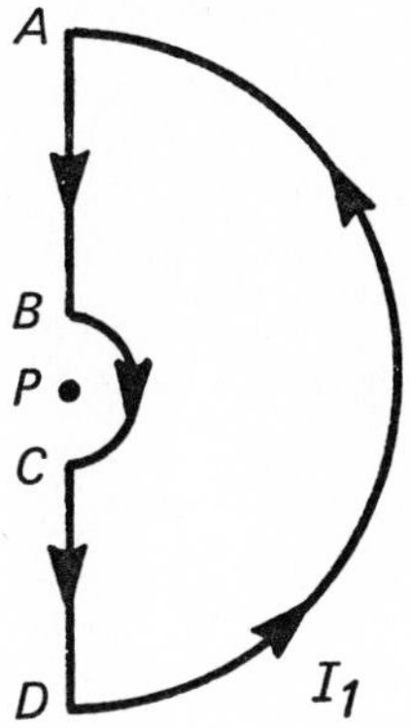

12 Find the torque on the loop of the previous problem.

13 Design a solenoid which could be placed over a cylindrical vacuum tube to keep a 100-eV electron circling the axis of the tube in a circle of 1 cm radius.

14 A long belt carries a surface charge of σC/m^2, is 3.0 cm wide, and moves at a rate of 2 m/sec. Find the magnetic field generated by the belt 3 m away from it.

11 ☐ Zero

The field of I_2 circles P and so is parallel to the two arcs, thereby causing no force on them. Below P the field is to the right, causing an upward force on CD. Above P, the field is to the left, causing an equal and opposite force. The sum of these forces is zero.

12 ☐ $\dfrac{\mu_0 I_1 I_2 (b-a)}{\pi}$

The force on the element $d\ell$ is out of the page and is $B_\ell I_1\, d\ell$ where $B_\ell = \mu_0 I_2/2\pi\ell$ is the field at $d\ell$ due to I_2. Taking torques about P,

$$d\tau = \ell\,(B_\ell I_1\, d\ell) = \frac{\mu_0 I_1 I_2\, d\ell}{2\pi}$$

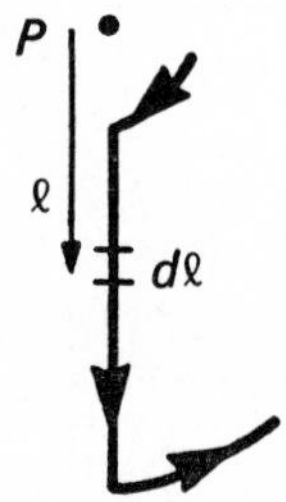

a

24
answers
11-14

Summing from $\ell = a$ to $\ell = b$ gives $\tau = (\mu_0 I_1 I_2/2\pi)\,(b - a)$. A similar torque exists upon the upper segment and both torques cause rotation in the same direction (outward at D), so the total torque is twice this value.

13 ☐ $nI = 2700$ A/m

The electron's velocity is (from $\dfrac{mv^2}{2}$ = energy) 6×10^6 m/sec. Using $qvB = mv^2/r$, one finds $B = 3.4 \times 10^{-3}$ T. For a long solenoid, $B = \mu_0 nI$ and so $nI = 2700$ A/m. For a current of 1 A, the solenoid would have to have 2700 loops per meter.

14 ☐ $4\sigma \times 10^{-9}$

The total current $\Delta Q/\Delta t$ carried by the belt will be the belt area passing a point per second multiplied by σ.

$I = (2 \times 0.03)\,\sigma = 0.06\,\sigma$ A. At 3 m away, the long, relatively thin belt can be considered a long wire and so $B = \mu_0 I/2\pi r = 0.06\,\sigma\mu_0/6\pi$, a very small field indeed for reasonable σ.

25 magnetic induction effects

1 State the mathematical relation expressing Faraday's and Lenz's laws.

2 How does one compute the magnetic flux through an area?

3 When the switch is suddenly closed in circuit A, a current flows momentarily in circuits B and C. In what direction does the induced current flow through the resistor in each case?

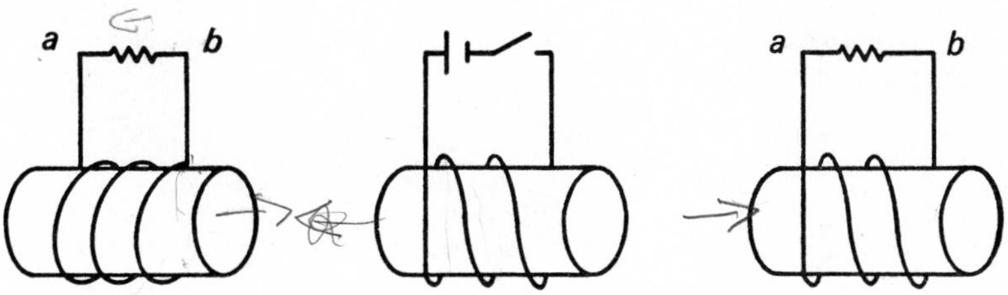

25
questions
1-6

4 Repeat the previous problem if the switch is suddenly opened.

5 A coil of N loops and area A is held fixed in a magnetic field $B = B_0 \sin(2\pi f t)$ as shown. Find the induced emf in the coil.

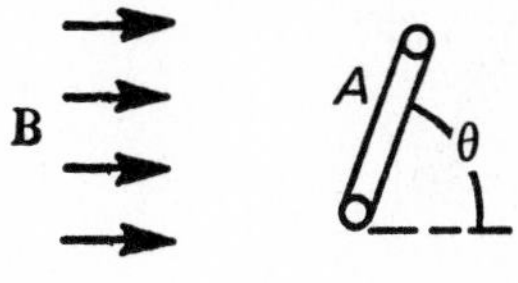

6 Suppose the loop of the previous problem was rotating in such a way that $\theta = 2\pi f t$ and the field was also changing with the same frequency. Find the induced emf.

1 $\mathcal{E} = -d\phi/dt$ where $\mathcal{E}$ is the emf induced in a loop through which the magnetic flux ϕ is changing at a rate $d\phi/dt$. The negative sign tells us the emf is in such a direction as to oppose the change in flux.

2 $\phi = \int \mathbf{B} \cdot d\mathbf{A}$ where the integral is to extend over the entire area.

3 ☐ $b \rightarrow a$ in B and $a \rightarrow b$ in C

The current flows so as to set up a flux to cancel out the change in flux caused by A. Use the right-hand rule to find the flux set up by the current in each single loop.

4 ☐ $a \rightarrow b$ in B and $b \rightarrow a$ in C

Same reasoning as in problem 3. Now, however, the flux due to A is dropping to zero.

5 ☐ $-2\pi fNAB_0 \sin\theta \cos(2\pi ft)$

The flux through a loop is $\phi = \int \mathbf{B} \cdot d\mathbf{A} = BA \cos(B,A) = BA \sin\theta$. Now θ is constant and so is A. Therefore

a

$$\mathcal{E} = -N\frac{d\phi}{dt} = -NA \sin\theta \frac{dB}{dt} = -2\pi fNAB_0 \sin\theta \cos(2\pi ft)$$

25
answers
1-6

6 ☐ $-2\pi fNAB_0 \sin(4\pi ft)$

As before, $\phi = BA \sin\theta$, but now both B and θ vary. Since $\phi = AB_0 \sin(2\pi ft) \sin(2\pi ft)$, we find

$$\mathcal{E} = -4\pi fNAB_0 \sin(2\pi ft) \cos(2\pi ft) = -2\pi fNAB_0 \sin(4\pi ft)$$

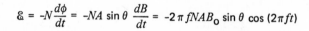

7 The rectangular loop of wire shown is moving with speed $\nu = 10^4$ m/sec to the right. It is moving in a nonuniform magnetic field B which is perpendicular to and into the page. If the value of B at the position shown is B_o and if B decreases uniformly by 2.0 G for each meter moved to the right, find the induced emf in the loop.

(a) To do this we make use of ________ law, namely ________, where N is unitv in this case. (b) The flux through the loop in its original position is ________. (c) After a certain time, t for example, the loop will have been displaced a distance ________ m and the flux through it will be ________. (d) Hence $\mathcal{E}$ = ________. (e) In this case, the induced current will flow through the resistor from ________.

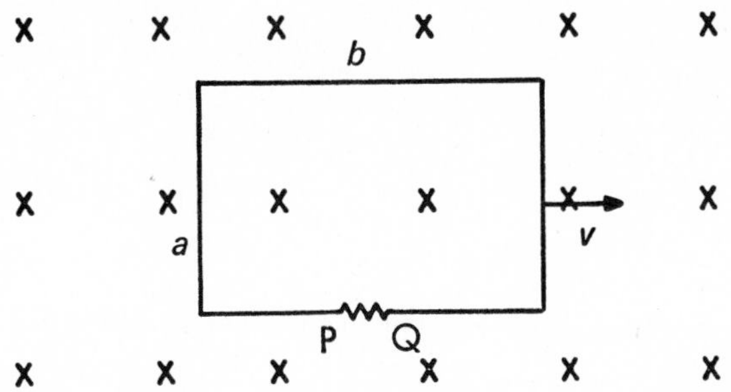

8 (a) Considering the situation of the previous problem in terms of motional emfs, the emf induced between the ends of the horizontal wires is ________ since these wires do not cut lines of **B**. (b) If the magnetic field at the left end of the loop is B_o, the value of the field at the right end is ________. (c) Since the induced emf for a wire of length a moving with speed ν in a magnetic field B (all quantities being mutually perpendicular) is ________, the induced emf in the left end of the loop is ________ and in the right end it is ________. (d) In both cases, the upper end of the wire is ________, and so the emfs tend to cancel. (e) As a result, the net induced emf in the loop is ________. This is the same value as was obtained in the previous problem.

q

25
questions
7-10

9 The current in an air-core solenoid is increasing at a rate of 2.0 amperes/sec. There are 10^6 turns of wire on the solenoid for each meter of its length, and its cross-sectional area is $(2)(10^{-4})$ m^2. A secondary coil of 10^4 turns is wound over the solenoid. How large an emf is induced in it?

10 What is the mutual inductance of the coils of the previous problem?

7 (a) Faraday's ; $\mathcal{E} = -N\,d\phi/dt$

(b) $B_0\,(ab)$

(c) vt; $(B_0 - 2 \times 10^{-4} vt)\,ab$

(d) $\frac{d}{dt}\,(B_0 - 2 \times 10^{-4}\,vt)\,ab = -2\,ab$

(e) Q to P

8 (a) Zero

(b) $B_0 - 2 \times 10^{-4} b$

(c) vBa; $vB_0 a$; $v(B_0 - 2 \times 10^{-4} b)\,a$

(d) Positive

(e) $-2 \times 10^{-4} vba = -2ba$

a

9 ☐ 5.0 V

Assuming the solenoid to be long enough so that B inside it is given by $B = \mu_0 nI$, the flux through the secondary will be BA where A in this case is $2 \times 10^{-4}\ m^2$. Hence the induced emf is

$$\mathcal{E} = -N_{sec}\frac{d}{dt}\,(\mu_0 nIA) = -N_{sec}\,n\mu_0 A\,\frac{dI}{dt}$$

Since $dI/dt = 2$ amperes/sec, $\mathcal{E} = 5.0$ V

25
answers
7-10

10 ☐ 2.5 H

Since $\mathcal{E} = -M\,dI/dt$ we see

$M = N_{sec}\,n\mu_0 A = 2.5$ H

11 What would have to be the current in the primary of the previous problem to give a secondary emf of 5 sin $(360t)$ V?

12 A coil has a self-inductance of $L = 20$ mH. What is the peak induced emf in this inductor when a current $i = 0.50 \sin (360t)$ A is sent through it?

13 If the inductance coil of the previous problem has a resistance of 40 Ω, how long will it take for the current to reach 0.990 of its maximum value when a 6-V battery is suddenly connected across it?

14 How much energy is stored in a 2-H inductor when a current of 3 A is flowing in it?

15 The earth's magnetic field is about 1 G. How much energy is stored in 1 m^3 of the atmosphere because of this field?

11 ☐ $I = 0.0056 \cos(360t)$ A

We know $\mathcal{E} = -M\, dI/dt$

and so

$$5 \sin(360t) = -2.5 \frac{dI}{dt}$$

from which

$dI = -2 \sin(360t)\, dt.$

Integrating, and setting the constant = 0 since it represents a steady current, gives the result above.

12 ☐ 3.6 V

One has $\mathcal{E} = -L\, di/dt$ and so

$$\begin{aligned}\mathcal{E} &= -(20 \times 10^{-3})(0.50 \times 360) \cos(360t)\\ &= -3.6 \cos(360t) \text{ V}\end{aligned}$$

The peak voltage is 3.6 V.

a

25
answers
11-15

13 ☐ 2.3×10^{-3} sec

One has (see Bueche, Sec. 25.4):

$$i = i_{max}\,(1 - e^{-Rt/L})$$

In our case, $i/i_{max} = 0.990$ and so $e^{-Rt/L} = 0.010$. Taking logs of both sides, and since $\ln x = 2.30 \log x$, we find $Rt/L = 2 \times 2.30$, and so $t = 2.3 \times 10^{-3}$ sec.

14 ☐ 9 J

The energy stored in an inductor is $W = \frac{1}{2}LI^2 = 9$ J in the present case.

15 ☐ 4×10^{-3} J

The energy density is $B^2/2\mu_0$. In the present case this is $(1 \times 10^{-4})^2/8\pi \times 10^{-7} = 4 \times 10^{-3}$ J.

16 A flat coil of area A and N turns has a resistance of $R\,\Omega$ and hangs in a uniform magnetic field $B = B_0 \sin(\omega t)$. If the field is perpendicular to the surface of the coil, find an expression for the torque on the coil.

17 Justify physically why the torque has twice the frequency of the applied field in the previous problem.

18 Find the magnitude of the electric field at the orbit of a betatron whose orbit diameter is 80 cm and whose average magnetic field increases at the rate of 10^3 G/sec.

16 ☐ $-\dfrac{N^2A^2B_o^2\omega}{2R}\sin(2\omega t)$

If i is the current induced in the coil, then torque = $BNiA$. To find i, we note it is $\mathcal{E}/R$

where

$$\mathcal{E} = -\frac{N\,d\phi}{dt} = -\frac{NA\,dB}{dt} = -NAB_o\omega\cos(\omega t).$$

Substitution gives

$$\text{torque} = -\left(\frac{N^2A^2B_o^2\omega}{R}\right)\cos(\omega t)\sin(\omega t)$$

Then use $\sin(2\theta) = 2\sin\theta\cos\theta$.

17 After *half* a field cycle *both* B and i are reversed, so that Bi, and hence the torque, has recovered its original value.

a

25
answers
16-18

18 ☐ 0.020 V/m

We use the basic relation

$$\oint \mathbf{E}\cdot d\mathbf{s} = \frac{d}{dt}\int \mathbf{B}\cdot d\mathbf{A}$$

taking the integral around the circular orbit. Then since **E** is tangential and constant, the relation becomes

$$E(2\pi r) = \pi r^2\frac{dB}{dt}$$

where B is the average value through the area of the orbit. Then

$$E = \frac{r}{2}\frac{dB}{dt} = \left(\frac{0.80}{4}\right)(10^{-1}) = 0.020\ \text{V/m}$$

26 dielectric and magnetic materials

1 When a dielectric is placed between the charged plates of a capacitor, the electric field (*increases, decreases*) because ____.

2 When is Gauss' law in the form $\epsilon_0 \int \mathbf{E} \cdot d\mathbf{A} = \Sigma\,(q_b + q_f)$ valid?

When is the form $\epsilon_0 \int k\mathbf{E} \cdot d\mathbf{A} = \Sigma\, q_f$ valid?

3 A capacitor has a capacitance of 2.000×10^{-9} F when empty. When filled with benzene, it has a capacitance of 4.570×10^{-9} F. What is the dielectric constant of benzene?

4 The plates in a parallel-plate capacitor are 0.20 mm apart and a potential difference of 100 volts exists across it. If $k = 3.0$ for the dielectric which fills the space between the plates, find E in the dielectric.

1 Decreases; charge of opposite sign to that on the plate is induced on the adjacent side of the dielectric, and this acts to cancel part of the field of the original charge.

2 The first form is always true under electrostatic conditions. The second form is restricted to the case of homogeneous, isotropic dielectrics.

3 ☐ 2.285

By definition, $k = C/C_0 = 2.285$.

4 ☐ 5×10^5 volts/m

From the definition of potential difference $|V_B - V_A| = \int_A^B \mathbf{E} \cdot \mathbf{ds} = E\,d$ in this case.

Therefore

$100 = E(2 \times 10^{-4})$

so

$E = 5 \times 10^5$ volts/m.

a

26
answers
1-4

5 For the capacitor of the previous problem, find the surface density of free charge on the capacitor plate.

6 Find the capacitance of the illustrated parallel-plate capacitor if the plate areas are all A.

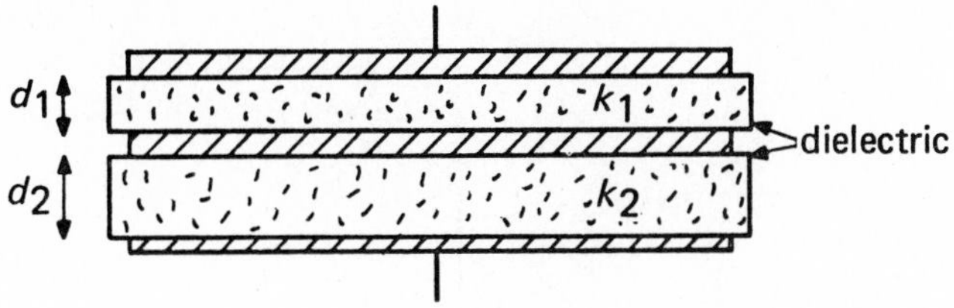

26
questions
5-6

5 Applying Gauss' law to the pillbox shown $\epsilon_0 \int k\,\mathbf{E} \cdot d\mathbf{A} = \Sigma q_f$; $0 + 0 + \epsilon_0 kEA = \sigma_f A$ from which $E = \sigma_f/k\epsilon_0$. Notice that for fixed σ_f, the dielectric reduces the field by the factor $1/k$.

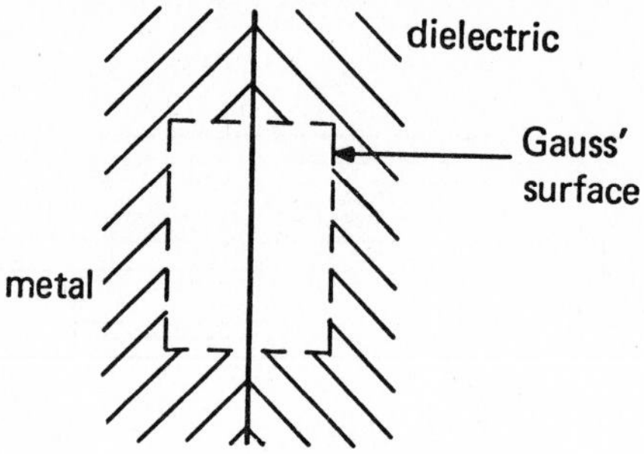

6 □ $\dfrac{\epsilon_0 A k_1 k_2}{d_1 k_2 + d_2 k_1}$

This is really two capacitors in series. One has $C_1 = \epsilon_0 k_1 A/d_1$ and $C_2 = \epsilon_0 k_2 A/d_2$.

So

$$\frac{1}{C} = \frac{1}{C_1} + \frac{1}{C_2}$$

gives

$$C = \frac{\epsilon_0 A k_1 k_2}{d_1 k_2 + d_2 k_1}$$

7 A large flat uncharged piece of dielectric (constant k) is placed in an electric field **E** with **E** perpendicular to the face. Find E inside the dielectric.

8 For the dielectric sheet of the previous problem, what is the density of induced charge on its faces?

q

26
questions
7-8

7 ☐ $\frac{E}{k}$

Applying Gauss' law to the pillbox,

$$\epsilon_0 \int k\mathbf{E} \cdot d\mathbf{A} = \Sigma q_f = 0$$

$$\epsilon_0 \left[\int_{\text{left}} + \int_{\text{side}} + \int_{\text{right}}\right] = 0$$

$$\epsilon_0 \left[-EA + 0 + kE_dA\right] = 0$$

where E_d is E in the dielectric. Solving, $E_d = E/k$. Thus, here too E is decreased by $1/k$.

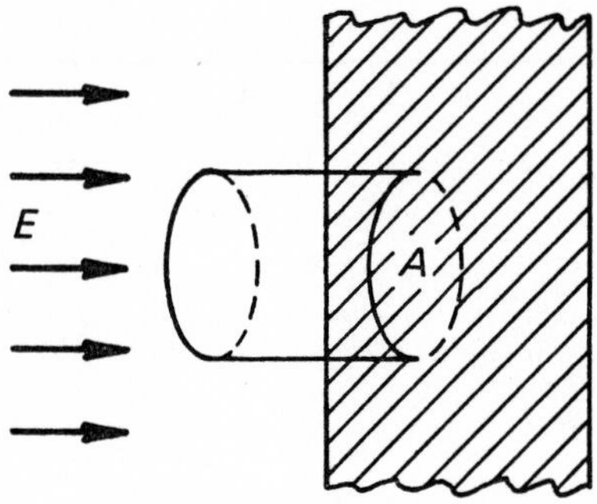

a

26
answers
7-8

8 ☐ $\frac{\pm \epsilon_0 E(k-1)}{k}$

If we apply the basic form of Gauss' law to the pillbox, we have

$$\epsilon_0 \int \mathbf{E} \cdot d\mathbf{A} = \Sigma (q_f + q_b)$$

Then

$$\epsilon_0 [-EA + E_dA] = \sigma_f A + \sigma_b A = \sigma_b A$$

From which

$$\sigma_b = \epsilon_0 (-E + E_d) = \epsilon_0 (-E + \frac{E}{k})$$

or

$$\sigma_b = \frac{-\epsilon_0 E(k-1)}{k}$$

9 What is P in the dielectric of the previous problem?

10 A dielectric sheet of constant k contains a free volume charge ρ C/m^3. The sheet has a thickness d. Find the electric field outside the sheet.

9 ☐ $\frac{\rho d}{2\epsilon_0}$

Applying Gauss' law to the pillbox, one has

$$\epsilon_0 \int k\mathbf{E} \cdot d\mathbf{A} = \Sigma q_f$$

which is

$$\epsilon_0 \left[\int_{\text{left}} + \int_{\text{right}} + \int_{\text{sides}} \right] = A d\rho$$

Now by symmetry, **E** is directed outward on the left and right ends and is constant. Then

$$\epsilon_0 \; [EA + EA + 0] = A\, d\rho$$

or $E = \frac{\rho d}{2\epsilon_0}$.

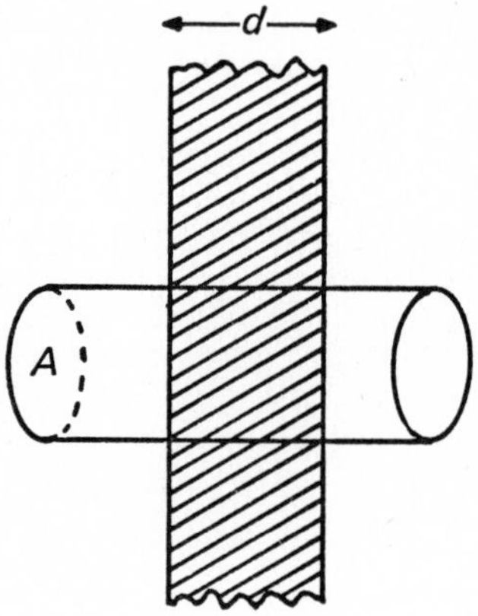

a

26
answers
9-10

10 ☐ $\frac{\rho x}{\epsilon_0}$

From symmetry, E is the same on the left and right faces and is outward. Therefore, Gauss' law yields

$$\epsilon_0 \; [EA + EA + 0] = A(2x)\rho$$

from which $E = \rho x/\epsilon_0$.

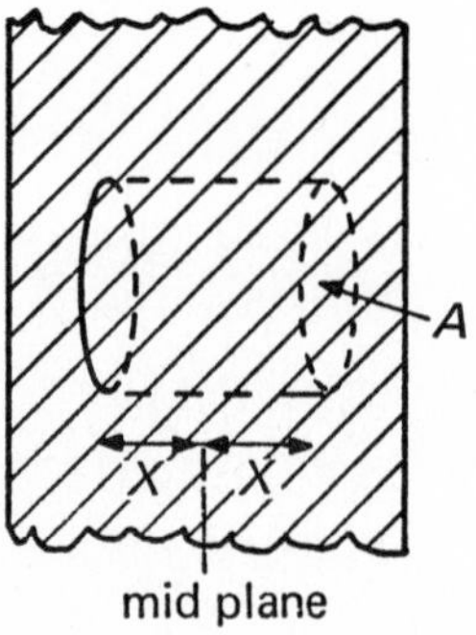

11 Distinguish between diamagnetic, paramagnetic, and ferromagnetic materials by stating what changes they cause in the field inside a toroid.

12 A certain narrow toroid has an average diameter of 20 cm and has 100 loops of wire per centimeter of its mean circumference. Find the magnetic field at the center of its interior when it is wound on an aluminum core. Take the current to be 3 A.

13 Repeat the previous problem for the case when the core is filled with a steel whose relative permeability is 100 at this value of B_0.

14 What is the basic idea behind the statement "all materials are, in part at least, diamagnetic"?

15 What atomic property is responsible for paramagnetism?

16 In the Bohr picture of the hydrogen atom, the electron rotates at a frequency of $\sim 7 \times 10^{15}$ sec^{-1} in an orbit with radius 0.5 Å. Find the magnetic dipole moment which results from this motion.

11 The field inside a toroid is decreased slightly (~10^{-3} percent) by diamagnetic, increased slightly (~10^{-3} to 1 percent) by paramagnetic, and increased greatly (factor of a few hundred) by ferromagnetic materials.

12 ☐ 3.77×10^{-2} T

Using Ampere's circuital law we find $\oint \mathbf{B} \cdot d\mathbf{s} = \mu_0$ (current) gives $B_0\,(2\pi r) = \mu_0\,(2\pi rnI)$ or $B_0 = \mu_0 nI$, provided the toroid is filled with vacuum. χ for aluminum is 2.1×10^{-5} and so in our case $k_m = 1.000021$.

Therefore,

$$B = 1.000021\,\mu_0 nI = 3.77 \times 10^{-2}\ \text{T}.$$

13 ☐ 3.77 T

From the previous problem, $B_0 \cong 3.77 \times 10^{-2}$ T. With a steel core, the field will be $100B_0 = 3.77$ T provided $\mu/\mu_0 = k_m = 100$.

a

14 If one uses the Bohr model of the atom in which the atom consists of electrons orbiting around the nucleus, the electronic currents in the atom obey Faraday's law. When a magnetic field is impressed on a substance, the induced emf due to the change in flux through the electronic loops causes the electronic motion to alter so as to set up a flux in the reverse direction. This causes a (very small) decrease in the total field. This effect, a diamagnetic contribution, occurs in all materials.

15 If an atom possesses a permanent magnetic dipole (resulting from orbital motion of the electrons and/or spin), these dipoles orient in an applied magnetic field and augment the field.

16 ☐ 9×10^{-24} ampere-m^2

The magnetic dipole moment of a current I is IA where A is the area of the current loop. In the present case, I = charge/sec $= 1.6 \times 10^{-19} \times 7 \times 10^{15} = 1.1 \times 10^{-3}$ ampere. The area is $\pi r^2 = 0.8 \times 10^{-20}$ m^2 and so $M = IA = 0.9 \times 10^{-23}$ ampere-m^2.

17 In our study of heat we found that the average energy of a particle is of the order of kT. How large must the external magnetic field be for an atom with $M = 1 \times 10^{-23}$ ampere-m^2 to have this energy difference between its aligned and antialigned positions?

18 An atom has three distinct causes for its magnetic dipole. What are they and how do their magnitudes compare?

19 What materials are ferromagnetic, and what is special about the atoms of these materials?

20 What is meant by the Curie temperature?

21 What is a magnetic domain?

22 Why should the area of the hysteresis curve for a transformer iron be small?

23 What is Gauss' law for magnetism and in what way does it differ from Gauss' law in electrostatics?

17 □ 207 T

The torque on the dipole is $MB \sin\theta$ where θ is the angle between M and B. To turn the dipole from $\theta = 0$ to $\theta = \pi$, one does work given by

$$\int_0^{\pi} MB \sin\theta \, d\theta = 2\mu B$$

We want this to be equal to kT. Using $k = 1.38 \times 10^{-23}$ J/°K and $T = 300$°K we find $B = kT/2M = 207$ T. Clearly, since ordinary fields are much less than this, the atoms will not be completely aligned.

18 Each electron has a magnetic dipole, called its spin magnetic moment. Usually these dipoles align in pairs so that they cancel in pairs. Atoms having an odd number of electrons must have a net dipole because of spin. Motion of the electrons within the atom causes them to act as current loops. This orbital moment is comparable to the spin moment of an electron. The nucleus acts as a magnetic dipole. Its moment is about 10^{-3} as large as the electron spin moment.

a

19 Iron, nickel, and cobalt, plus alloys and a few others of less importance. These atoms have more than one unpaired electron (i.e., more than one electron in the atom has its magnetic moment unpaired with another opposite moment). Further, the filling of the electron shell structure of the atom is such that outer shells begin to fill before the inner shells are completed.

26
answers
17-23

20 Above this temperature the unpaired atomic moments are not ordered in magnetic domains as they are at lower temperatures. The ordering is broken up by the thermal motion at these high temperatures.

21 It is an aggregate of a large number of atoms, so ordered that the atomic magnetic dipoles within the domain are aligned. Domains large enough to be seen under a microscope are easily obtained.

22 The area of the hysteresis curve represents the energy loss within the material as the domain direction is reversed under an oscillating magnetic field. Since transformers are used in oscillating magnetic fields, a large hysteresis curve area would lead to heat buildup and wasteful energy loss in the transformer.

23 It is $\int_{\text{closed surface}} \mathbf{B} \cdot d\mathbf{A} = 0$. The analogous relation in electrostatics is

$$\epsilon_0 \int \mathbf{E} \cdot d\mathbf{A} = \Sigma q$$

Since there are no free magnetic poles, the right side of the magnetic equation is zero.

24 Prove that a radial magnetic field cannot exist.

25 Prove that the tangential component of **H** is continuous across a boundary between two magnetic materials, provided that no current is flowing along the boundary.

q

26
questions
24-25

24 If a radial field exists, it must appear as shown. Take a gaussian sphere concentric to its center.

We have

$$\int \mathbf{B} \cdot d\mathbf{A} = \int B\, dA = B \int dA = 4\pi r^2 B$$

From Gauss' law, this must equal zero and so B itself must be zero. The field does not exist.

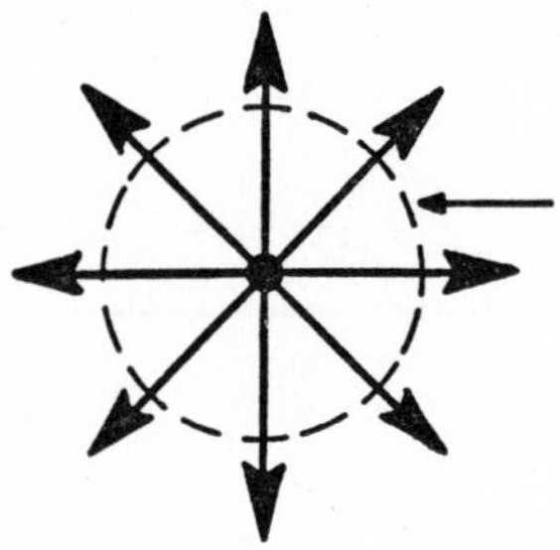

a

26
answers
24-25

25 Let us apply Ampere's circuital law in the form $\oint \mathbf{H} \cdot d\mathbf{s} = \int \mathbf{J} \cdot d\mathbf{A}$ to a rectangular path on the boundary as shown. H_1 and H_2 being the components of **H** parallel to the boundary, we have

$$H_1 a - H_2 a = \int \mathbf{J} \cdot d\mathbf{A}$$

where the integrals over the two ends are made zero by taking b very small. But no current flows through the enclosed area so $H_1 a - H_2 a = 0$ and $H_1 = H_2$.

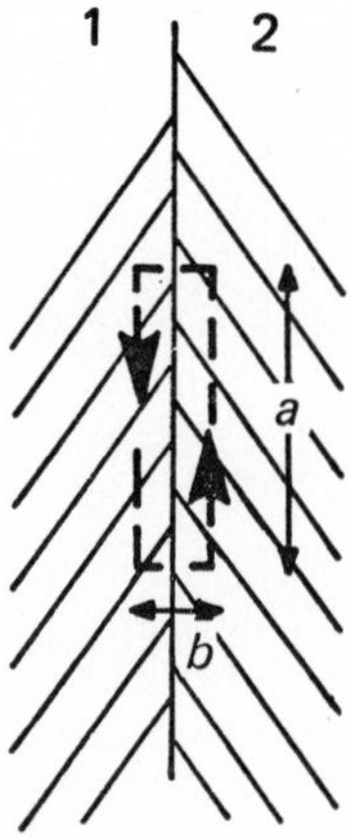

27 alternating current circuits

1 What is meant by the rms (or effective) voltage and current supplied by an ac power source? Why is it important?

2 Most alternating current voltmeters and ammeters are calibrated to read what when the current and voltage are sinusoidal functions of time?

3 When a current with effective value I passes through a resistor R, what is the rms voltage across the resistor? Repeat for an inductance L and capacitance C.

4 A 100-Ω resistor, 0.010-H inductor, and 0.50-μF capacitor are connected in series with a 3180-Hz oscillator. The current through the circuit is 0.20 A. Find the voltage drop across the three elements.

5 For the situation of the previous problem, find the source voltage.

1 The root-mean-square value is, as its name implies, the square root of the average of the voltage squared (or current squared) over one cycle. It is important because power delivered to a resistor is given by I^2R or V^2/R where I and V are rms values.

2 They read the rms values. The maximum value of a sinusoidal voltage V_m (or current I_m) is related to the effective value by $V = \dfrac{V_m}{\sqrt{2}}$ or $I = \dfrac{I_m}{\sqrt{2}}$

3 These values are (see Bueche, Eqs. 27.5 and 27.7):

$$V_R = IR$$

$$V_L = IX_L \qquad \text{with } X_L = 2\pi fL$$

$$V_C = IX_C \qquad \text{with } X_C = \frac{1}{2\pi fC}$$

where f is the frequency of the sinusoidal current. X_L is called the inductive reactance while X_C is the capacitive reactance. Both are measured in ohms.

4 ☐ $V_R = 20$ volts; $V_L = 40$ volts; $V_C = 20$ volts

$$V_R = IR = (0.20)\,(100) = 20 \text{ volts}$$

To find V_L and V_C we need X_L and X_C.

$$X_L = 2\pi fL = 200\ \Omega \qquad \text{and} \qquad X_C = \frac{1}{2\pi fC} = 100\ \Omega$$

So

$$V_L = IX_L = 40 \text{ volts and } V_C = IX_C = 20 \text{ volts.}$$

5 ☐ 28.2 volts

This is most easily approached in terms of the vector diagram shown. One has that the source voltage $V = \sqrt{V_R^2 + (V_L - V_C)^2}$ which is $\sqrt{400 + 400}$ $= 20\sqrt{2}$ volts.

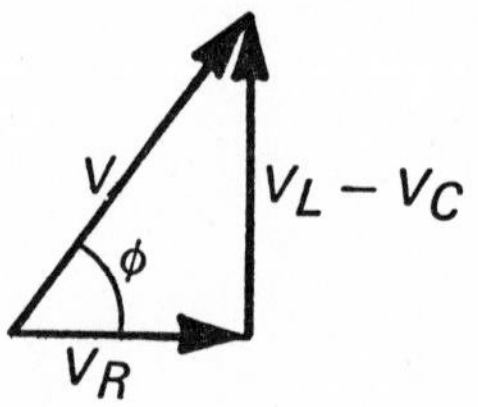

6 If the equation of the current in the previous example is $i = i_0 \sin(2\pi f t)$, what is the equation for the source voltage?

7 Explain why the sinusoidal current through an inductor is out of phase with the voltage across it. Use physical rather than mathematical arguments.

8 Explain why the sinusoidal current through a capacitor is out of phase with the voltage across it.

9 What is the current in a series circuit consisting of

(1) an inductance coil having a resistance of 200 Ω and an inductance of 0.20 H,

(2) a 0.50-μF capacitance, and

(3) a 60-V, 318-Hz source?

10 How much power is expended in the resistance of the circuit of problem 9? Find the result without using the phase angle ϕ.

6 ☐ $v = 40 \sin (20{,}000t + \frac{\pi}{4})$

Since the phase angle ϕ in the figure for the previous example is given by tan $\phi = \frac{(V_L - V_C)}{V_R} = 1$, one has $\phi = \pi/4$ rad.

Therefore

$$v = v_0 \sin (2\pi ft + \frac{\pi}{4})$$

In this case $v_0 = (20\sqrt{2})\sqrt{2} = 40$ volts and $2\pi f = 20{,}000$.

7 We know from Faraday's law that the voltage drop across an inductor is $L\,(di/dt)$. This means that the voltage will reach its maximum when the rate of change of the current (rather than the current itself) is maximum. Since a sine function has its greatest slope when the function is zero, the voltage is maximum when the current is zero, i.e., they are 90° out of phase.

a

8 The voltage is Q/C and so the voltage is maximum when the charge is largest. However, when the charge is largest the current into the capacitor (the derivative of the charge) is reversing from + to - and is zero. As a result, the voltage and current are 90° out of phase.

9 ☐ 0.095 A

The Ohm's law analog for this circuit is $V = IZ$ with $Z^2 = R^2 + (X_L - X_C)^2$. We note that $X_L = 2\pi fL = 400\ \Omega$ and $X_C = \frac{1}{2\pi fC} = 1000\ \Omega$. Hence

$$Z = \sqrt{4 \times 10^4 + 36 \times 10^4} = 633\ \Omega.$$

Therefore,

$$I = \frac{V}{Z} = \frac{60}{633} = 0.095\ \text{A}.$$

10 ☐ 1.8 W

We use $P = I^2R = (0.009)(200) = 1.8$ W since power is lost only in the resistor.

11 Find the power expended by the source in problem 9. Make use of the phase angle ϕ.

12 Prove that no power is lost in a pure inductor or in a pure capacitor.

13 At what frequency will the current in an LRC series circuit reach its maximum value? What is this frequency called?

14 Draw an analogy between the free oscillation of a pendulum and the free oscillation of an LC circuit.

11 ☐ 1.8 W

The power expended by the source is $P = VI \cos \varphi$ where V is the source voltage. To find ϕ we use the vector triangle shown together with the data of problem 9. We have $\tan \phi = \dfrac{X_L - X_C}{R} = -3.0$

so $\phi = -71.5°$ and $\cos \phi = 0.315$. Therefore $P = (60)\ (0.095)\ (0.315) = 1.8$ W.

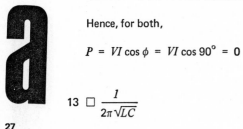

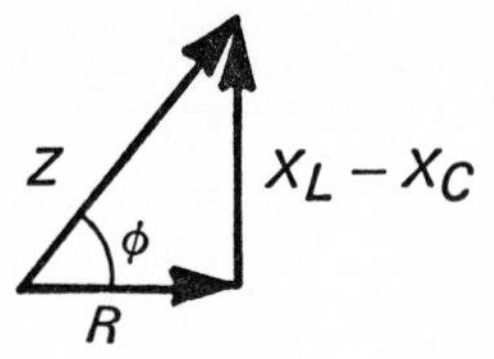

12 In each of these cases $/\phi/ = 90°$ as one can see from the vector diagram (since $R = 0$). This is also clear from the discussion given previously about the phase relations between V and I in these elements.

Hence, for both,

$$P = VI \cos \phi = VI \cos 90° = 0$$

13 ☐ $\dfrac{1}{2\pi\sqrt{LC}}$

27
answers
11-14

This is the resonance frequency and occurs when $X_L = X_C$ so Z is a minimum. Equating $2\pi fL = \dfrac{1}{2\pi fC}$ and solving gives $2\pi f = 1/\sqrt{LC}$.

14 In a pendulum, the energy alternates between kinetic and potential as the pendulum alternately swings through the lowest position and then rises to stop at its highest position. In the LC circuit, the current oscillates back and forth. When the current is a maximum, the inductance has its maximum energy $\frac{1}{2} LI^2$. When the current stops, the energy is all stored in the capacitor, $\dfrac{Q^2}{2C}$. In both systems the energy oscillates back and forth between two forms.

15 What in an oscillating circuit corresponds to the damping down of a free pendulum?

16 What is meant by critical damping in an electrical circuit and to what does it correspond in the motion of a pendulum or spring system?

15 The pendulum damps down because energy is slowly lost doing friction work. Oscillations in an LC circuit damp down because there is always some resistance present and energy loss occurs as the current flows through it. The damping mechanism in both cases leads eventually to the production of heat energy.

16 A pendulum or spring system usually swings back and forth with decreasing amplitude and eventually stops. However, if it is in a high-viscosity medium, the system does not oscillate at all but, when displaced and released, slowly swings back to its rest position. The transition point between these two cases is the case of critical mechanical damping. A similar situation exists in an oscillating electrical circuit where resistive loss replaces the viscous loss mechanism. The transition point occurs when $(R/2L)^2 = (1/LC)$ (see Bueche, Sec. 27.8).

a

27
answers
15-16

28 electromagnetic interactions and fields

1 Maxwell's four equations are composed of two pairs of analogous equations. What are they?

2 Consider the two isolated parallel plates shown with charge q. Charge slowly leaks through the space between the plates from the upper plate to the lower. Show that the displacement current is equal and opposite to the regular current flowing.

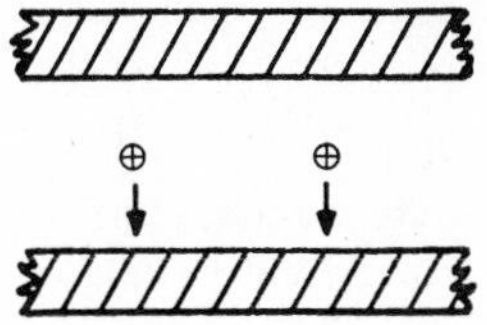

3 When does the displacement current term in Maxwell's equations become important? Why was it not discovered earlier?

4 Draw a typical sinusoidal wave as a function of x, give its equation, and indicate, by labeling, the wave crests, troughs, amplitude, and wavelength.

q

28 questions 1-4

1 The two Gauss' law equations (for vacuum)

$$\epsilon_0 \int \mathbf{E} \cdot d\mathbf{A} = \Sigma q \qquad \text{and} \qquad \int \mathbf{B} \cdot d\mathbf{A} = 0$$

and the two circuital equations

$$\oint \mathbf{B} \cdot d\mathbf{s} = \mu_0 \int \mathbf{J} \cdot d\mathbf{A} + \mu_0 \epsilon_0 \frac{d}{dt} \int \mathbf{E} \cdot d\mathbf{A}$$

and

$$\oint \mathbf{E} \cdot d\mathbf{s} = -\frac{d}{dt} \int \mathbf{B} \cdot d\mathbf{A}$$

2 The current between the plates is $-A\,(d\sigma/dt)$ while the displacement current is $[\epsilon_0\,(d/dt)]\,(EA)$. But $E = \sigma/\epsilon_0$ and so the displacement current is also

$$\epsilon_0 \frac{d}{dt}\left(\frac{A\sigma}{\epsilon_0}\right) = A\frac{d\sigma}{dt}$$

except with a positive sign. Therefore the two currents cancel and the magnetic field, given by $\oint \mathbf{B} \cdot d\mathbf{s} = \mu_0 \cdot$ (real current + displacement current), will be zero.

3 The term in question is usually much smaller than the quantity $\int \mathbf{J} \cdot d\mathbf{A}$. As a result, the observed magnetic field near a current is almost entirely due to the regular current and so the small effect of the displacement current is not noticed. However, as experimenters became capable of generating very high frequency fields, the displacement current effects, being proportional to dE/dt, became noticeable.

4 ☐ $y = A \sin (2\pi x/\lambda)$

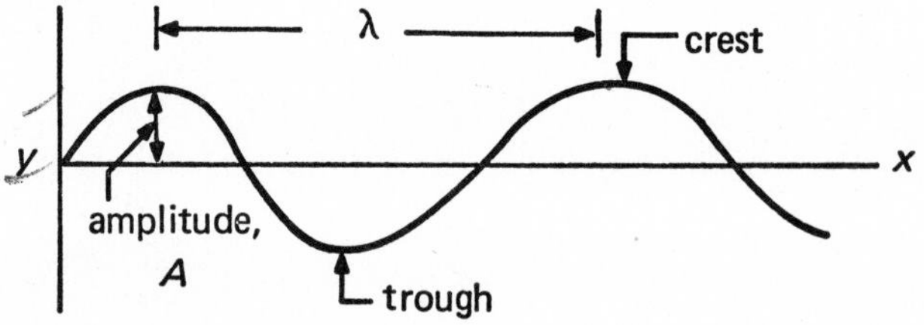

5 At time $t = 0$ a wave is given by $y = y_0 \sin (2\pi x/\lambda)$. Write the equation of the wave at time t if the wave moves to positive x values with speed v.

6 What is meant by a *plane wave*?

7 What is the basic relation between frequency, wavelength, and speed?

8 How are E and B related in a plane electromagnetic wave?

9 A certain wave is given by the relation

$$E = E_0 \cos (40x + 5t)$$

What are (a) the direction of motion, (b) speed, (c) frequency and period, and (d) wavelength of the wave?

5 ☐ $y = y_0 \sin[\frac{2\pi}{\lambda}(x - vt)]$

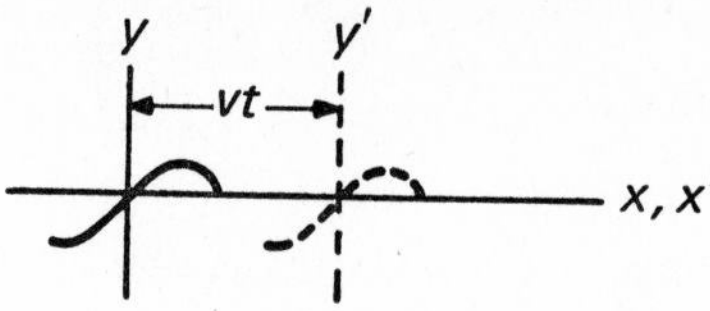

After time t the wave must have the same equation in the $x'\,y'$ system as it had in the original xy system, namely,

$y' = y_0 \sin(2\pi x'/\lambda)$.
But,

$x' = x - vt, y' = y$; and hence the answer.

6 Suppose a point source sends out a series of spherical wave crests. As these spheres expand, their radius of curvature becomes very large and any small section of the surface is nearly flat. If the wave crests actually form planes (i.e., spheres of infinite radius), then the waves are said to be plane waves.

a

7 ☐ $f = \frac{v}{\lambda}$

8 E and B are mutually perpendicular and both are perpendicular to the direction of propagation of the wave. They are in phase. Their magnitudes are related by $B = \sqrt{\epsilon\mu_0}\,E = E/c$.

28
answers
5-9

9 ☐ (a) $-x$ direction; (b) 1/8 m/sec; (c) 0.795 Hz, 1.26 sec; (d) 0.157 m

The standard wave equation is

$$y = y_0 \cos\left[2\pi\left(\frac{x}{\lambda} - \frac{vt}{\lambda}\right)\right]$$

Therefore, by comparison, $\lambda = \pi/20$ and $v/\lambda = -5/2\pi$. Solving, one finds $v = \frac{-1}{8}$ m/sec, which indicates that the wave is going towards $-x$ values. Since $f = v/\lambda$, we can use $1/\lambda = 20/\pi$ to find $f = 0.795$ Hz. Since $T = 1/f$, the period is 1.26 sec.

10 What is the wave equation, and how does it lead to a value for the speed of electromagnetic waves?

11 A typical radio station sends out waves of frequency near 10^6 Hz. Find the wavelength of waves having this frequency.

10 ☐ $$\frac{\partial^2 E_y}{\partial x^2} = \mu_o \epsilon \frac{\partial^2 E_y}{\partial t^2}$$

Since E_y is of form

$$E_o \sin [2\pi f(t - \frac{x}{v})]$$

this can be substituted in the above equation. After canceling out like terms, one finds

$$\frac{1}{v^2} = \mu_o\epsilon \qquad \text{so that } v = \frac{1}{\sqrt{\mu_o\epsilon}}$$

11 ☐ 300 m

Since $\lambda = v/f$ and since $v = 3 \times 10^8$ m/sec, one finds $\lambda = 3 \times 10^2$ m.

29
waves

1 Repeat questions 4, 5, 6, 7, 9, and 11 for Chap. 28.

2 An electromagnetic wave in space or a wave on a string can be thought of as two waves, a wave in time and a wave in space. Explain why.

3 A transverse wave along a string is given by the following equation: $y = 2.0 \cos (120t - 4.0x)$ cm with t in sec and x in cm. Find the amplitude, period, frequency, and speed of the wave.

4 For the wave on a string discussed in the previous problem, find the displacement, velocity, and acceleration of the piece of string at $x = 3.0$ cm as a function of time.

1 Answers in Chap. 28.

2 If one observes a fixed point in space or on a string, a plot of the electric field E or displacement y is the function of time shown. It is therefore a wave in time. Alternately one could plot the electric field or displacement at a given instant as a function of distance. This is a wave in space.

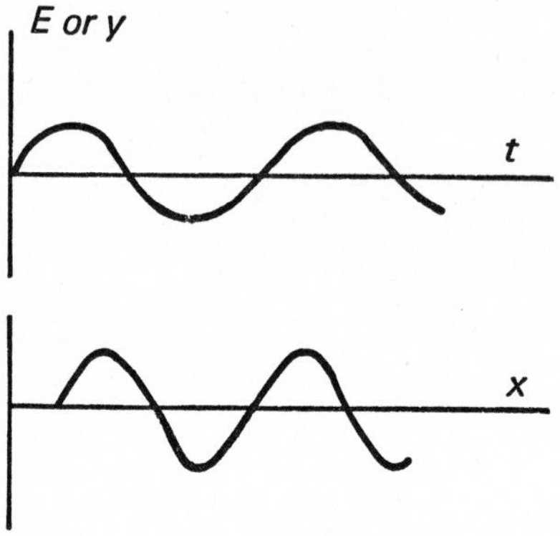

3 □ 2.0 cm; 0.053 sec; 19 Hz; 30 cm/sec

The standard wave form is

$$y = y_0 \cos\left(2\pi f t - 2\pi \frac{x}{\lambda}\right)$$

By comparison, the amplitude $y_0 = 2.0$ cm. Also, since $2\pi f = 120$, $f = 19$ Hz. The period $= 1/f = 0.053$ sec. We note that $2\pi/\lambda = 4.0$ and so $\lambda = 1.57$ cm. Then, using $\lambda = v/f$, we find $v = 30$ cm/sec.

4 We seek the transverse displacement, velocity, and acceleration; that is, y, dy/dt, and d^2y/dt^2. At $x = 3.0$ cm they are

$$y = 2.0 \cos(120t - 12) \text{ cm}; \quad \frac{dy}{dt} = -240 \sin(120t - 12) \text{ cm/sec}$$

$$\frac{d^2y}{dt^2} = -28{,}800 \cos(120t - x) \text{ m/sec}^2$$

5 Show that each small piece of the string in problem 3 is acted upon by a Hooke's law force. What is the spring constant?

6 Still considering the wave on a string from problem 3, find the maximum velocity and acceleration of any particle of the string. Where is it when it has these values?

7 Arrange the following in a table of decreasing wavelength, indicating the approximate wavelength range of each: radar, visible light, x rays, heat, radio, ultraviolet, and infrared.

8 State the approximate colors of the following visible wavelengths: 4000 Å, 7000 Å, 4358 Å, 5460 Å, 5790 Å, and 6200 Å.

9 Convert the following lengths to meters: 20 μ, 5000 Å, and 600 mμ.

a

29
answers
5-9

5 ☐ $14{,}400m$ N/m

Since $F_y = ma_y$ for each segment of the string and since

$$a_y = \frac{d^2y}{dt^2} = -288 \cos (120t - 4x) \text{ m/sec}^2,$$

one has

$$F_y = -288m \cos (120t - 4x)$$

Substituting $y = 0.020 \cos (120t - 4x)$ in this relation gives

$F_y = -(14{,}400m)y$ which is of the Hooke's law form with $k = 14{,}400m$ N/m.

6 ☐ 240 cm/sec, $y = 0$; 28,800 cm/sec^2, $y = y_0$

From the results of problem 4 we see $v_{max} = 240$ cm/sec when $\sin (120t - 12) = 1$. At that instant, $y = 0$. Also $a_{max} = 28{,}000$ cm/sec^2 when $\cos (120t - 12) = 1$ and so y has its maximum value, y_0.

7 Radio ($\gtrsim 100$ cm); radar ($\gtrsim 1$ cm); infrared and heat ($\gtrsim 7 \times 10^{-5}$ cm); light ($\gtrsim 4 \times 10^{-5}$ cm); ultraviolet ($\gtrsim 10^{-6}$ cm); and x rays. Each group is bracketed on the long-wavelength side by its predecessor.

8

4000	→	violet	5790	→	yellow
4358	→	blue	6200	→	orange-red
5460	→	green	7000	→	deep red

9 ☐ 2×10^{-5} m; 5×10^{-7} m; 6×10^{-7} m

Since 1 $\mu = 10^{-6}$ m and 1 m$\mu = 10^{-9}$ m.

10 Consider a radio station which sends out 80,000 W uniformly distributed on a sphere. What is the electric field strength (that is, E_0) at a distance of 20 km from the station?

11 Referring to the radio wave of problem 10, how large an emf would be induced in a 10^3-loop coil of area 1 cm^2 wound on a rod of relative permeability 1000? Consider only the point 20 km from the station and assume the frequency to be 10^6 Hz.

12 Two speeds are of importance for a transverse wave moving down a string: the speed of the disturbance traveling down the string, v, and the cross-wise motion of the particles of the string, dy/dt. Are they at all related?

10 □ 0.11 V/m

To find the power going through unit area at 20 km we must divide 80,000 by the area of the sphere of radius 20 X 10^3 m.

Therefore

$$\frac{\text{Power}}{\text{Area}} = \frac{8 \times 10^4}{4\pi 4 \times 10^8} = 1.6 \times 10^{-5}\ \text{W/m}^2$$

But (from Bueche, Eq. 29.5), this is $\frac{1}{2}\, c\epsilon_o E_o^2$. Solving gives $E_o = 0.11$ V/m. In practice, the beam will be directional and E would be larger in the area covered by the station.

11 □ 0.23 V

The magnetic field

$$B_o = \frac{E_o}{c} = 3.7 \times 10^{-10}\ \text{T}$$

a

29
answers
10-12

If the coil is oriented with its axis parallel to the field, $\phi = BA$.

But

$$B = k_m B_o \cos(2\pi f t) = 3.7 \times 10^{-7} \cos(6.28 \times 10^6\, t)$$

Then

$$\mathcal{E} = -N\frac{d\phi}{dt} = 10^3\,(3.7 \times 10^{-7}) \cdot (6.28 \times 10^6)\,(1 \times 10^{-4}) \cdot \sin(6.28 \times 10^6 t).$$

from which $\mathcal{E}_o = 0.23$ V.

12 □ v influences only the phase of dy/dt

A wave moving down a string is given by

$$y = y_o \sin\left(\omega t - \omega\frac{x}{v}\right)$$

from which

$$\frac{dy}{dt} = y_o\omega \cos\left(\omega t - \omega\frac{x}{v}\right)$$

As we see, the speed of the wave v influences only the phase of dy/dt and not its magnitude.

13 What is the primary difference between transverse and longitudinal waves?

14 Compute the speed of sound in copper from the facts that the density is 9 g/cm^3 and the isothermal bulk modulus is 1.2 X 10^{11} N/m^2.

15 An object emitting a sound of frequency f_0 approaches a stationary observer with speed V_s. Before the object passes, the observer notices the sound to have a frequency f_1, and after passing the sound has a frequency f_2 with $f_1/f_2 = 1.20$. Find the speed of the object.

13 In transverse waves, the oscillating particle or field vector moves in a plane which is perpendicular to the line of transmission of the wave. In longitudinal waves, the vibration occurs in a direction parallel to the direction of transmission of the wave.

14 □ 3650 m/sec

The speed of sound is $\sqrt{E/\rho}$. Placing in the values $\rho = 9 \times 10^3$ kg/m^3 and $E = 1.2 \times 10^{11}$ N/m^2 gives $v = 3650$ m/sec. This should be compared with the value of 3560 m/sec found by experiment.

15 □ $V_s = 0.091v$

According to the doppler effect equation,

$$f_1 = f_0 \frac{v}{v - V_s}$$

and

$$f_2 = f_0 \frac{v}{v + V_s}$$

from which

$$\frac{f_1}{f_2} = \frac{v + V_s}{v - V_s} = 1.20$$

Solving, one has $V_s = 0.091v$, where v is the speed of sound.

a

29
answers
13-15

30 reflection and refraction

1 A light bulb without reflector is used to illuminate the yard outside a house. Compare the light intensity at distances of 3 and 20 m from the bulb.

2 A very long fluorescent light tube would correspond to an infinite cylindrical light source. Show that in this case, for points near the tube, $I_1/I_2 = r_2/r_1$.

3 An object is placed in front of a plane mirror. What can one say about the image one sees of this object?

4 For a concave mirror, show the three rays one can draw with straight edge to locate the image of an object which is at an object distance $>R$. What can one say about the image?

5 Repeat problem 4 if $R>p>f$.

1 ☐ $44 = \frac{I_3}{I_{20}}$

Since the bulb is free to radiate in all directions, it will correspond approximately to a source of spherical waves.

Then

$$\frac{I_3}{I_{20}} = \frac{(20)^2}{(3)^2} = 44$$

2 We proceed in analogy to the point source, replacing concentric spheres by cylinders.

Then

Energy through cylinder 1 = energy through cylinder 2

Assuming no flux lost through the ends,

$$I_1\,(2\pi r_1 L) = I_2\,(2\pi r_2 L)$$

from which

$$\frac{I_1}{I_2} = \frac{r_2}{r_1}$$

a

30
answers
1-5

3 The image is virtual (or imaginary). It is right side up. Its size is the same as the object's size. The image is as far behind the mirror as the object is in front of it. If the object is a right-handed man (i.e., if he eats and writes with his right hand), the image will be a man who is left-handed.

4 ☐ Real, inverted, smaller

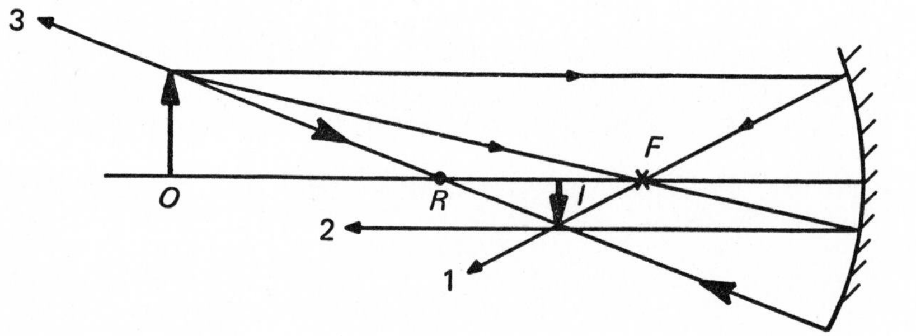

5 ☐ Real, inverted, larger

The image in problem 4 is now the object and the object becomes the image. Simply reverse the directions of the three rays.

6 Repeat problem 4 if $p<f$.

7 Repeat problem 4 for a convex mirror. Show that the answer will remain much the same for all positions of a real object.

8 What is the mirror relation and what sign conventions apply to it? How is the image size I related to the object size O?

9 A convex mirror of 40-cm radius of curvature forms an image of an object, the object distance being 60 cm. Describe the image.

6 ☐ Imaginary, erect, larger

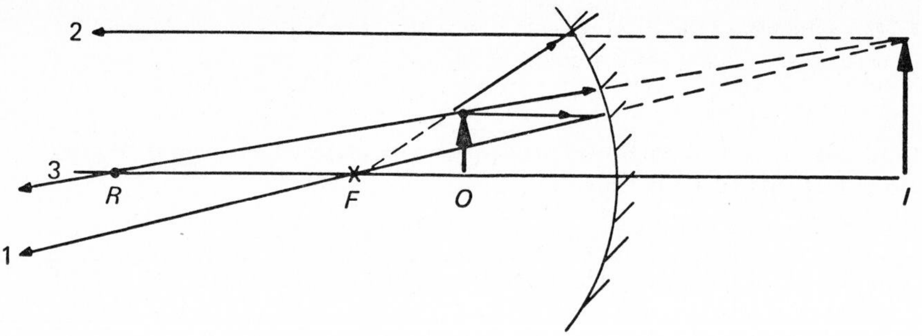

7 ☐ Imaginary, erect, smaller

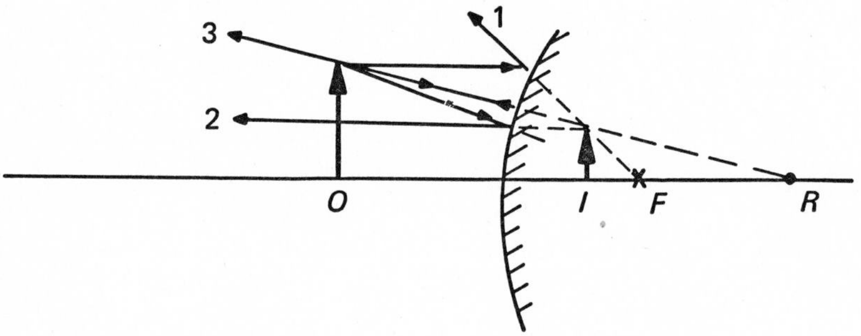

a

30
answers
6-9

8 ☐ $\frac{1}{p} + \frac{1}{p'} = \frac{1}{f} = \frac{2}{R}; \quad \frac{I}{O} = \frac{p'}{p}$

Where p = object distance, positive when on the lighted side of the mirror; p' = image distance and is positive when on the lighted side of mirror; f is the focal length $R/2$ where R is the radius of curvature. Both f and R are positive for a concave mirror and negative for convex.

9 ☐ p' = -15 cm; virtual; $\frac{1}{4}$ size; erect

$$\frac{1}{p} + \frac{1}{p'} = \frac{2}{R} \Rightarrow \frac{1}{60} + \frac{1}{p'} = -\frac{2}{40} \qquad \text{so } p' = -15 \text{ cm}$$

Since p' is negative, the image is on the dark side of the mirror and is virtual. $I/O = p'/p = 15/60 = \frac{1}{4}$. A ray diagram shows the object to be erect.

10 It is desired to use a concave mirror ($R = 60$ cm) to form a real image which is three times as large as the object. Where should the object be placed?

11 For a converging thin lens, show the three rays one can draw with a straight edge to locate the image if $p>f$. What can one say about the image?

12 Repeat problem 11 if $p<f$.

13 Repeat problem 11 for a diverging thin lens.

10 ☐ $p = 40$ cm

Since $I/O = 3$, $p'/p = 3$. The mirror equation becomes

$$\frac{1}{p} + \frac{1}{3p} = \frac{2}{60}$$

$p' = 3p$ and is positive since the image is to be real. Solving, $p = 40$ cm.

11 ☐ Real; inverted

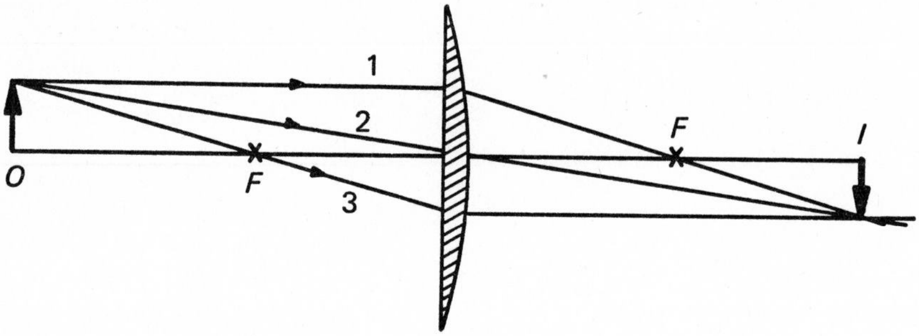

12 ☐ Imaginary; upright; enlarged

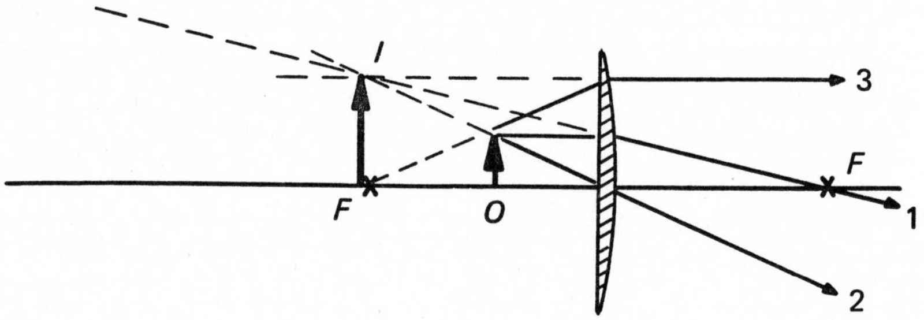

13 ☐ Imaginary; upright; smaller

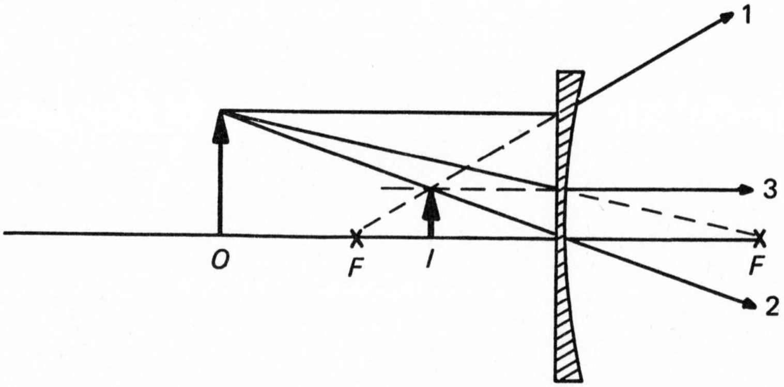

a

30
answers
10-13

14 Repeat problem 11 for a diverging lens but with $p<f$.

15 What is the thin lens formula and what are the sign conventions to be used with it?

16 An object is placed 80 cm in front of a 60-cm focal length diverging lens. Where is the image and what can one say about it?

17 Using a 60-cm focal length converging lens, one wishes to obtain a virtual image which is four times as large as the object. Where will the object and image be?

14 ☐ Imaginary; upright; smaller

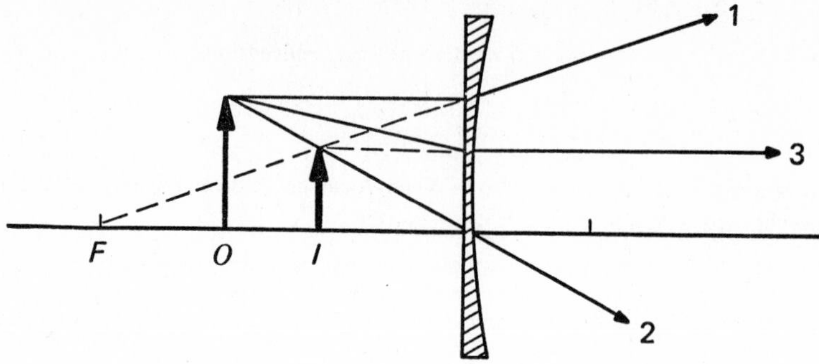

15 ☐ $\frac{1}{p} + \frac{1}{p'} = \frac{1}{f}$

p is positive if the object is on the side of the lens from which light is coming. p' is positive if the image is on the side of the lens to which light is going. f is positive for converging lenses. In the opposite cases, the signs are negative.

a

16 ☐ $p' = -34$ cm; imaginary; $\frac{I}{O} = 0.43$; erect

$$\frac{1}{p} + \frac{1}{p'} = \frac{1}{f} \Rightarrow \frac{1}{80} + \frac{1}{p'} = -\frac{1}{60}$$

30
answers
14-17

which gives $p' = -34$ cm. The minus sign tells us the image is on the same side as the object and is thus virtual. Also $I/O = p'/p = 34/80 = 0.43$. A ray diagram shows that the image is erect.

17 ☐ $p = 45$ cm; $p' = -180$ cm

Since $I/O = p'/p = 4$, one has $p' = -4p$, the minus sign being necessary because the image will be on the same side of the lens as the object, as shown in problem 12.

Then

$$\frac{1}{p} - \frac{1}{4p} = \frac{1}{60}$$

which gives $p = 45$ cm and $p' = -180$ cm.

18 The boundary between material 1 (refractive index μ_1) and material 2 (index μ_2) is a portion of the surface of a sphere. What is the relation between object and image distance for light passing through the boundary?

19 A glass sphere (radius = 20 cm) has an index of refraction of 1.50. Where will a bubble at the center of the sphere appear to be to an observer outside the sphere?

20 Find the image position for the system shown below.

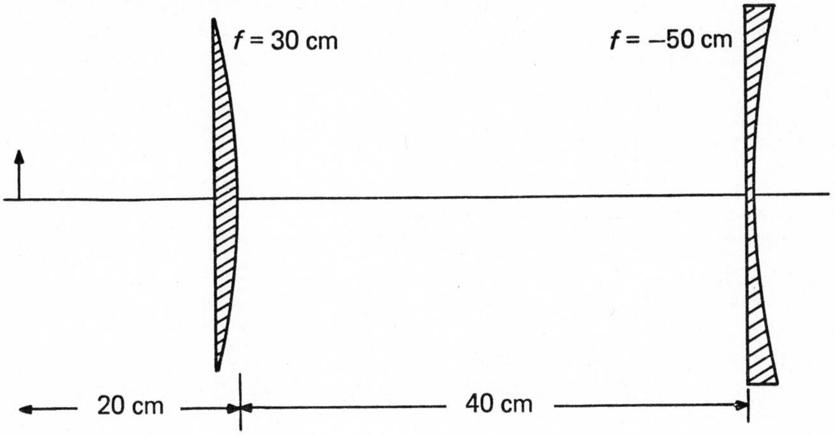

q

30
questions
18-20

18 ☐ $\frac{\mu_1}{p} + \frac{\mu_2}{p'} = \frac{\mu_2 - \mu_1}{R}$

The usual sign convention used for thin lenses applies to p and p'. The radius of curvature of the surface R is positive if the center of the sphere (of which the boundary is a part) lies on the side of the boundary to which light is going.

19 ☐ At the center

Use the bubble as an illuminated object immersed in glass. Considering the light to shine from the bubble out through the surface of the sphere and using the equation of the previous problem with $\mu_1 = 1.50$ and $\mu_2 = 1.00$, one finds

$$\frac{1.50}{20} + \frac{1}{p'} = -\frac{0.50}{-20}$$

Notice that both R and $\mu_2 - \mu_1$ are negative.

$$\frac{1}{p'} = \frac{-1}{20} \qquad \text{so } p' = -20 \text{ cm}$$

The image is at the center of the sphere. What is the meaning of the minus sign? Can you show why this answer must be correct by considering the effect of the surface on the wavefronts?

20 ☐ 33 cm to left of second lens

Using the lens formula for the first lens,

$$\frac{1}{20} + \frac{1}{p'} = \frac{1}{30}$$

from which $p' = -60$ cm. The image is to the left of the first lens. It acts as an object for the second lens with $p = 60 + 40 = 100$ cm.

Then

$$\frac{1}{100} + \frac{1}{p'} = -\frac{1}{50}$$

gives $p' = -33$ cm so the final image is virtual and 33 cm to the left of the diverging lens.

31 interference of waves

1 Why is it generally sufficient to study the behavior of a sinusoidal wave even though most waves encountered in practice are more complicated?

2 What is the superposition principle as applied to waves?

3 What does it mean to say that two simple sine waves of the same type are coherent?

4 What does it mean to say that two *complex* waves are coherent?

5 A sound wave of speed 330 m/sec and 1000 Hz frequency is split and sent into two tubes. The far ends of the tubes are brought together again at a detector. By how much must one of the tubes be elongated between successive loud points at the detector? (The length of each tube can be adjusted independently of the other.)

q

31
questions
1-7

6 A sound beam of 20-cm wavelength is sent into the tubes shown. What must be the circle radius R so that the two component beams will cancel when they reach the detector?

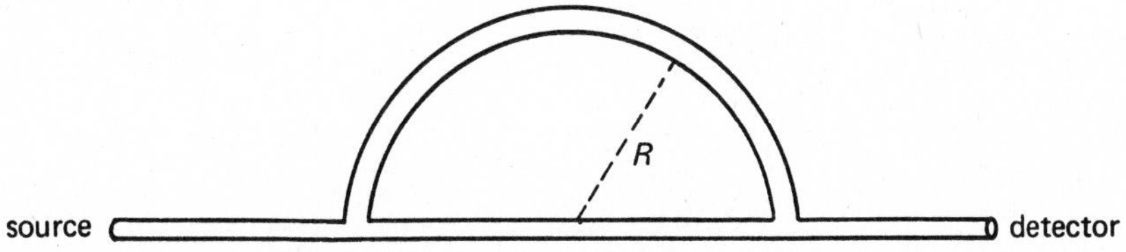

7 Suppose that the path-length difference for the two beams is $\lambda/6$ in the situation outlined in problem 6. If each beam has an amplitude A, find the amplitude of the resultant disturbance at the detector.

1 If the superposition principle holds, then a wave can be considered as the sum of sinusoidal waves. The behavior of the complicated wave can thus be inferred from the behavior of its component waves.

2 "When several wave disturbances arrive at a point simultaneously, the resultant disturbance is the vector sum of the separate disturbances."

3 The two waves are of the same frequency and maintain a fixed phase difference.

4 The waves must have exactly the same shape and must maintain the same phase relationship to each other. This means that each of the individual sinusoidal waves which are superposed to form the complex wave must be the same for the two waves except for a proportionality constant and a constant phase difference.

5 ☐ 33 cm

As the path length is increased one wavelength, the sound goes from loud to weak to loud. But $\lambda = v/f = (330 \text{ m/sec})/1000 \text{ Hz} = 33 \text{ cm}$.

a

31
answers
1-7

6 ☐ $8.77(2n + 1)$ cm; $n = 0, 1, \ldots\ldots$

For cancellation, the two paths must differ by $\frac{1}{2}\lambda$, $(3/2)\lambda, \ldots$ $\lambda(2n + 1)/2$ with n equal to 0, 1, 2, ... Therefore

$$\pi R - 2R = \frac{(20)(2n + 1)}{2}$$

Solving,

$$R = \frac{(2n + 1)10}{1.14} = 8.77(2n + 1) \text{ cm}$$

7 ☐ $1.73A$

A path-length difference of $\lambda/6$ is equivalent to a phase angle difference of $360°/6 = 60°$. Therefore, the two disturbances are

$$y_1 = A \sin(\omega t) \text{ and } y_2 = A \sin(\omega t - 60°)$$

Using the formula for the sum of two sines, one then finds

$$y = y_1 + y_2 = 2A \cos(30°) \sin(\omega t - 30°) = 1.73A \sin(\omega t - 30°)$$

8 Show how one would find the amplitude of the sum of $y_1 = 0.5A \sin(\omega t)$ and $y_2 = A \sin(\omega t + 37^\circ)$ using the concept of phasors.

9 In order to obtain a resultant wave $y = 2.0 \sin[\omega t + (\pi/2)]$, what wave must one add to $y_1 = 3.0 \sin(\omega t)$?

q

31
questions
8-9

8 ☐ $1.43A$

The vector diagram for the two disturbances is shown.

From the diagram, the amplitude R is given as

$R^2 = (1.3A)^2 + (0.6A)^2 = 2.05A^2.$

Incidentally, the phase angle ϕ is given by $\tan\phi = 0.6/1.3$.

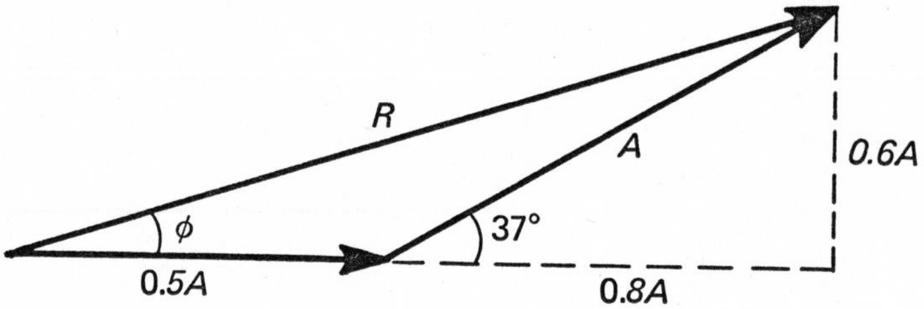

9 ☐ $3.6 \sin(\omega t + 146°)$

The phasor diagram is as shown. Notice $y_1 + y_2 = y$ and we wish to find y_2. Clearly, its amplitude is $\sqrt{4 + 9} = 3.6$. The phase angle ϕ is such that $\tan\phi = -0.67$ and $\phi = 146°$. Therefore

$y_2 = 3.6 \sin(\omega t + 146°)$

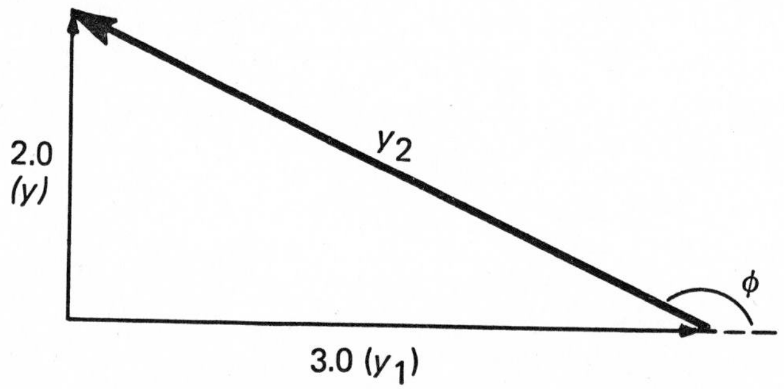

10 Suppose one wished to do a Young's double-slit experiment with the radio waves from a station whose frequency was 10^6 Hz. What should be the slit separation so that the first maximum would occur at an angle of 37° to the undeviated beam when observed at a great distance from the slits?

11 Show that in a Young's double-slit experiment when the screen is far from the slits, the angle at which the minima occur relative to the undeviated beam is given by

$$\sin\theta = \frac{[n + (1/2)]\lambda}{d}$$

with $n = 0, 1, \ldots$. How is this related to the usual expression $\Delta/d = x/D$?

q

31
questions
10-11

10 ☐ 500 m

The first maximum occurs when the path difference is λ as shown. But

$\lambda = c/f = 3 \times 10^8/10^6 = 300$ m.

From the figure,

$\sin 37^\circ = \lambda/d$ and so $d = 300/0.60 = 500$ m.

It appears that this experiment is impractical. However, using microwaves for which $\lambda \cong 10$ cm, the experiment is easily carried out.

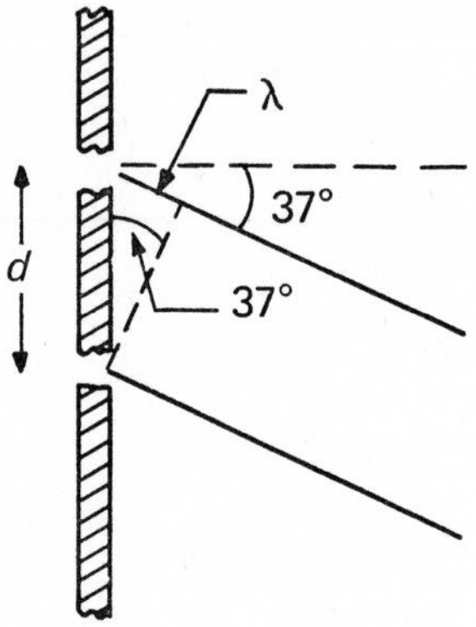

a

31
answers
10-11

11 The situation is as shown. Since the screen is far away, the two rays are essentially parallel. For a minimum,

$$\Delta = \lambda/2, 3\lambda/2, \ldots \left(n + \frac{1}{2}\right)\lambda.$$

As seen from the figure, $\sin\theta = \Delta/d$ and so $\sin\theta = (n + 1/2)\lambda/d$. Now in the large triangle from the slit to the screen, one has $\tan\theta = x/D$. If θ is small, the sine and tangent are equal and the usual relation follows.

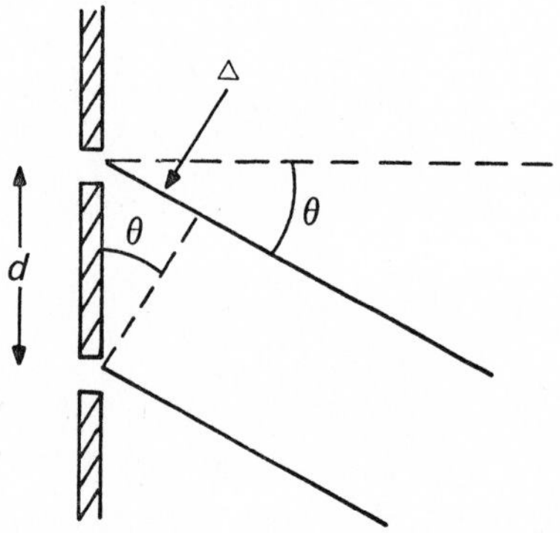

12 Show by means of a phasor diagram how the amplitude and intensity of the light varies with angle in a double-slit experiment.

13 Show that the result of the previous problem agrees with the facts that maxima occur when $\Delta = 0, \lambda, 2\lambda, \ldots, n\lambda$ and minima when $\Delta = [n + (1/2)]\lambda$.

12 The beams from the two slits are represented by phasors as shown. To find the phase angle ϕ we note that if $\Delta = \lambda$, where Δ is shown in problem 11, then $\phi = 360° = 2\pi$. Thus, $\phi = 2\pi(\Delta/\lambda)$. But from the figure of problem 11 one has $\Delta = d \sin\theta$ and so $\phi = (2\pi\, d/\lambda) \sin\theta$ which is, for θ small, $\phi = 2\pi(\theta\, d/\lambda)$. Now $R^2 = A^2 \sin^2\phi + (A\cos\phi + A)^2$ so that $R^2 = 2A^2 + 2A^2 \cos\phi = 2A^2 \cos^2(\phi/2)$. Therefore, the light intensity, which is proportional to R^2, is

$$I = I_0 \cos^2 \frac{\pi\theta\, d}{\lambda}$$

Of course, the amplitude is proportional to $\sqrt{I}$.

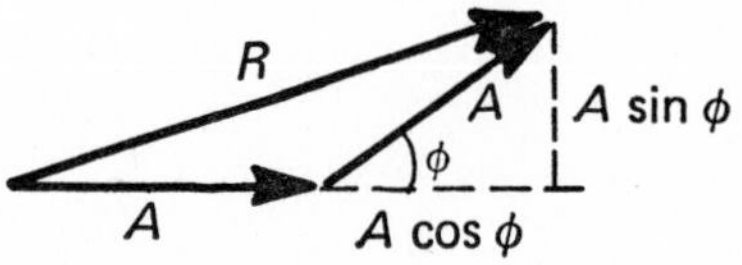

13 To do this we note from the figure of problem 11 that $\sin\theta = \Delta/d$, and, for θ small, $\theta = \Delta/d$. Now from problem 12, $I \sim \cos^2(\pi\theta\, d/\lambda)$ which is maximum when the argument of the cosine is $0, \pi, 2\pi, \ldots, n\pi$; that is, when $\pi\theta\, d/\lambda = 0, \pi, \ldots, n\pi$ or when $\Delta/\lambda = 0, 1, \ldots, n$. Similarly, the cosine is zero when $\pi\theta\, d/\lambda = \pi/2, 3\pi/2, \ldots, (n + 1/2)\pi$, which gives the condition sought for the minima. Notice from the above figure that $R = 0$ when $\phi = \pi, 3\pi, 5\pi$, etc. We could use this together with the fact that $\phi = 2\pi\,(\theta\, d/\lambda)$ to arrive at the same result.

a

31
answers
12-13

14 Using the phasor method, find the intensity of the light in a triple-slit experiment as a function of angle θ, assuming the slit separations to be d and the viewing screen to be far from the slits.

15 Two identical 2000-Hz sound sources A and B send waves to the detector as shown, the intensity at the detector being a maximum for the position indicated. As B is moved backwards very slowly, alternate high and low readings are recorded by the detector. At what positions are these maxima and minima observed? Speed of sound is 330 m/sec.

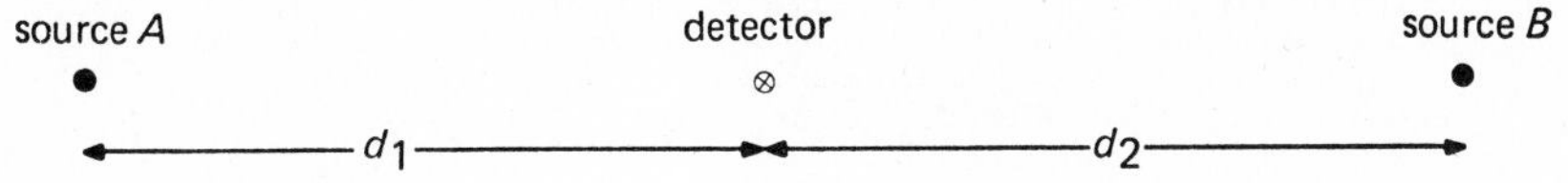

a

14 □ $I = (I_0/9)\,[3 + 4\cos\phi + 2\cos(2\phi)]$ with $\phi = 2\pi(\theta\, d/\lambda)$

We note that the phase angle of each adjacent slit is $\phi = 2\pi(\Delta/\lambda)$ with $\Delta = d\sin\theta \cong \theta\, d$. The phasor diagram is as shown and so the amplitude of the resultant wave

$$R = A\sqrt{(1 + \cos\phi + \cos 2\phi)^2 + (\sin\phi + \sin 2\phi)^2}$$

so that

$$R = A\sqrt{3 + 2\cos 2\phi + 2\cos\phi + 2\cos\phi\cos 2\phi + 2\sin\phi\sin 2\phi}$$

$$= A\sqrt{3 + 2\cos 2\phi + 2\cos\phi + 2\cos\phi}$$

where use has been made of $\cos(A - B) = \cos A\cos B + \sin A\sin B$. Or, since the intensity I is proportional to R^2,

$$I = \frac{I_0}{9}(3 + 4\cos\phi + 2\cos 2\phi)$$

where the factor $\frac{1}{9}$ has been introduced to make $I = I_0$ when $\theta = 0$.

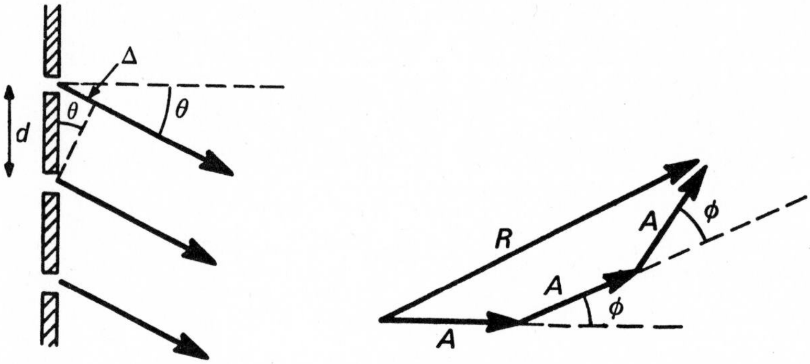

15 □ Max: $d_2 \pm 16.5n$ cm; Min: $d_2 \pm 16.5\left(n + \frac{1}{2}\right)$ cm

The sounds from the two sources are in phase at the detector. When d_2 is increased or decreased by $n\lambda$, they will also be in phase. Since $\lambda = v/f = 16.5$ cm, the maxima occur for $d_2 \pm 16.5n$ cm. Similarly, the minima occur for $d_2 \pm (n + 1/2)\lambda$.

16 The two coherent sources shown send waves of wavelength $\lambda << L$ towards each other along the line joining them. If the sources are

in phase, find the locations of the points of maximum intensity between A and B.

17 If the wavelength of a wave is λ in vacuum, how great is it in a material of refractive index μ? What is the optical path-length equivalent to an actual path length L when the material has a refractive index μ?

18 When Newton's rings are seen in reflected light, why is the center region dark rather than bright?

19 For the air-filled wedge shown, find the wavelength of the light which gives rise to the set of fringes indicated. Assume the light beam to be nearly vertical.

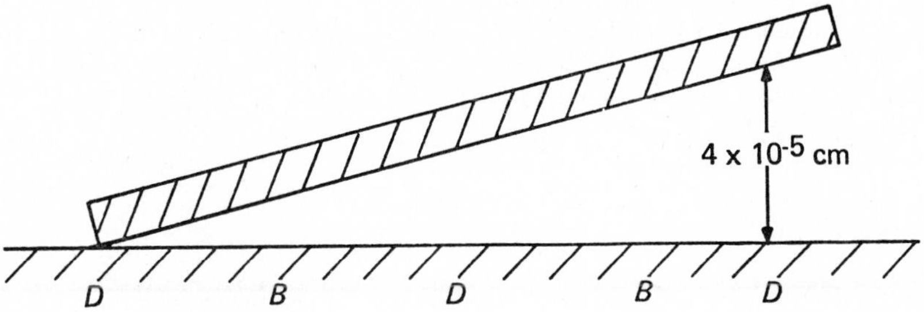

31
questions
16-20

20 Repeat the previous problem if the wedge space is filled with water, $\mu = \frac{4}{3}$.

16 □ $x = (1/2)(L - n\lambda);\ n = 0, \pm 1, \pm 2, \ldots$

For a maximum at x, the difference in the two path lengths, x and $L - x$, must be $n\lambda$, with $n = 0, \pm 1, \pm 2, \ldots$. Therefore, the points in question are

$$(L - x) - x = n\lambda \quad \text{or} \quad x = \frac{1}{2}(L - n\lambda)$$

Notice, as one would expect, that one maximum is at the center point, $L/2$, and the others are $n(\lambda/2)$ on either side.

17 □ $\frac{\lambda}{\mu};\ \mu L$

Since $\mu = c/v$ and $\lambda = c/f$, one has $\lambda_{mat} = v/f = \lambda/\mu$. Optical path length is measured in terms of wavelengths. For vacuum, the optical path length is $(L/\lambda_v)\lambda_v = L$ and in any other case, the length is $(L/\lambda_m)\lambda_v = L(\lambda_v/\lambda_m) = \mu L$.

a

18 Although the distances traveled by two reflected rays from the center are essentially the same, a ray reflected by a high-μ material suffers a 180° phase change. As a result, the beam reflected from the lower surface is, in effect, held back through $\lambda/2$ and therefore interferes destructively with the beam reflected from the upper surface.

19 □ 4×10^{-5} cm

31
answers
16-20

We know that between regions of darkness and brightness, one ray must be retarded by $\lambda/2$. In this case the beam is retarded $4(\lambda/2)$ at one end relative to the other. Hence, $2(4 \times 10^{-5}\text{cm}) = 4(\lambda/2)$ from which $\lambda = 4 \times 10^{-5}$ cm. The extra factor of 2 occurs since the beam goes through the air space of the wedge twice, once up and once down. (The light is violet in color.)

20 □ 5.3×10^{-5} cm

The value for λ found in the previous problem is the wavelength in the material filling the wedge, air in that case. Now, however, $\lambda_{H_2O} = 4 \times 10^{-5}$ cm and since $\lambda_{vac} = \lambda_{H_2O}\mu$, one has $\lambda_{vac} = 5.3 \times 10^{-5}$ cm for the light used. The light is bluish-green in color.

32
diffraction

1 Distinguish between the terms interference and diffraction.

2 What is Huygen's principle?

3 What is the difference between Fraunhofer and Fresnel diffraction?

4 Show that the extra path length in glass of a ray focused in a Fraunhofer diffraction experiment is just canceled by the refraction in the lens.

5 Refer to the figure. A plane light wave strikes a single slit which we artificially consider to be four slits as shown. For simplicity, consider point P to be much farther away than indicated. (a) Then the four rays from the four (artificial) slits will be essentially______ to one another. (b) If $\Delta_1 = \lambda/2$, then the light from (artificial) slit 2 will_________ the light from slit 1. (c) In addition, since the rays are essentially parallel, $\Delta_2 =$______, and $\Delta_3 =$ _________ . (d) Then $\Delta_3 - \Delta_2 =$ _________, and therefore the light from (artificial) slit 4 will _________ that from slit 3. (e) As a result, point P will be a point of _________ .

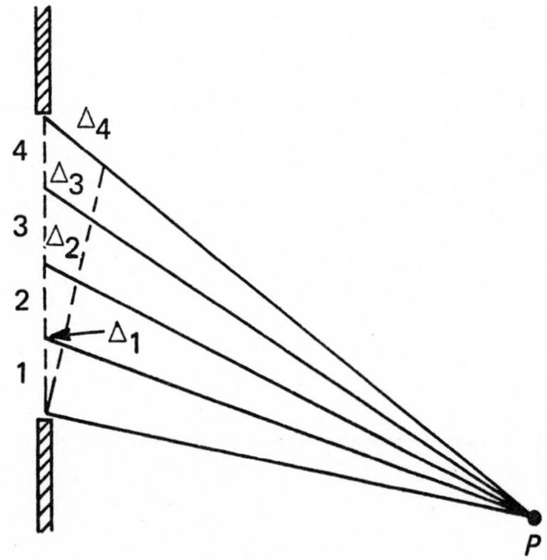

1 Diffraction is the phenomenon in which wave motion propagates into regions which should be shadow if the propagation were strictly rectilinear. This phenomenon is the result of interference between the various waves sent out by an advancing wavefront.

2 Each point on an advancing wavefront acts as a point source for a new wave.

3 In Fraunhofer diffraction the incident beam is a plane wave disturbance and the exiting rays are observed at a great distance or using a lens system focused for infinity so that parallel light is used. Fresnel diffraction is used to designate all other cases.

4 The action of the lens is best seen in terms of wavefronts. As shown in the diagram, the lens causes the plane waves to become spherical and to converge on a point. All points of the wave (i.e., all of the rays), reach the focal point at the same time and so their relative phase is not disturbed by the focusing action of the lens.

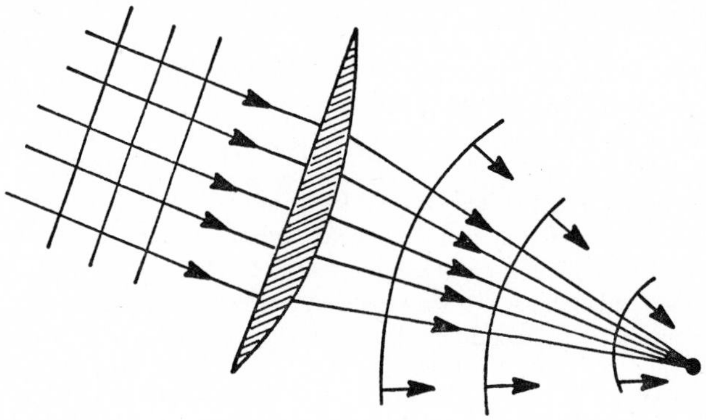

5 (a) parallel

(b) cancel

(c) λ; $3\lambda/2$

(d) $\lambda/2$; cancel

(e) darkness

6 Suppose that point P in the previous problem moves somewhat farther below the slit. The new situation is shown where now the actual slit is artificially divided into five artificial slits, such that succeeding Δs differ by $\lambda/2$. (a) Then the light from (artificial) slit 1 will __________ that from slit 2 and light from 3 will __________ that from slit 4. (b) However, the light from (artificial) slit 5 has no slit to cancel it, and so point P in this case shows __________. (c) The intensity of the bright spot at P will be much __________ than that of the central bright spot since only a fraction, namely __________, of the slit contributes to its brightness. (d) This type of interference pattern resulting from a single slit is called __________.

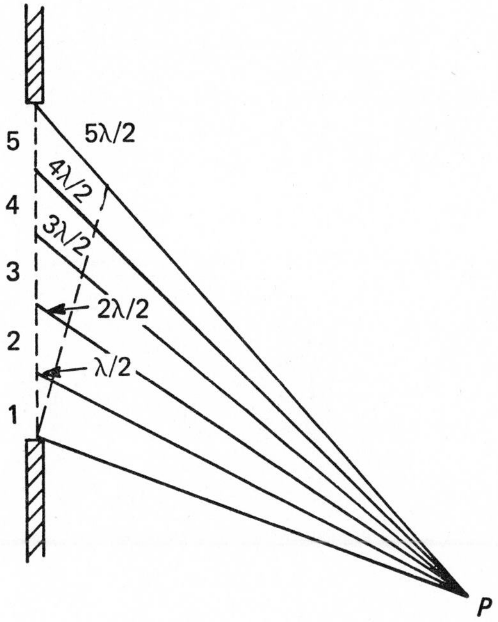

32
questions
6-7

7 Plane water waves with crests 10 cm apart strike a wall squarely. The disturbance enters the region of still water beyond the wall through a hole of width 50 cm. The waves in this region eventually strike a distant wall. Find the angle from the hole to the first side point of zero disturbance on this second wall.

6 (a) cancel; cancel

(b) brightness

(c) less; 1/5

(d) a diffraction pattern

7 ☐ 11.5°

This is clearly a case of Fraunhofer diffraction since the source and screen are at essentially infinite distances. At the first point of no disturbance, the disturbance from the top half of the hole must cancel that from the bottom half. Therefore, Δ on the diagram must be $\lambda/2 = 5.0$ cm. Since the slit width is 50 cm, one has $\sin\theta = \Delta/(b/2) = 5/25 = 0.20$ from which $\theta = 11.5°$.

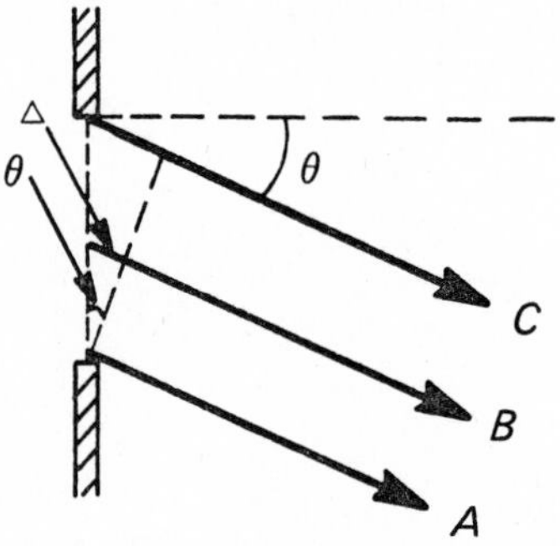

a

32
answers
6-7

8 For the situation of the previous problem, find the angle at which the point P in the disturbance pattern indicated below occurs.

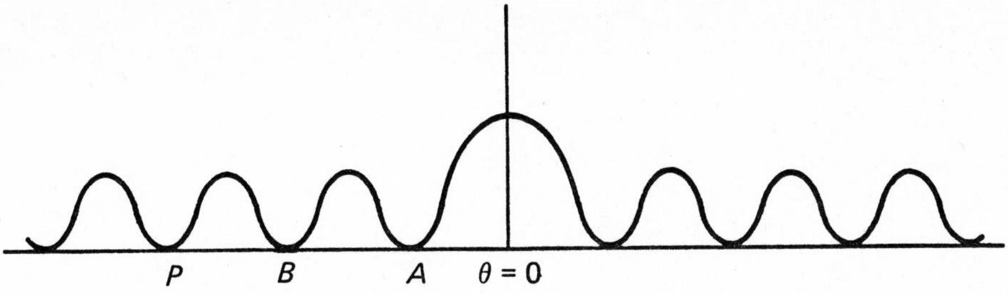

9 In a Fraunhofer single-slit diffraction experiment the pattern is focused by a lens of 80-cm focal length placed just behind the slit. For light of $\lambda = 5000$ Å, the distance between the two minima which bound the central maximum is 0.020 cm. Find the width of the slit.

q

32
questions
8-9

8 □ 37°

At point A, the two halves of the slit cancel, as in the previous problem. At B the slit, divided into fourths, cancels, fourth by fourth. At P the slit, divided into sixths, cancels sixth by sixth. From the diagram, $\Delta = \lambda/2$ to obtain cancellation of adjacent slit portions so

$$\sin\theta = \frac{6\Delta}{b} = \frac{3\lambda}{50}$$

$$= \frac{3}{5} = 0.60$$

Therefore, θ for point P is 37°.

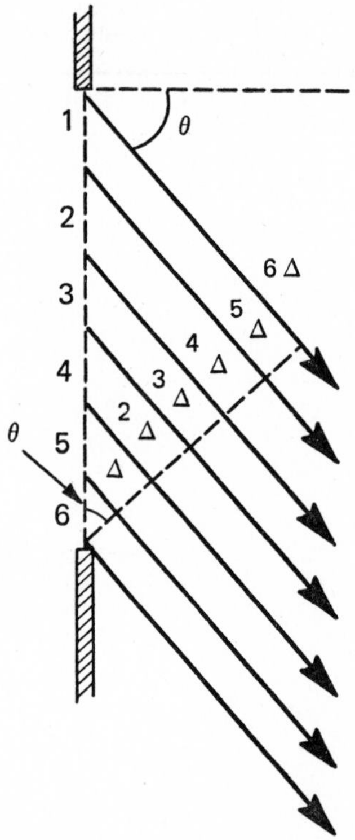

a

32
answers
8-9

9 □ 0.40 cm

At the position of the first minimum, the figure for problem 7 gives us $\Delta = \lambda/2$ and $\sin\theta = 2\Delta/b = \lambda/b$ where b is the slit width. In the present case, using the triangle with its vertices at the slit, central maximum, and first minimum, one has $\sin\theta = 0.010/80$. Equating these two expressions for $\sin\theta$ and setting $\lambda = 5 \times 10^{-5}$ cm, one finds $b = 0.40$ cm.

10 Sketch the Fraunhofer diffraction patterns for single slits of width 4×10^{-2} cm, 4×10^{-4} cm, and 4×10^{-5} cm when using $\lambda = 400$ mμ light.

11 How do the diagrams of the previous problem explain the fact that two slits, closely spaced, cannot be seen as distinct if the slits are too narrow? What is the limiting condition for resolving them?

12 How far away could one be from a person whose eyes are separated by a distance of 7 cm and still see his eyes as two distinct objects? Assume the size of the pupil of the observer's eye is the limiting factor for resolution.

13 According to the work of this chapter, superimposed upon the Young's double-slit pattern treated in the previous chapter, there is a diffraction pattern due to each slit separately. Under what condition would the single-slit diffraction pattern be of only secondary importance?

10 The first side minimum occurs at $\sin\theta = \lambda/b$, which is 10^{-3}, 0.10, and 1.0 for the three cases of concern. Hence the patterns will be as shown (not to scale).

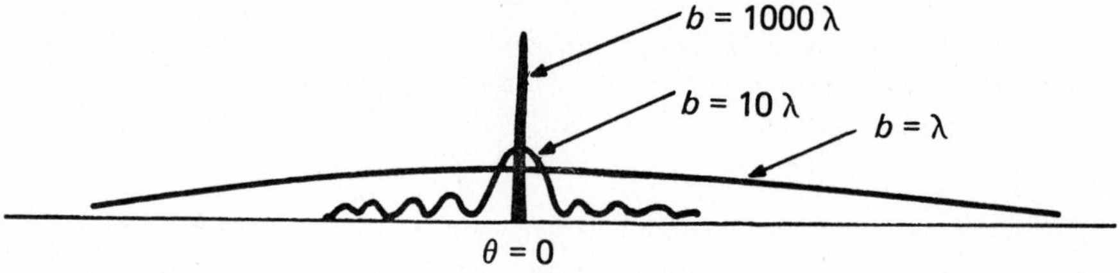

11 If the images of the slits are not sharp enough, they will just give rise to a continuous blur. For example, in the diagrams of problem 10, slits for which $\sin\theta = 1$ could not give rise to distinct images. If the central maximum of one slit's pattern falls on the first minimum of the other's pattern as shown, then the angle subtended by the slits at the screen is $\theta_c \cong \lambda/b$ where b is the slit width. In this case, one has reached the limit of resolution.

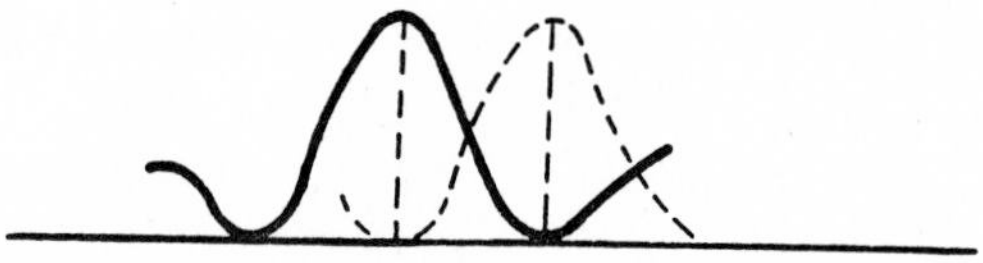

a

12 ☐ ~300 m

32
answers
10-13

We know that the limiting angle of resolution $\theta_c = 1.22\lambda/D$ where D is the diameter of the pupil of the observer's eye and θ_c is the angle subtended at the observer by the eyes of the person being observed. Calling the distance between observer and observed L, one has $\sin\theta_c \cong \theta_c = 7/L$ where L is in centimeters. Estimating the diameter of the pupil to be 0.3 cm, one has $7/L = 1.22\,(5 \times 10^{-5})/0.3$, where 5000 Å has been used as an average wavelength for the light. Solving gives $L \cong 300$ m.

13 If the slits are extremely narrow, then the first minimum in the diffraction pattern will not exist; the pattern will spread so much that the central maximum will cover the whole field of view. In that case the diffraction pattern will be missing.

14 Draw the phasor diagrams at the first minimum for the following cases: 4 slits, 6 slits, and 8 slits. Assume the slit separations to be b in each case. What is the angle between adjacent phasors?

15 For each of the cases of the previous problem, find the angle at which the first minimum occurs when the slits are used as a grating. What implication does this have for the sharpness of images formed by diffraction gratings?

16 A certain diffraction grating gives its first-order image of the mercury blue line (λ = 4360 Å) at an angle of 37°. At what angle will the image occur if the whole apparatus is immersed in water, $\mu_{H_2O} = \frac{4}{3}$?

14

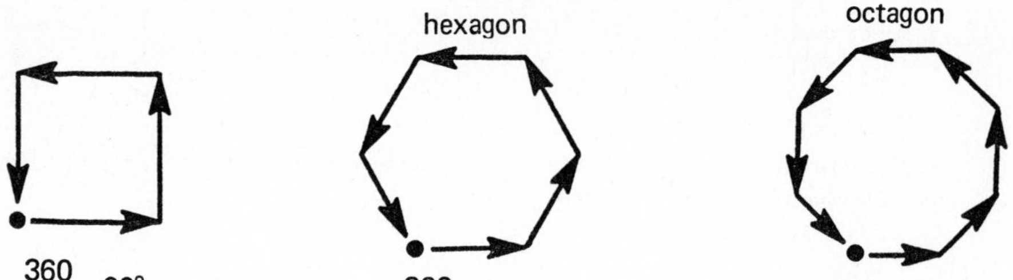

$\frac{360}{4} = 90°$ $\frac{360}{6} = 60°$ $\frac{360}{8} = 45°$

15 From the diagram, $\sin\theta = \Delta/b$. But in each case

$$\Delta = (\text{phasor angle})\ \frac{\lambda}{360°} \quad \text{and so}$$

$$\sin\theta = \frac{(\text{phasor angle})}{360°}\left(\frac{\lambda}{b}\right)$$

Therefore, for 4, 6, and 8 slits one has

$$\sin\theta = \left(\frac{1}{4}\right)\left(\frac{\lambda}{b}\right), \quad \left(\frac{1}{6}\right)\left(\frac{\lambda}{b}\right), \quad \left(\frac{1}{8}\right)\left(\frac{\lambda}{b}\right)$$

As one sees, the images narrow as the number of slits increases providing the slit spacing is held constant.

a

32
answers
14-16

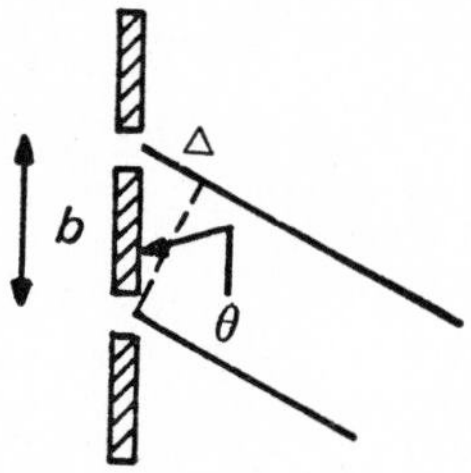

16 □ $\theta = 27°$

The only effect observed will be that due to the change in λ. For vacuum (or air) one has $n\lambda_a = d \sin 37°$ with $n = 1$. For water, $n\lambda_w = d\sin\theta$. Taking ratios of the two equations,

$$\frac{\lambda_a}{\lambda_w} = \frac{0.60}{\sin\theta}$$

But

$$\frac{\lambda_a}{\lambda_w} = \mu = 4/3 \text{ and so } \sin\theta = 0.45.$$

33 optical instruments

1 Illustrate the function of a simple magnifier by two diagrams, one showing the image formed on the retina when the object is viewed as close to the naked eye as one can see, and one with the magnifying glass.

2 A common box-type camera consists of a single lens 10 cm from the film. The lens' focal length is 10 cm so distant objects are focused on the film. How far from the film will an object 3 m away from the camera be imaged?

3 A point source of light 3 m in front of the camera described in problem 2 will be imaged as a circular spot on the film. Show, by means of a diagram, why it is enlarged and find the diameter of the spot. The lens diameter is 1.0 cm.

1 In the second case, the eye actually looks at the virtual image indicated.

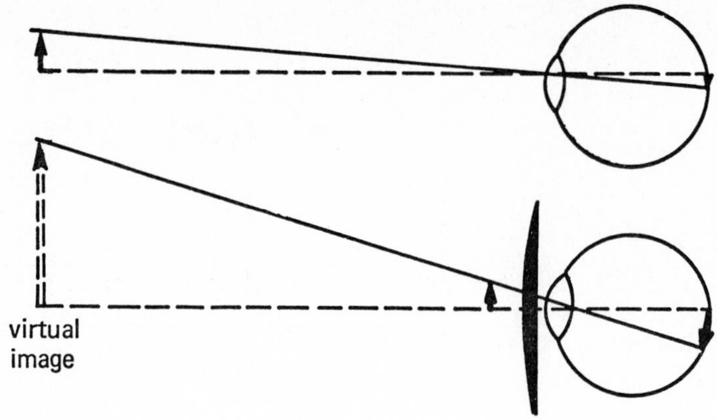

2 ☐ 3.4 mm

We have

$$\frac{1}{p}+\frac{1}{p'}=\frac{1}{f}$$

which gives

$$\frac{1}{300}+\frac{1}{p'}=\frac{1}{10}$$

resulting in $p' = 10.34$ cm. Therefore the image is 3.4 mm behind the film.

a

33
answers
1-3

3 ☐ 0.34 mm

The lens forms a point image as shown. Since it is not focused on the screen, the spot on the screen is rather large. Calling the spot diameter D, one has, from similar triangles, $1/10.34 = D/0.34$ from which $D = 0.034$ cm.

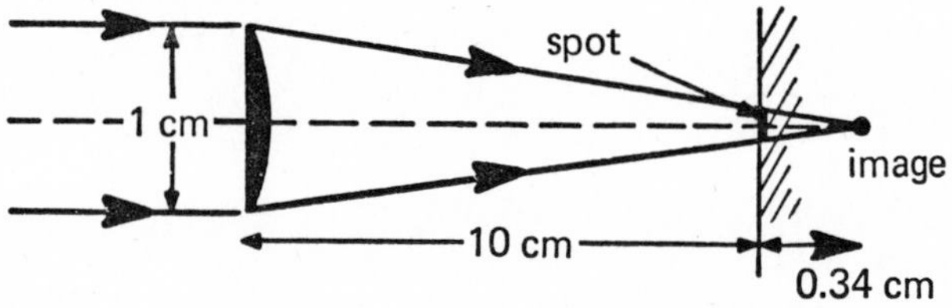

4 Compare the diameter of the spot found in the previous problem with the size of the diffraction ring formed by the diffraction effect of the lens opening. (An approximate answer is sufficient.)

5 Show that for the out-of-focus situation described in problem 3 the spot diameter D is given by

$$D = \left(\frac{L - L_o}{L}\right) d$$

where L_o is the image distance, d is the diameter of the opening, and L is the lens to film distance.

6 How do we know that it is impossible to design a light microscope which will be capable of seeing small molecules?

7 The so-called *opera glass* has an optical system like that shown. Find the image formed of a distant object.

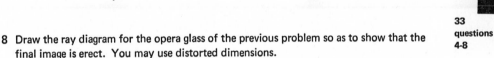

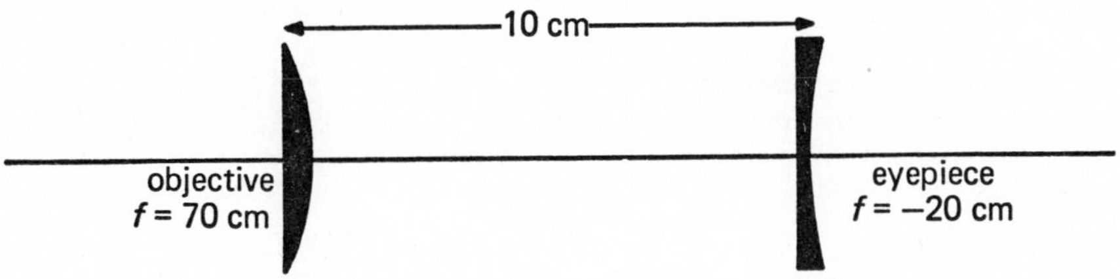

33
questions
4-8

8 Draw the ray diagram for the opera glass of the previous problem so as to show that the final image is erect. You may use distorted dimensions.

4 □ 10^{-3} cm versus 34 X 10^{-3} cm

As an approximation, consider the opening to be a slit of width 1 cm. From the diagram, for the first minimum in the pattern, $\Delta = \lambda$ and so $\sin\theta \cong \theta = \lambda/1 \cong 5 \times 10^{-5}$. Also, $\sin\theta \cong \tan\theta \cong \theta = (D/2)/10$. Equating gives $D = 10^{-3}$ cm as compared to 34 X 10^{-3} cm found in problem 3. The diffraction effect is small in comparison.

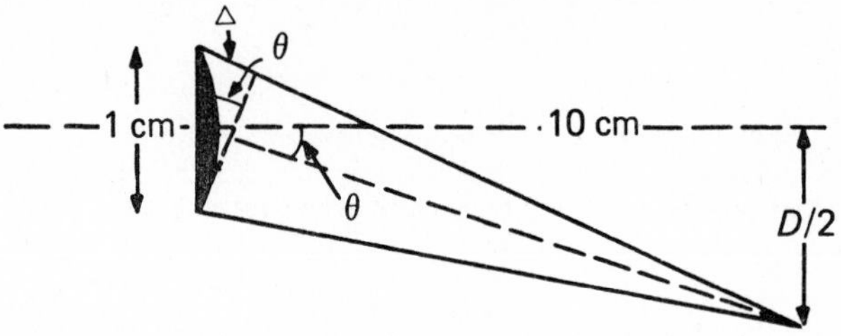

5 Using the same method as in problem 3 but replacing the numbers by symbols, one finds $d/L = D/(L - L_0)$. Notice that if the aperture diameter d is made very small, the lack of proper focus will be negligible. This fact is used in the pinhole camera which has no lens at all.

6 Detail smaller than the wavelength of radiation used is not observable because of diffraction effects (see Bueche, Sec. 33.2). Since λ for light is ~ 5 X 10^{-5} cm and since molecules have sizes in the range ~ 5 X 10^{-8} cm, diffraction effects preclude observation in this way.

a

33
answers
4-8

7 The image of a distant object formed by the objective is 60 cm to the right of the diverging lens. This constitutes a virtual object for that lens and so the lens equation gives

$$\frac{1}{-60} + \frac{1}{p'} = \frac{1}{-20}$$

from which $p' = -30$ cm. In other words, the final image is 20 cm to the left of the first lens. It is, of course, virtual.

8

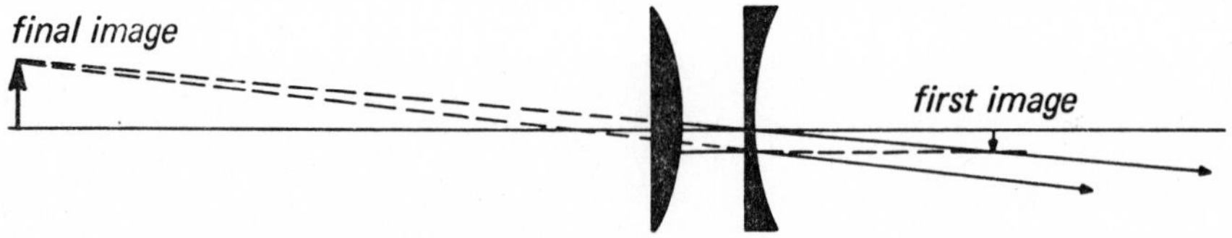

9 The density of the air above the earth varies approximately with height y as $\rho_0 e^{-0.0001\,y}$ when y is in meters. The index of refraction of air at sea level is about 1.003. Find the increase in optical path length for light from a star resulting from the atmosphere.

10 What is a spectral line and why, in a spectrometer, does it appear as a bright line?

11 What is meant by the resolving power of a grating? Why does it depend upon N, the number of lines in the grating?

12 Prism spectrometers using glass prisms are not usable below about 3500 Å and above about 25,000Å. Why? Does this same restriction apply to grating spectrometers? Can prism spectrometers be used outside this range?

9 □ 30 m

The excess optical path length over that in vacuum will be $\mu_{air} - 1$ per meter of path. Assuming $(\mu - 1)$ to vary in the same way as ρ the total optical path difference Δ will be

$$\Delta = \int_0^\infty \left(\mu_{air} - 1\right) dy = \int_0^\infty 0.003e^{-0.0001y}\, dy$$

$$= \frac{0.003}{0.0001} = 30 \text{ m}$$

10 In a spectrometer, the optical system forms a final image which is the image of the entrance slit of the spectrometer. If a continuous band of wavelengths is given off by the light source, then these slit images for the various wavelengths appear at different angles and give rise to a continuous colored band. If the source gives off only a distinct set of λs, then the slit images are separated and one sees a single image (or line) for each separate λ.

11 By definition, if $\Delta\lambda$ is the minimum separation between the wavelengths of two lines which are just resolvable, then resolving power = $\lambda/\Delta\lambda$. It is shown in Bueche, Sec. 33.6, that this is also Nn where n is the order of the spectrum. We recall that the diffraction pattern narrows with increasing N and therefore the lines are better separated when N is large.

12 (a) Glass absorbs radiation (i.e., does not transmit well) outside these wavelength limits.

(b) Grating spectrometers which do not use lenses made of glass are not restricted by this.

(c) Prisms made of quartz transmit much further into the ultraviolet, and other materials can be used as prisms in the infrared.

13 Metal reflection gratings are sometimes made as concave mirrors. Draw a diagram for a spectrometer which would need no lenses if this type of grating were used.

q
33
question
13

13 The entrance slit at $p = 2f$ acts as the object for the mirror. The diffraction line at angle θ is imaged at $p' = 2f$ on a photographic film. No lens is needed.

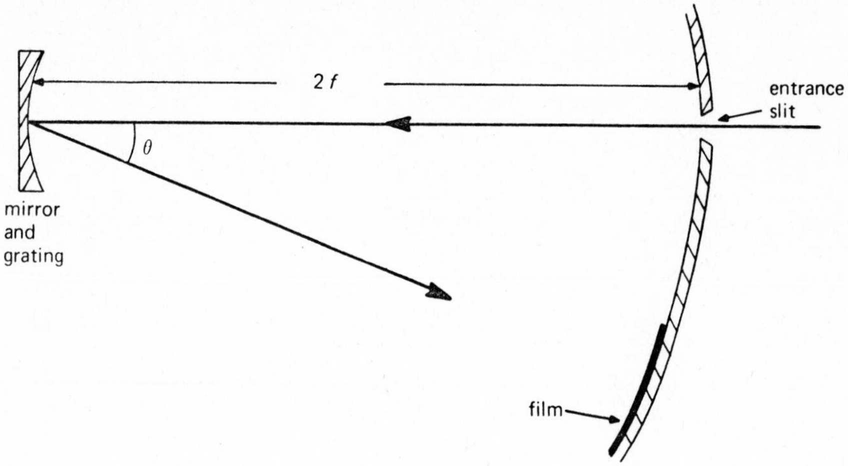

a

33
answer
13

34
resonance of waves

1 What principle governs the combination of waves?

2 Two identical sources a distance L apart send out waves toward each other. The sources are in phase. How large must L be in terms of λ if there are to exist stationary points between the sources where the resultant disturbance is always zero? What are these points called?

3 A series of sharp pulses is sent down a string as shown. Upon reflection, the pulses are inverted. Describe the combined incident and reflected wave, giving the location of nodes and antinodes, if any exist.

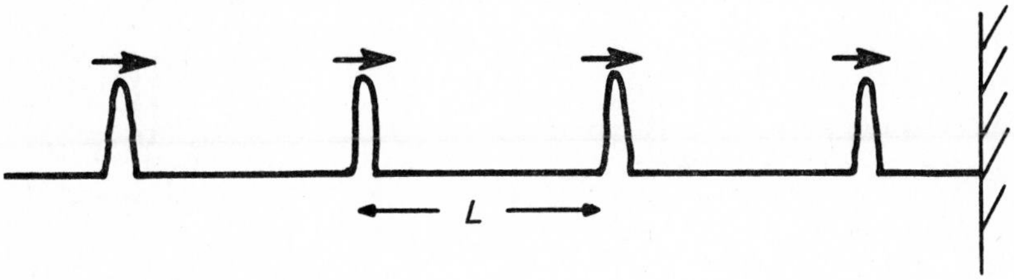

1 The superposition principle. It is assumed that several wave disturbances passing through a given point can be added linearly to give the resultant disturbance at the point.

2 □ $L > \frac{\lambda}{2}$; nodes

The points are called nodes. They will occur at points where the waves from the two sources are $\lambda/2$, or $3\lambda/2$, or $5\lambda/2$, etc., out of phase. For this to be true, the distance of one source from the point x must be related to the distance of the other source from the point $L - x$ in the following way: $(L - x) - x = (n + 1/2)\lambda$ with $n = 0, 1, \ldots$. Therefore $L = 2x + (n + 1/2)\lambda$ and so $L > \lambda/2$ for such a point to exist.

3 The fastened end of the string is a node. It is this fact which demands inversion of the pulse on reflection. Whenever an incident and reflected pulse are at the same point, they cancel. As seen from the diagram, this will occur at distance $L/2$, $3L/2$, . . ., $(n + 1/2)L$ from the fixed end. These points will be nodes. There are no distinct antinodes.

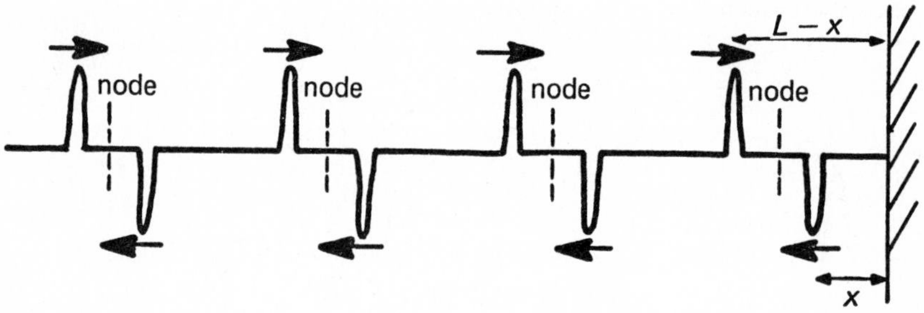

a

34
answers
1-3

4 A sine wave is reflected without phase change from the end of a string. Find the positions of the nodes relative to the end of the string in terms of λ.

5 Where are the antinode positions in the previous problem?

4 □ $\frac{\lambda}{4}, \frac{3\lambda}{4}, \frac{5\lambda}{4}, \ldots$

Qualitative reasoning using the diagrams is sufficient to show that they occur at

$$\frac{\lambda}{4}, \quad \left(\frac{\lambda}{2} + \frac{\lambda}{4}\right), \quad \left(\frac{2\lambda}{2} + \frac{\lambda}{4}\right), \ldots$$

Or, mathematically,

$$y = y_0 \sin \left[2\pi\left(ft - \frac{x}{\lambda}\right)\right] + y_0 \sin \left[2\pi\left(ft + \frac{x}{\lambda}\right)\right]$$

giving

$$y = 2y_0 \sin (2\pi ft) \cos \left(2\pi \frac{x}{\lambda}\right)$$

which has zeros at

$$\frac{2\pi x}{\lambda} = \frac{\pi}{2}, \frac{3\pi}{2}, \ldots, \text{etc.}$$

a

34
answers
4-5

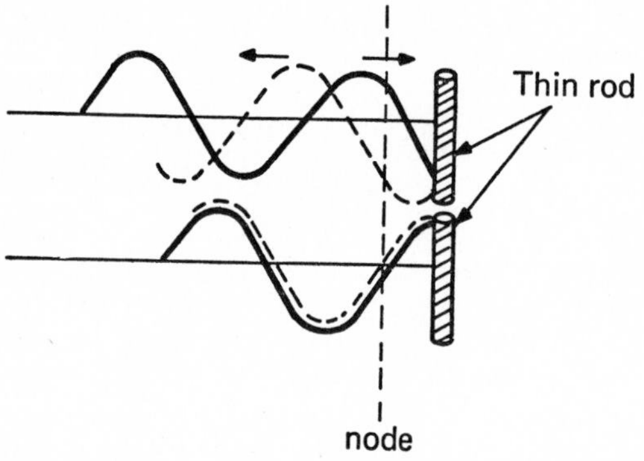

5 □ $n\frac{\lambda}{2}$ with $n = 0, 1, \ldots$

From the second diagram (or from the fact that the antinode-to-node distance is always $\lambda/4$), one sees that the antinodes occur at $x = 0, \lambda/2, 2\lambda/2, \ldots$.

6 Repeat problem 4 if the reflected wave is held back by $\pi/2$ as a result of the reflection.

7 In problems 4 and 6 we obtained equations similar to the following: $y = A \sin (2\pi f t) \cos (2\pi x/\lambda)$. By the aid of a diagram, illustrate the meaning of each of the factors in this expression for the case of a string.

q

34
questions
6-7

6 □ $\frac{\lambda}{8} + n\frac{\lambda}{2}$

From the diagram, the first node is at $\lambda/8$. Or mathematically

$$y = y_0 \left\{ \sin\left[2\pi\left(ft - \frac{x}{\lambda}\right)\right] + \sin\left[2\pi\left(ft + \frac{x}{\lambda}\right) - \frac{\pi}{2}\right] \right\}$$

$$= 2y_0 \sin\left(2\pi ft - \frac{\pi}{4}\right) \cos\left(2\pi\frac{x}{\lambda} + \frac{\pi}{4}\right)$$

from which the first zero occurs when

$2\pi(x/\lambda) + \pi/4 = \pi/2$ so $x = \lambda/8$.

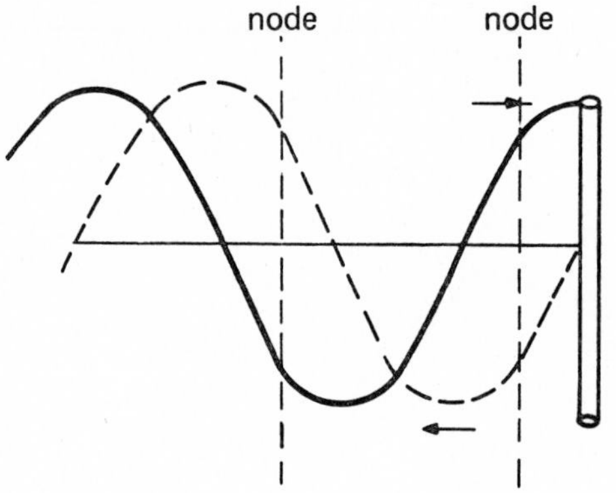

7 The position of the string at a particular instant is shown by the solid line. It oscillates back and forth with amplitude A. The dotted curves are $\pm A \cos(2\pi x/\lambda)$. The plus curve, when multiplied by $\sin(2\pi ft)$, gives a cosine function (such as the full line) which represents the string. It oscillates back and forth between the dotted curves with frequency f to form a standing wave.

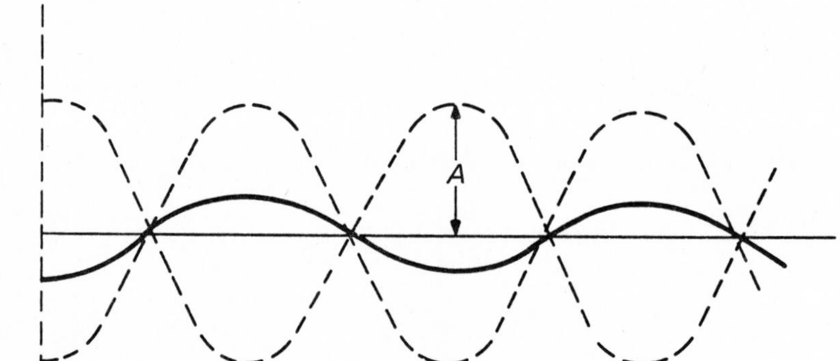

8 Resonance is achieved in a system in which waves are repeatedly reflected back and forth upon each other, provided what condition is satisfied?

9 Any one-dimensional resonating system which has nodes at its two ends must be how many wavelengths long?

10 Repeat problem 9 for a system having antinodes at its two ends.

11 Repeat problem 9 if the system has a node at one end and an antinode at the other.

q

34
questions
8-11

8 The waves traveling in the same direction along the resonating system must all be in phase or be $n(2\pi)$ radians out of phase where n is an integer.

9 □ $n\frac{\lambda}{2}$

The resonant modes of motion of the system must be similar to those shown. Since the distance between nodes is always $\lambda/2$, one has that $L = n(\lambda/2)$ with $n = 1, 2, \ldots.$

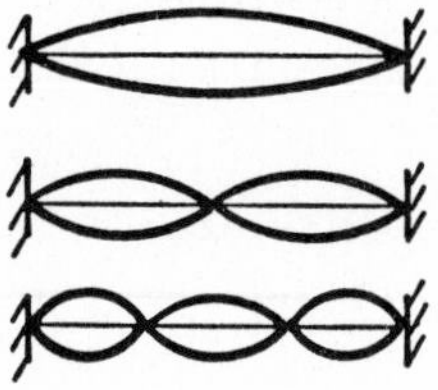

10 □ $n\frac{\lambda}{2}$

The resonant modes of motion are similar to the ones shown. Since the distance between antinodes is $\lambda/2$, one has $L = n(\lambda/2)$ with $n = 1, 2, \ldots.$

11 □ $(n + 1/2)\ \frac{\lambda}{2}$

Since the distance between adjacent node and antinode is $\lambda/4$, the diagrams indicate $L = \left(n + \frac{1}{2}\right)\left(\frac{\lambda}{2}\right)$ with $n = 0, 1, \ldots.$

12 A string (fixed at both ends) resonates to a frequency of 20 Hz in three segments (i.e., two nodes plus the ends). Find the speed of the wave if the string is 100 cm long.

13 A certain string resonates to frequencies of 200 and 250 Hz but to no frequencies in between. Find its fundamental resonance frequency.

14 A tube open at one end and closed at the other shows resonance every 20.0 cm as the piston closing the tube is moved in. Using 330 m/sec as the speed of sound in air, find the frequency of the sound source used to resonate the tube.

15 The coil spring illustrated lies on an essentially frictionless surface. It is 10.0 m long. At point A is a driving mechanism which pushes and pulls sinusoidally on the spring. If a pulse sent down the spring returns to A in a time of 0.80 sec, find the frequencies to which the spring will resonate.

12 ☐ 13.3 m/sec

From the diagram, the string is $3(\lambda/2)$ long. So $100 = 1.5\lambda$. Using the fact that $\lambda = v/f$, one finds $v = 13.3$ m/sec.

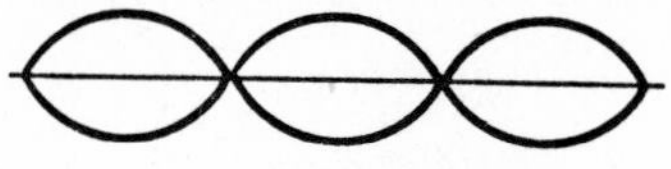

13 ☐ 50 Hz

For a string fixed at both ends, the resonance frequencies are such that (see problem 9) $L = n\lambda/2 = nv/2f$. Writing this twice for two adjacent frequencies gives $f_1 = nv/2L$ and $f_2 = (n + 1)v/2L$. Taking ratios and putting in values for f_1 and f_2 gives $n = 4$. Also, the fundamental frequency $= v/2L = f_1/n$ and so it is 50 Hz.

14 ☐ 825 Hz

a

34
answers
12-15

The tube will resonate whenever the closed end is at the position of a node, as illustrated. The distance between resonance positions is the distance between nodes and so $\lambda/2 = 20.0$ cm. Use of $f = v/\lambda$ gives $f = 825$ Hz.

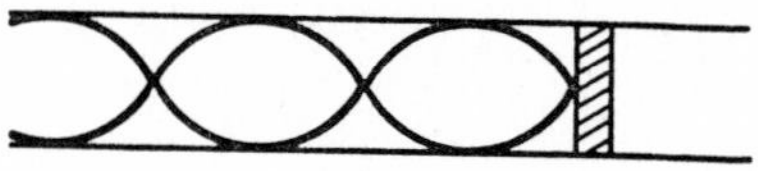

15 ☐ $1.25n$ Hz

Because of the way it is constrained, the spring will have displacement nodes near its ends. Therefore, at resonance, $L = n(\lambda/2)$. Now the speed of the wave is $v = s/t = 20.0/0.80 = 25$ m/sec. Then, since $f = v/\lambda$, we have $f = v(n/2L) = (25/20)n$ Hz.

35 quantum phenomena

1 A sphere covered with lampblack acts nearly like a black body; i.e., it absorbs nearly all the radiation incident on it. When it is in an oven at equilibrium, it radiates as much energy as it receives. Hence, the power/per square meter received from its surroundings at temperature T_0 is equal to the power it radiates. Using this fact, prove that the net loss from the sphere is $\sim (T - T_0)$ where T and T_0 are the slightly unequal temperatures of sphere and surroundings.

2 A black body has its maximum radiation energy at $\lambda \cong 20{,}000$ Å, when the body is at 1500°K. What must be its temperature if the radiation maximum is to be at 5000 Å? For comparison purposes, the melting point of tungsten is 3643°K and that of copper is 1356°K.

3 What is meant by the "ultraviolet catastrophe"?

1 At equilibrium

$$U_{radiated} = U_{received} = (const) T_o^4$$

If the temperature of the sphere is raised slightly to $T = T_o + \Delta$, then

$$U_{radiated} = (const)\,(T_o + \Delta)^4$$

The net power loss per square meter of sphere area will be

$$(const)\,[(T_o + \Delta)^4 - T_o^4]$$

After factoring, this becomes

$$(const) \left[T_o^4 (1 + \frac{\Delta}{T_o})^4 - T_o^4\right] \cong (const) \left[4T_o^3 \Delta\right]$$

where the expansion for $(1 + x)^4$ has been used. Therefore the power loss is proportional to Δ or $T - T_o$. This is called Newton's law of cooling.

a

35
answers
1-3

2 ☐ 6000°K

According to Wien's displacement law,

$$\lambda_m T = const$$

Therefore

$$(20{,}000)\,(1500) = 5000T$$

from which $T = 6000°K$.

3 The classical theory for the power radiated by a black body predicts $U \sim 1/\lambda^2$ as a function of wavelength. Hence it predicts (incorrectly) infinite power radiation as $\lambda \rightarrow 0$. Since this catastrophe (for the theory) occurs at subultraviolet wavelengths, the name was given.

4 What limiting forms does Planck's radiation law take on at long wavelengths ($f \rightarrow 0$) and at short wavelengths ($f \rightarrow \infty$)?

5 In order to obtain his radiation law, what fundamental assumption did Planck make?

6 In what way did Einstein modify Planck's ideas in order to describe the photoelectric effect?

7 How did Einstein explain the existence of a critical wavelength λ_c, above which wavelength electrons would not be emitted?

8 What is Einstein's interpretation of the photoelectric equation,

$$\frac{1}{2} mv^2_{\text{max}} = Af - B$$

where the LHS is the kinetic energy of the fastest electron emitted by radiation of frequency f.

4 □ f^2T; $f^3 \exp \frac{-hf}{kT}$

Planck's radiation law is

$$U(f) \sim \frac{f^3}{\exp\left(\frac{hf}{kT}\right) - 1}$$

(a) Limit $hf/kT \ll 1$: Expanding the exponential and dropping the third and higher terms

$$U(f) \sim f^2 T$$

(b) Limit $hf/kT \gg 1$: In this case the exponential overpowers the -1 and so

$$U(f) \sim f^3 \exp \frac{-hf}{kT} \to 0$$

5 He assumed that the atomic oscillators which existed in the black body could only take on certain discrete energies, namely, nhf. In this expression, n is an integer, h is a constant of nature (Planck's constant = 6.63×10^{-34} J-sec), and f is the natural frequency of the oscillator.

6 Reasoning from the concept of Planck that oscillators which radiate waves of frequency f can only have energies of hf, $2hf$, $3hf$, . . . , Einstein postulated that the radiated energy came in energy quanta or packets equal to hf, the energy difference between two allowed energy states for the Planck oscillators.

7 A light photon or quantum has an energy $hf = h(c/\lambda)$. The minimum energy needed to tear an electron loose from the material is ϕ, the work function. If the photon energy is greater than this, electrons will be emitted; if less, they will not. Therefore λ_c is given by $hc/\lambda_c = \phi$, or $\lambda_c = hc/\phi$.

8 Einstein postulated that the fastest emitted electron had a kinetic energy equal to that of a light quantum, hf, minus the energy needed for the electron to free itself, ϕ.

Therefore

$$\frac{1}{2} mv^2{}_{max} = hf - \phi$$

Comparison shows h must equal A and this is confirmed by experiment.

9 When light of 4000 Å is used, the stopping potential for the electrons from a certain surface is 0.20 V. Find the work function for the material and λ_c.

10 Light of λ = 4000 and 5400 Å is incident simultaneously on the surface described in problem 9. What will be the stopping potential in this case?

11 Suppose a photon of wavelength λ strikes a resting atom head-on and is absorbed by the atom. Find the final velocity v of the atom in terms of its mass M.

12 A photon (λ = 663 Å) is moving in the $+x$ direction when it strikes a free electron at rest and rebounds elastically. Find the subsequent velocity of the electron (assumed in the $+x$ direction) and the wavelength of the reflected photon.

9 ☐ 2.9 eV; 4280 Å

Since the stopping potential is the voltage needed to stop the fastest photoelectrons,

$$\frac{1}{2}mv^2_{max} = hf - \phi$$

yields $\phi = 4.7 \times 10^{-19}$ J = 2.9 eV

Since $hf_c = hc/\lambda_c = \phi$, one has $\lambda_c = 4280$ Å.

10 ☐ 0.20 V

The energy of the fastest electron will be determined by the energy of the highest energy photon. Since $\lambda = 4000$ Å gives the highest energy photon, we need only consider this wavelength. As pointed out in the previous problem, the stopping potential is 0.20 V for this wavelength and this surface.

11 ☐ $v_x = \frac{h}{M\lambda}$; $v_y = v_z = 0$

a

The photon has a momentum hf/c. From the law of momentum conservation, assuming the photon to be moving in the $+x$ direction,

momentum before = momentum after

$$\frac{hf}{c} = Mv_x$$

35
answers
9-12

Replacing f by c/λ yields $v_x = h/M\lambda$.

Of course, $v_y = v_z = 0$ since the photon had no momentum components in those directions. Notice that the rest mass (and final momentum) of the photon is zero.

12 ☐ 2.2×10^4 m/sec; $\lambda + 0.049$ Å

From the conservation of momentum, assuming the electron initially at rest,

$$\frac{h}{\lambda} + 0 = -\frac{h}{\lambda'} + mv_x$$

At the given wavelength $v_x \ll c$ and so $m = 9 \times 10^{-31}$ kg. Also, from the (non-relativistic) conservation of energy,

$$\frac{hc}{\lambda} = \frac{hc}{\lambda'} + \frac{1}{2}mv_x^2$$

Solving these two equations simultaneously gives $v_x = 2.2 \times 10^4$ m/sec and $\lambda' = \lambda + 0.049$ Å.

13 An electron moving in the $-x$ direction with a speed $0.99c$ is to be stopped by a head-on, elastic collision with a photon going in the $+x$ direction. Find λ and λ'.

14 Suppose that one wishes to make a realistic scale model of a hydrogen atom. Using a 2-cm-diameter ball to represent the size of the nucleus, how far away from the center of the ball should the "electron" be placed? (The orbit radius of the hydrogen electron is about 5×10^{-11} m.)

13 □ $3.7 \times 10^{-13}\,m$; $5.2 \times 10^{-12}\,m$

The electron is relativistic and so its momentum is $mv = 0.99\,mc$ and its kinetic energy is $(m - m_0)c^2$ with $m = m_0/\sqrt{1 - (0.99)^2} \approx 7m_0$. From the conservation of momentum,

$$\frac{h}{\lambda} - mv = -\frac{h}{\lambda'} \qquad \text{or} \qquad \frac{1}{\lambda} + \frac{1}{\lambda'} = \frac{mv}{h}$$

and from the law of conservation of energy,

$$\frac{hc}{\lambda} + (m - m_0)\,c^2 = \frac{hc}{\lambda'} \qquad \text{or} \qquad \frac{1}{\lambda} - \frac{1}{\lambda'} = \frac{(m - m_0)c}{h}$$

Solution of these two equations simultaneously leads to $\lambda = 3.7 \times 10^{-13}\,m$ and $\lambda' = 5.2 \times 10^{-12}\,m$.

14 □ ~100 m

Assuming the diameter of a proton to be about 2.5×10^{-15} m, the diameter of the electron's orbit should be $5 \times 10^{-11}/2.5 \times 10^{-15} = 2 \times 10^4$ times larger than the nuclear diameter. The electron should therefore be placed about 100 m from the center of the model nucleus. Clearly, the atom has vast expanses of open space.

a

35
answers
13-14

36 introduction to atoms and spectra

1 Describe the emission spectrum of hydrogen atoms and give the empirical relationships which represent it.

2 How did Bohr obtain an expression for the total energy of an electron in its circular orbit in his model of the hydrogen atom?

3 In order to obtain agreement with experiment, what condition did Bohr find necessary for a stable orbit?

4 In addition to the assumption mentioned in problem 3, what other assumption did Bohr make?

1 The spectrum consists of several series of spectral lines such as the one illustrated. Each one of these can be represented by an equation

$$\frac{1}{\lambda} = R\left(\frac{1}{p^2} - \frac{1}{q^2}\right) \quad p < q$$

with p and q integers. The Lyman, Balmer, and Paschen series have $p = 1, 2,$ and 3, respectively.

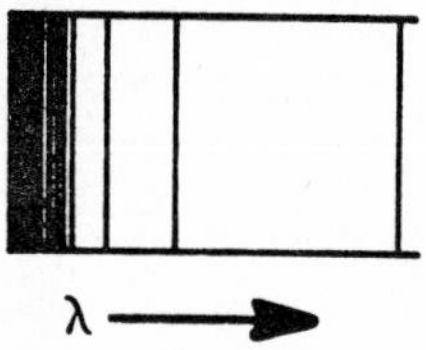

2 To find the kinetic energy, he equated centripetal and coulomb forces to give

$$\frac{mv^2}{r} = \frac{1}{4\pi\epsilon_0}\frac{q^2}{r^2} \rightarrow \frac{1}{2}mv^2 = \frac{1}{8\pi\epsilon_0}\frac{q^2}{r} = \text{KE}$$

The potential energy is that of a negative charge in the field of a positive charge,

$$\text{PE} = -\frac{1}{4\pi\epsilon_0}\frac{q^2}{r}$$

Taking the sum of these two gives the total energy

$$-\frac{1}{3\pi\epsilon_0}\frac{q^2}{r}$$

a

36
answers
1-4

3 Bohr had to assume that only those orbits were stable in which the angular momentum of the electron about the nucleus was given by

$$mv_n r_n = \frac{nh}{2\pi}$$

where h = Planck's constant

$n = 1, 2, \ldots,$

v_n = electron's speed in the nth orbit

4 He assumed that when the electron fell from an outer orbit to an inner orbit it emitted a photon of energy $hf = E_p - E_j$, where E_p is the electron's energy in the outer orbit and E_j is the energy in the inner orbit.

5 How could these two assumptions be used to find the previously empirical formulas for the hydrogen spectral series?

6 How did Bohr explain the Balmer series of spectral lines? The Lyman series?

7 When a continuous spectrum of wavelengths is sent into a gas of atomic hydrogen, only certain wavelengths are absorbed. What are they and how does Bohr's model explain them?

8 When the gas of problem 7 is excited by shining light of wavelength equal to that of the Lyman series limit upon it, it is noticed that not only the Lyman series of lines is emitted by the gas but the Balmer and Paschen series as well. Explain why.

q

36
questions
5-8

5 In problem 2 we had $E_n = -\left(\frac{1}{8\pi\epsilon_o}\right)(q^2/r_n)$ and

$v_n = \sqrt{q^2/4\pi\epsilon_o m r_n}$. Combining the latter with the result from problem 3, namely,

$v_n = nh/2\pi m r_n$, gives $\frac{1}{r_n} = \frac{\pi q^2 m}{\epsilon_o h^2 n^2}$

and so

$$hf = E_p - E_j = \frac{q^4 m}{8\epsilon_o{}^2 h^2}\left(\frac{1}{j^2} - \frac{1}{p^2}\right)$$

Rewriting $hf = hc/\lambda$ gives the desired result.

6 He showed that the Balmer series corresponded to the light emitted as the electron made transitions to the second orbit. The longest λ of the series corresponds to a transition from $n = 3$ to $n = 2$ while the series limit corresponds to a transition from $n = \infty$ (outside the atom) to $n = 2$. In the same way, the Lyman series corresponds to transitions ending in the first orbit.

a

7 The Lyman series of wavelengths is absorbed. Since the vast majority of the hydrogen atoms are in the ground state (i.e., in the $n = 1$ level), light photons which have an energy exactly equal to the energy difference between this state and a higher state will be absorbed by the atom. The photon's energy is used to throw the electron into the higher state. When the electron falls back to the $n = 1$ state from this excited state, it will give off a line in the Lyman series, a photon with exactly the same energy and λ as the photon which was absorbed.

8 Consider the energy-level diagram shown. A Lyman series limit photon excites an electron from the $n = 1$ to the $n \to \infty$ state. As the electron falls back down to the $n = 1$ state, it may do so by many paths. Three possible ones are shown. Consequently, photons of energy $E_p - E_j$ for all p and j will be emitted, and so the entire hydrogen spectrum will be emitted.

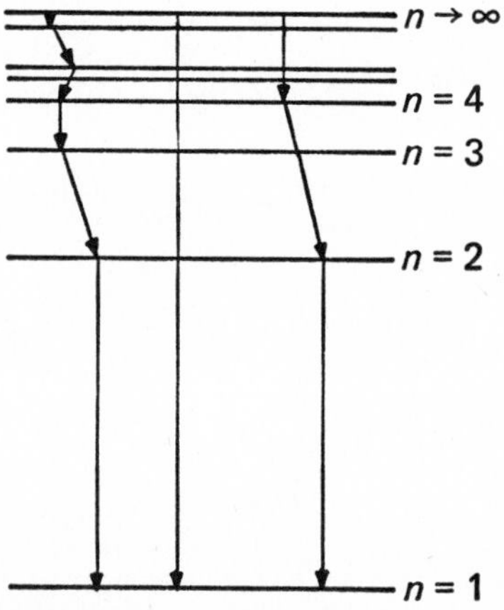

9 List the five lowest energy levels (in electron volts) for hydrogen.

10 What wavelength radiation is emitted by a hydrogen atom when an electron falls from the $n = 10$ level to the $n = 9$ level?

11 Is it correct to say that an electron is a wave?

12 (a) A material particle of mass m moving with speed v behaves like a wave with $\lambda =$ ________ when moving through space. (b) The wavelike motion of the particle can be described in terms of a wave function or disturbance ψ which satisfies ________'s equation. (c) Although the amplitude of the ψ wave has only limited physical meaning, the amplitude squared (more correctly $\psi\psi^*$ where ψ^* is the complex conjugate), the intensity of the wave, represents (in the case of a beam of particles) ________ ; (d) in the case of a single particle, it represents ________.

13 Why does one ordinarily not notice the wavelike properties of laboratory-size objects?

q

36
questions
9-13

9 □ -13.6, -3.4, -1.5, -0.85, -0.544 eV

They are given by $E_n = -13.6/n^2$ eV.

10 □ 39 μ

The energy difference is

$$13.6\left(\frac{1}{81} - \frac{1}{100}\right) = 0.032 \text{ eV}$$

But

$$hf = \Delta E = 0.032 \times 1.6 \times 100^{19} \text{ J.}$$

So

$$hc/\lambda = 5.12 \times 10^{-21} \text{ J and } \lambda = 3.9 \times 10^{-5} \text{ m}$$

which is 39 μ and is in the infrared.

11 Not unless you are willing to argue with many people! In the last analysis, this is a matter of semantics. Unless you are willing to define a "wave" to include such diverse things as light, baseballs, water ripples, etc., it is incorrect to say that an electron is a wave. It is probably preferable to say that the electron has wavelike characteristics and exhibits these when in motion. This statement is correct for all objects which have rest mass, as well as for photons (which do not).

12 (a) h/p or h/mv

(b) Schrödinger

(c) the density of the particles in space, that is, the relative number of particles in the beam at various positions

(d) the probability of finding the particle at various positions

13 Since $\lambda = h/mv$ and since $h = 6.63 \times 10^{-34}$ J-sec, the momentum of the particle must be very small if λ is to be even as large as atomic size. We know that to observe wave effects (interference and diffraction), λ must be comparable to the size of the measuring slits, etc. This is impossible to achieve for such small λ values as one has for h/mv of laboratory objects. Only when m is very small (atomic masses for example) does λ become large enough to be measured directly.

14 A 2.0-g ball sits on a table at 300°K. Find the average of the magnitude of its momentum and compute its associated wavelength.

15 In discussions of the Bohr atom it is found that the first Bohr orbit has a radius 0.53×10^{-10} m and the speed of the electron in this orbit is 2.2×10^{6} m/sec. Compare the wavelength of the wave associated with the electron to the circumference of the orbit.

14 ☐ 5×10^{-12} kg-m/sec; 1.3×10^{-22} m

At thermal equilibrium, energy $= \frac{3}{2} kT = 6.2 \times 10^{-21}$ J.

Therefore

$$\frac{1}{2} mv^2 = 6.2 \times 10^{-21}$$

so that mv, in this case where $m = 2 \times 10^{-3}$ kg, is 5×10^{-12} kg-m/sec.

As a result $\lambda = h/p = 1.3 \times 10^{-22}$ m. Under faster motion, λ would be still smaller.

15 ☐ They are both equal to 3.3×10^{-10} m

One has $\lambda = h/mv = 3.3 \times 10^{-10}$ m. The orbit's circumference is $2\pi r = 3.3 \times 10^{-10}$ m. Therefore, the path along the orbit is one wavelength long.

37 atoms and molecules

1 A beam of protons is shot with speed 4×10^3 m/sec at a crystal with planes as indicated. At what angles will strong reflection occur?

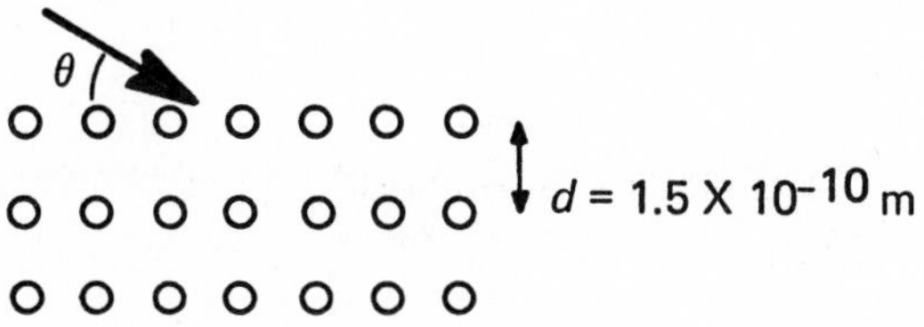

2 Through how large a potential would the protons of problem 1 have been accelerated in order to achieve the given speed? How large a voltage would be required for a 1 Å electron wave?

3 What further data would one need to apply Schrödinger's equation to the situation outlined in problem 1? If this were available, what else could one compute for this situation?

4 When one solves the Schrödinger equation for the motion of an electron with total energy E, and potential energy V, one arrives at the wave function ψ. What information does the ψ function give us?

5 What properties must the ψ function have to be an acceptable solution to the Schrödinger equation?

6 When Schrödinger's equation is solved for the electron in the hydrogen atom, the condition that ψ remain finite as $r \to \infty$ leads to integer values for the principal quantum number n. What information does this quantum number provide?

1 □ 19°, 42°, 90°

This is simply Bragg reflection of protons rather than x rays. The value of $\lambda = h/p = h/mv = 1 \times 10^{-10}$ m. Now we make use of Bragg's law

$$n\lambda = 2\, d \sin\theta$$

which gives $\sin\theta = n/3$ from which $\theta = 19°, 42°$, and $90°$.

2 □ 0.084 volt; 150 volts

One has $Vq = \frac{1}{2}mv^2$. Placing in the values gives

$$V = \frac{(1.67 \times 10^{-27})\,(16 \times 10^{6})}{(1.6 \times 10^{-19})\,(2)} = 0.084 \text{ volt}$$

Clearly, it is difficult to obtain a proton beam of this long a wavelength. In the case of an electron, $v = h/m\lambda = 7.3 \times 10^{+6}$ m/sec and $V = 150$ volts.

a

37
answers
1-6

3 One would need the potential energy and kinetic energy of the proton as it passes into the crystal. This would be extremely difficult to find exactly since the motion and structure of the crystal atoms would need to be known too. Given these, the intensity of the beam reflected at any angle could be found, although machine computation methods would have to be used to obtain even an approximate answer.

4 The ψ function, when squared (or multiplied by its complex conjugate if it is not a real number), gives the fraction of times (or probability) one would find the electron in various regions when the position of the electron is determined in a large number of independent observations.

5 Since ψ^2 (or $\psi\psi^*$) is simply a number proportional to the chance of finding a particle at a given point, it must (a) be single valued. This follows because the chance of finding the particle is a single-valued function of position. Also, (b) it must be finite since physically the probability of finding the particle is bounded.

6 This is the quantum number basic to the Bohr atom. Schrödinger's equation, too, determines the electron energy levels as $E_n = -13.6/n^2$ eV. However, no definite orbits are found, in contradiction to the Bohr model.

7 Indicate on a diagram the system of coordinates r, θ, and ϕ used in the Schrödinger treatment of the hydrogen atom. In terms of these coordinates, what form does the ψ function take on? If an external magnetic field exists, in what direction is it taken?

8 In order that the function $\psi_2(\theta)$ in problem 7 be single valued, a quantum number l, called the orbital quantum number, must be introduced. What is its significance?

9 Clearly, if ψ (ϕ) is to be single valued, it must repeat itself every 360°. This gives rise to a third quantum number, m_l, called the magnetic quantum number. What values can it take on and what does it specify?

10 Suppose that $l = 2$ so that $L = \hbar\sqrt{6}$. Show by means of vector diagrams the possible values of L_z.

7 The resultant ψ function has three factors, thus, $\psi = \psi_1(r)\, \psi_2(\theta)\, \psi_3(\phi)$ where each factor is a function of only one variable, as indicated. **B** is taken along the $+z$ axis.

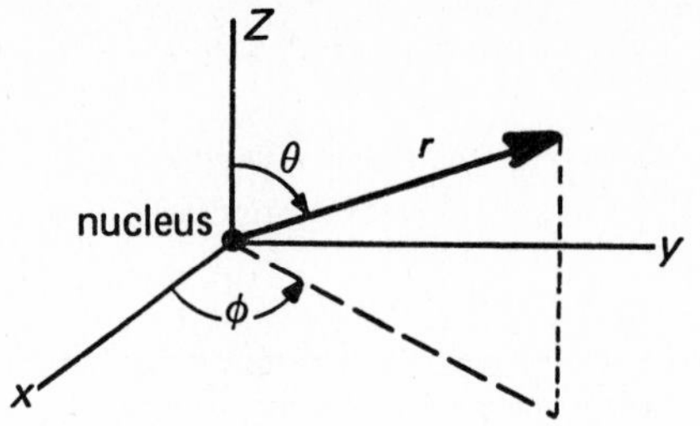

8 The orbital quantum number l specifies that the orbital angular momentum **L** of the electron about the nucleus, which was $mv_n r_n$ in the Bohr theory, can only have magnitude $L = (h/2\pi)\sqrt{l(l+1)}$ with $l = 0, 1, \ldots, (n-1)$ for each value of n. Therefore, for a given energy E_n, the orbital angular momentum can have values $(h/2\pi)\cdot 0 = 0$, $(h/2\pi)\sqrt{2}$, $(h/2\pi)\sqrt{6}, \ldots, (h/2\pi)\sqrt{(n-1)n}$. Clearly, a fixed orbit for each n is untenable.

a

9 □ $m_l = 0, \pm 1, \pm 2, \ldots, \pm l$

It determines the component of the orbital angular momentum vector **L** which lies along the z axis, L_z. The relation is

$$L_z = m_l \frac{h}{2\pi}$$

10 As stated in problem 9, m_l can be 0, ± 1, ± 2, and so L_z can be 0, $\pm \hbar$, ± 2. The diagrams are

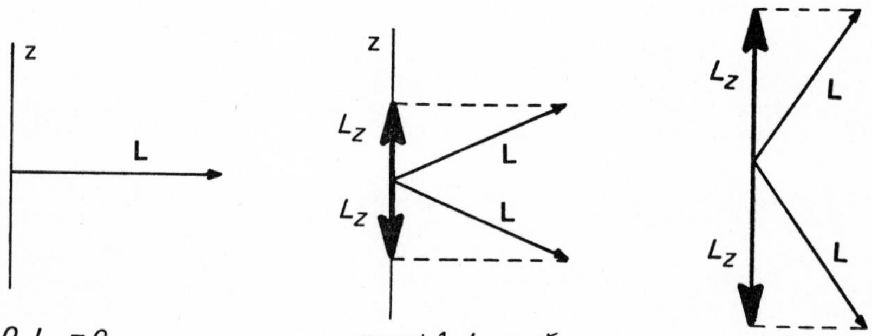

$m_l = 0,\ L_z = 0$ $\qquad$ $m_l = \pm 1,\ L_z = \pm\hbar$ $\qquad$ $m_l = \pm 2,\ L_z = \pm 2\hbar$

11 How large is the z component of the electron's spin angular momentum? How is the spin quantum number defined?

12 State the Pauli exclusion principle as applied to atoms.

13 List the quantum numbers for the electrons in neon.

14 In reference to the tabulation of the previous problem, why is the next element after neon, namely sodium, univalent?

15 State in mathematical form the Heisenberg uncertainty principle.

11 S_z = z component of spin angular momentum = $m_s\hbar$ where

$m_s = \pm\frac{1}{2}$ is the spin quantum number.

12 "In a system containing several electrons, no two electrons can be in the same state characterized by the same four quantum numbers, n, l, m_l, and m_s."

13

Electron	n	l	m_l	m_s
1	1	0	0	$\frac{1}{2}$
2	1	0	0	$-\frac{1}{2}$
3	2	0	0	$\frac{1}{2}$
4	2	0	0	$-\frac{1}{2}$
5	2	1	0	$\frac{1}{2}$
6	2	1	0	$-\frac{1}{2}$
7	2	1	1	$\frac{1}{2}$
8	2	1	1	$-\frac{1}{2}$
9	2	1	-1	$\frac{1}{2}$
10	2	1	-1	$-\frac{1}{2}$

14 The eleventh electron would have to go into the $n = 3$ level, which is the next higher energy state. It is therefore considerably easier to tear loose from the atom than are the electrons for which $n = 2$.

15 ☐ $(\Delta p_x)(\Delta x) \geqslant \hbar$

$(\Delta E)(\Delta t) \geqslant \hbar$

(See Bueche, Sec. 37.5.)

16 An electron is moving along the x axis at a speed of $(5.000 \pm 0.002) \times 10^7$ m/sec. What is the smallest possible uncertainty with which its x position could be located?

17 The electromagnetic radiation given off and absorbed by molecules can be grouped into three different types. What are they and in what range of wavelengths are they found?

18 The moment of inertia of a typical diatomic molecule such as O_2 is of the order of 2.5×10^{-46} kg-m^2. What will be the wavelength of the radiation emitted by such a molecule as a result of rotational energy transitions?

19 Referring to the previous problem, about what value would j have for a molecule at 300°K?

16 □ 2.9×10^{-9} m

We have the uncertainty relation

$$(\Delta p)\,(\Delta x) \geqslant \hbar$$

In the present case, $\Delta p = m(\Delta v) = m(0.004) \times 10^7$

and so

$$\Delta x \geqslant \hbar / m(0.004 \times 10^7) = 2.9 \times 10^{-9}\ \text{m}$$

17 The spectrum emitted by the electrons in the atoms constituting the molecules is similar to that of the free atoms, at least insofar as the inner electrons are concerned. It lies in the x-ray, ultraviolet, and visible range. The vibration of the atoms (constituting the molecules) against springlike restoring forces gives rise to a set of lower-energy transitions, frequently in the infrared. Finally, there exist energy levels of the molecule associated with molecular rotation. They are of very low energy and appear in the infrared or microwave regions.

a

37
answers
16-19

18 □ $0.004/j$ m

The energy levels are, Eq. 37.10 from Bueche,

$$E_j = \frac{\hbar^2}{2I}\, j(j+1) \quad j = 0, 1, \ldots$$

Because of selection rules, j can only change by 1 during a transition so

$$hf = \frac{\hbar^2}{2I}\left[j(j+1) - (j-1)(j)\right] = \frac{\hbar^2 j}{I}$$

but

$$\lambda = \frac{c}{f} = \frac{4\pi^2 Ic}{hj} \cong \frac{0.4 \times 10^{-2}}{j}\ \text{m}$$

19 The rotational energy of the molecule, from the equipartition theorem, should be about $kT/2$. Therefore, $E_j \cong kT/2$. Using the value for E_j given in Eq. 37.10 of Bueche,

$$\frac{h^2}{8\pi^2 I}\, j(j+1) = \frac{kT}{2}$$

from which $j(j+1) \cong 93$ and so $j \cong 10$. As a result, λ of the previous problem would be about 0.04 cm.

38 nuclei of atoms

1 The z component of the spin angular momentum of the electron, proton, or neutron is $\pm \hbar/2$. Its total angular momentum is $\sqrt{3}\,\hbar/2$. Find the apex angle of the cone on which the total angular momentum vector rotates about the z axis.

2 Is it correct to say that the electron can have its spin oriented in only two directions, parallel or antiparallel to the applied magnetic field?

3 What is the relation between the spin angular momentum **S** of a particle and its magnetic dipole moment? What about the z component of each?

4 How can one rationalize the fact that $\mu = 0$ for the following nuclei:

$$_2He^4,\ _6C^{12},\ _8O^{16},\ \text{and}\ _{10}Ne^{20}?$$

5 The value of μ_z for deuterium nuclei is 0.86 μ_N. How can this be interpreted?

6 Estimate the radius of the nucleus of $_{88}Ra^{226}$.

1 □ 110°

The apex angle is 2θ. From the diagram, $\cos\theta = 1/\sqrt{3} = 0.578$ from which $2\theta = 110°$.

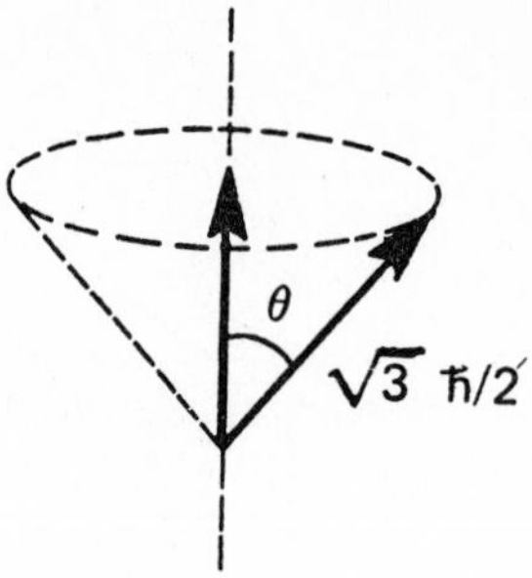

2 Not strictly correct. This should be clear from the diagram of problem 1. What is really meant is that the z component is

$$\pm\frac{1}{2}\hbar .$$

But as one sees, the total spin vector rotates on the surface of a cone.

a

3 Since μ and **S** are in line, and since for an electron, proton, or neutron, as seen in problem 1, $S = \sqrt{3}\, S_z$, then $\mu = \sqrt{3}\, \mu_z$. For an electron,

$$\mu_z = \frac{e\hbar}{2m} \equiv \mu_B$$

38 answers 1-6

and is called the Bohr magneton. The magnetic moments of the neutron, proton, and nuclei are much smaller. One has for the proton, $\mu_z = 2.79\ \mu_N$, and for the neutron, $\mu_z = 1.91\ \mu_N$. Here, the nuclear magneton μ_N is $(m/M_p)\ \mu_B$, with m being the electron mass and M_p being the proton mass.

4 Considering these nuclei to be composed of equal numbers of neutrons and protons, the magnetic moments (i.e., the z components thereof) cancel in pairs and give zero net magnetic moment from that source. Also, any magnetic effects due to the motion of the protons in these nuclei must also cancel.

5 Deuterium is $_1H^2$ and contains one proton and one neutron in the nucleus. Their moments are apparently antialigned. Therefore the resultant μ_z is the difference between the proton and neutron values, $(2.79 - 1.91)\,\mu_N = 0.88\ \mu_N$. The slight disagreement shows that some magnetic effect must exist due to motion of the proton in the nucleus.

6 The nuclear radius is given by (see Bueche, Sec. 38.3): $R \cong 1.2 \times 10^{-15} A^{1/3}$ m. In this case $A = 226$ and so $R = (1.2 \times 10^{-15})\ (6.1) = 7.3 \times 10^{-15}$ m.

7 Three major isotopes of silicon exist in nature with atomic masses 27.977, 28.976, and 29.974. The isotope having $A = 28$ has a percentage abundance of 92.27. Find the percentage abundance of the $A = 30$ isotope. In the atomic chart, $A_{Si} = 28.086$.

8 The tritium atom (i.e., H^3) has a mass 3.016049 amu. Find the energy, in million electron volts, needed to tear this nucleus into two neutrons and a proton. (One atomic mass unit is equivalent to 931 MeV of energy.)

9 The binding energy of the hydrogen electron is 13.6 eV. By what fraction does a hydrogen atom's mass change as the nearly free electron in the excited atom drops to the ground state? (1 amu → 931 MeV.)

10 Point out why, for large Z, the number of neutrons in the nucleus must exceed the number of protons.

7 □ 3.1

We know that

$$28.086 = (27.977)(0.923) + (28.976)(0.077 - x) + (29.974)x$$

where x is the fraction of the $A = 30$ isotope. Solving for x gives 0.031.

8 □ 7.7 MeV

The mass defect for this nucleus is

$$3.016049 - 2(1.007825) - 1.008665 = 0.00827 \text{ amu}$$

Since 1 amu corresponds to 931 MeV of energy, this mass loss is equivalent to 7.7 MeV. (Notice in this calculation that the mass of one electron is included in *both* the tritium and hydrogen mass and so it is canceled out.)

9 □ -1.5×10^{-8}

As the electron drops to the ground state, it radiates 13.6 eV of energy. This is equivalent to $13.6/931 \times 10^6$ amu of mass. Since the mass of the atom is 1 amu, the fractional mass loss is 1.5×10^{-8}.

a

38
answers
7-10

10 At high atomic numbers, the surface term of the binding energy equation (see Bueche Eq. 38.8) will be of little importance, so the binding energy per nucleon is

$$P\epsilon_N - \frac{C_c Z^2}{A^{4/3}}$$

The first term is constant (since it represents the nearest-neighbor contact energy). If $A \sim Z$, then the proton-repulsion term would increase as $Z^{2/3}$ and the binding energy would become zero. Clearly, A must increase faster than Z to maintain a suitable binding energy. In essence, the neutrons dilute the mutually repelling protons.

11 A 1-MeV beta particle enters a region perpendicular to a magnetic field of 500 G. Find the radius of the circular path which it follows.

q

38
question
11

11 □ 9.5 cm

The electron will be relativistic.

Therefore

energy = $(10^6)(1.6 \times 10^{-19}) = (m - m_0)c^2$

so

$m = 9.1 \times 10^{-31} + 17.8 \times 10^{-31} = 26.9 \times 10^{-31}$ kg.

But

$$\left(\frac{m}{m_0}\right)^2 = \left(1 - \frac{v^2}{c^2}\right)^{-1}$$

and so

$\frac{v^2}{c^2} = 0.885$ and $v = 2.82 \times 10^8$ m/sec.

a

Then since

$\frac{mv^2}{r} = qvB$ one has $r = \frac{mv}{qB} = 9.5$ cm.

38
answer
11

12 When the count rate for a particular radioactive material is plotted in the form

$$\ell n \left| \frac{dn}{dt} \right| \quad \text{versus } t$$

a straight line of slope $-3 \times 10^{-4}\ \text{sec}^{-1}$ results. Find the decay constant λ for the material.

13 What is the half-life of the material of the previous problem?

14 How long will it take for the material of problem 12 to decay to one-tenth its original value?

12 3×10^{-4} sec^{-1}

The usual decay law is

$$n = n_o e^{-\lambda t}$$

from which

$$\left|\frac{dn}{dt}\right| = +n_o \lambda e^{-\lambda t}$$

Taking logs of each side gives

$$\ell n \left|\frac{dn}{dt}\right| = -\lambda t + \ell n\,(n_o \lambda)$$

This is the equation of a straight line of form

$y = mx + b$ with $m = -\lambda$ being the slope.

Therefore

$$\lambda = 3 \times 10^{-4} \text{ sec}^{-1}$$

a

13 ☐ 2310 sec

The half-life τ is given by $\lambda\tau = 0.693$. From this and the λ value found in problem 12, $\tau = 2310$ sec.

14 ☐ 7700 sec

We have

$$\frac{n}{n_o} = \frac{1}{10} = e^{-\lambda t}$$

or

$$\ell n\,(10) = \lambda t$$

But

$\ell n\,(10) = 2.30 \log (10) = 2.30$ and since

$\lambda = 3 \times 10^{-4}$ sec^{-1} we find

$$t = \frac{2.30}{3} \times 10^{-4} = 7700 \text{ sec}$$

15 The shortest x-ray line emitted by a certain atom is 0.22 Å. When the radioactive nucleus of this atom causes an internal-conversion electron of energy 50 keV to be emitted, what energy γ-ray transition gives rise to the radiation

16 Referring back to problem 11, find the value of r without computing m and ν.

q

38
questions
15-16

15 □ 106 keV

The energy equation is as follows:

50 keV + binding energy = γ-ray energy
of electron

The binding energy of the electron in the atom is essentially the energy of its shortest x-ray line. It is therefore

$$h\frac{c}{\lambda} = 6.63 \times 10^{-34} \frac{3 \times 10^8}{2.2 \times 10^{-11}} = 9 \times 10^{-15}\ \text{J}$$

or

5.6×10^4 eV.

Therefore the γ-ray energy is 56 + 50 = 106 keV.

16 □ 9.5 cm

We may make use of the relation (Bueche, Eq. 38.14):

$$K = \sqrt{m_o{}^2c^4 + p^2c^2} - m_oc^2$$

to find p. Since $K = 1.60 \times 10^{-13}$ J and $m_oc^2 = 82 \times 10^{-15}$, one finds $p = 0.76 \times 10^{-21}$ kg-m/sec. Using this for mv in the expression for r again gives $r = 9.5$ cm.

39
high-energy physics

1 A beam of electrons is decreased 10 percent in intensity by passing through an aluminum sheet 0.010 cm thick. Find the effective cross section of each atom for electrons of this energy.

$(\rho_{A\ell} = 2.70\ \text{g/cm}^3;\ A = 13)$

2 Find the thickness of aluminum needed to decrease a beam to 0.10 of its original intensity if the effective cross section per atom is 2.0 barns.

3 When an α particle collides head-on with a gold nucleus, what fraction of its energy is available for reaction?

4 A particular reaction between a proton and a nucleus of 8.0 amu requires an energy of 7.0 MeV. What must be the energy of the proton in the laboratory reference frame?

1 ☐ 84 barns

One has $I/I_0 = e^{-\sigma nx}$ where n is the number of atoms in unit volume. But $n = (6 \times 10^{23}/\text{g-mole})\,(2.70\ \text{g/cm}^3)/(13\ \text{g/g-mole}) = 1.25 \times 10^{23}/\text{cm}^3$. Also, $\ln(I_0/I) = \sigma nx$, with $I/I_0 = 0.90$ and $x = 0.010$ cm. Solving for σ gives $84 \times 10^{-24}\ \text{cm}^2$.

2 ☐ 9.2 cm

One has (see Bueche, Eq. 39.3) that $I = I_0 e^{-\sigma nx}$ with $I/I_0 = 0.10$ and $\sigma = 2.0 \times 10^{-24}\ \text{cm}^2$. But for aluminum

$$n = (6 \times 10^{23}\ \text{molecules/g-mole}) \left(\frac{2.70\ \text{g/cm}^3}{13\ \text{g/g-mole}}\right) = \frac{1.2 \times 10^{23}}{\text{cm}^3}$$

Therefore,

$$\ln(0.10) = -(2 \times 10^{-24}\ \text{cm}^2) \left(\frac{1.2 \times 10^{23}}{\text{cm}^3}\right) x$$

from which $x \cong 9.2$ cm.

3 ☐ 0.98

The available energy is (see Bueche, Eq. 39.8): $m_{Au}/(m_\alpha + m_{Au})$.
But $m_{Au} = 197$ amu and $m_\alpha = 4$ amu so the fraction is $197/201 = 0.98$.

a

39
answers
1-4

4 ☐ 7.9 MeV

From problem 3, the fraction of the proton's energy which is available is eight-ninths. Therefore the proton must have an energy in the lab frame of $(9/8)(7.0) = 7.89$ MeV.

5 A radioactive nucleus of mass 9 amu (C^9) emits a proton with energy 9.3 MeV as measured in the laboratory. How much energy did the nucleus lose in the process?

6 What should be the ratio of initial velocities of two identical nuclei which collide and undergo reaction if the original kinetic energy is to be used most efficiently?

7 Repeat problem 6 if the two particles have masses m_1 and m_2.

5 □ 10.5 MeV

Since the resultant nucleus has a mass of 8 amu, the law of conservation of momentum requires

$$0 = m_p v - MV$$

where v and V are final velocities.

Also

$$K = \frac{1}{2} m_p v^2 + \frac{1}{2} M V^2$$

$$= \frac{1}{2} m_p v^2 + \frac{1}{2} M \left(\frac{m_p}{M}\right)^2 v^2$$

$$= K_p \left(1 + \frac{m_p}{M}\right)$$

Therefore

$$K = 9.3\ (1 + 1/8) = 10.5 \text{ MeV}$$

a

39
answers
5-7

6 □ Unity

It is possible to use all of the lab-frame kinetic energy if the two identical particles have equal and opposite velocities and collide head-on. Since the original momentum of the system is zero, there will be no kinetic energy tied up in the motion of the mass center after collision.

7 □ $\dfrac{v_1}{v_2} = \dfrac{m_2}{m_1}$

We wish $m_1 v_1 = m_2 v_2$ and so $v_1/v_2 = m_2/m_1$.

8 What fraction of its energy will a nonrelativistic proton lose as it shoots past a helium nucleus with a collision parameter of 10^{-14} m? Assume that the energy of the proton is large enough so it can undergo a collision of this type.

9 From the answer to problem 8 it is clear that $\Delta E/E$ becomes larger than unity for E small. This cannot be true physically. What approximations in the derivation of Eq. 39.9 in Bueche give rise to this difficulty?

10 For α particles in the range of 10 MeV, how much farther would the particles travel in aluminum than in lead?

(ρ_{Al} = 2.70 g/cm^3, ρ_{pb} = 11.3 g/cm^3; Z_{Al} = 13,

Z_{Pb} = 82; A_{Al} = 27, A_{Pb} = 207)

a

39
answers
8-10

8 □ $\dfrac{\Delta E}{E} = \dfrac{2.1 \times 10^{10}}{E^2 \text{ (in eV)}}$

According to Eq. 39.9 of Bueche

$$\Delta E = \frac{q_1{}^2 q_2{}^2}{8\pi^2 \epsilon_o{}^2 b^2 m_2 v^2}$$

In our case,

$q_1 = e,\ q_2 = 2e,\ b = 10^{-14}$

$m_2 = 4(1.67 \times 10^{-27})\text{kg}$ and $\frac{1}{2}mv^2 = E$

Therefore

$$\frac{\Delta E}{E} = \frac{4e^4}{8\pi^2 \epsilon_o{}^2 (10^{-14})^2 (6.68 \times 10^{-27}) (2E/1.67 \times 10^{-27})E}$$

from which

$$\frac{\Delta E}{E} = \frac{5.3 \times 10^{-28}}{E^2 \text{ (joules)}} = \frac{2.1 \times 10^{10}}{E^2 \text{ (in eV)}}$$

9 It is assumed in Eq. 39.9 of Bueche that the particle goes by the stationary particle in such a way that $\langle F_x \rangle = 0$. Further, it is assumed that θ varies from $-\pi/2$ to $\pi/2$ as the particle goes by. If b is too small, or if E is too small, or both, then the particle will rebound in such a way that these two assumptions are not even approximately valid.

10 □ $\dfrac{R_{\text{Al}}}{R_{\text{Pb}}} \cong 22$

As a rough rule, at a given energy the range varies as $A/Z^2 \rho$ and so

$$\frac{R_{\text{Al}}}{R_{\text{Pb}}} = \frac{27}{(13)^2(2.7)} \cdot \frac{(82)^2(11.3)}{207} = 22$$

A more exact value could be found by using the experimental data of Bueche's Fig. 39.9 directly.

review of some mathematics

POWERS OF TEN

It is often inconvenient to write numbers such as 1,420,000,000 and 0.00031. These numbers can be written $(1.42)(10^9)$ and $(3.1)(10^{-4})$, as we now show.

Let us consider the following identities:

$$
\begin{aligned}
10 &= 10^1 \\
100 &= (10)(10) = 10^2 \\
1000 &= (10)(10)(10) = 10^3 \\
1{,}000{,}000{,}000 &= 10^9
\end{aligned}
$$

If we wish to write the number 4,561,000,000, we have at once that this number is equivalent to multiplying 4.561 nine times by 10. (Each time we multiply by 10 we move the decimal point one place to the right.) Hence

$$4{,}561{,}000{,}000 = (4.561)(10^9)$$

In general, if we move the decimal place on a number q places to the left, we must multiply the number by 10^q if it is to remain unchanged. For the example just given, $q = 9$.

The procedure for writing numbers less than unity is somewhat similar. We make use of the fact that

$$
\begin{aligned}
0.1 &= \frac{1}{10} = 10^{-1} = (1)(10^{-1}) \\
0.01 &= \frac{1}{100} = \frac{1}{10^2} = 10^{-2} = (1)(10^{-2}) \\
0.001 &= \frac{1}{1000} = \frac{1}{10^3} = 10^{-3} = (1)(10^{-3}) \\
0.000{,}000{,}01 &= \frac{1}{10^8} = 10^{-8} = (1)(10^{-8})
\end{aligned}
$$

Clearly, when we move the decimal point q places to the right, we must multiply by 10^{-q}. In the case originally treated, $0.00031 = (3.1)(10^{-4})$, q was 4, since the decimal point was moved four places.

CONVERSION OF UNITS

Suppose we want to know how many inches are equivalent to 2 miles. Problems such as this are easily done provided we know the proper conversion factors. In this case we know there are 5280 ft/mile and 12 in./ft. We then proceed as follows:

$$
\begin{aligned}
s &= 2 \text{ miles} \\
&= (2\ \cancel{\text{miles}})\left(5280\ \frac{\text{ft}}{\cancel{\text{mile}}}\right) = 10{,}560 \text{ ft} \\
&= (10{,}560\ \cancel{\text{ft}})\left(12\ \frac{\text{in.}}{\cancel{\text{ft}}}\right) = 126{,}720 \text{ in.}
\end{aligned}
$$

Notice that the units of the conversion factors are treated like algebraic symbols.

As another example, let us find the number of hours in 60,000 sec.

$$
\begin{aligned}
t &= 60{,}000 \text{ sec} \\
&= (60{,}000 \cancel{\text{sec}})\left(\frac{1}{60}\frac{\text{min}}{\cancel{\text{sec}}}\right) = 1000 \text{ min} \\
&= (1000 \cancel{\text{min}})\left(\frac{1}{60}\frac{\text{hr}}{\cancel{\text{min}}}\right) = 16.7 \text{ hr}
\end{aligned}
$$

Here we have made use of the factor 60 sec/min, which has been inverted to give 1⁄60 min/sec.

TRIGONOMETRY

In this text we need only the basic definitions of trigonometry, together with a very few relations between functions. As shown in figure A3.1, the sine, cosine, and tangent functions are defined in terms of a right triangle.

$$\sin\theta = \frac{a}{c} \qquad \cos\theta = \frac{b}{c} \qquad \tan\theta = \frac{a}{b}$$

Although we seldom use them, the cosecant, secant, and cotangent are

$$\csc\theta = \frac{c}{a} \qquad \sec\theta = \frac{c}{b} \qquad \cot\theta = \frac{b}{a}$$

From the fact that in any right triangle such as the one shown, $a^2 + b^2 = c^2$, we have upon substitution

$$\sin^2\theta + \cos^2\theta = 1$$

A few other formulas are also used in the text, and we list them here:

$$
\begin{aligned}
\sin(x \pm y) &= \sin x \cos y \pm \cos x \sin y \\
\cos(x \pm y) &= \cos x \cos y \mp \sin x \sin y \\
\sin 2\theta &= 2 \sin\theta \cos\theta \\
\cos 2\theta &= \cos^2\theta - \sin^2\theta = 1 - 2\sin^2\theta
\end{aligned}
$$

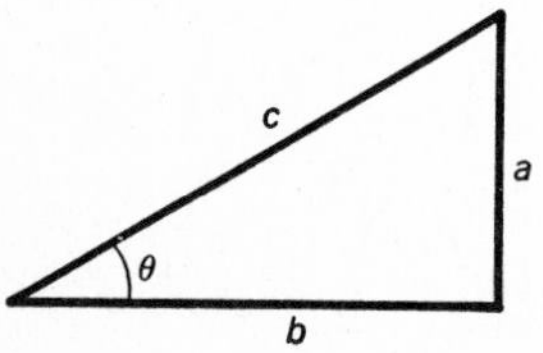

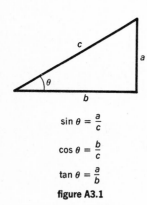

$\sin\theta = \frac{a}{c}$

$\cos\theta = \frac{b}{c}$

$\tan\theta = \frac{a}{b}$

figure A3.1

SERIES EXPANSIONS
($|x| < 1$ UNLESS OTHERWISE INDICATED)

$$(1 \pm x)^n = 1 \pm nx + \frac{(n)(n-1)}{2!}x^2 \pm \frac{n(n-1)(n-2)}{3!}x^3 + \cdots$$

$$(1 \pm x)^{-n} = 1 \mp nx + \frac{n(n+1)}{2!}x^2 \mp \frac{n(n+1)(n+2)}{3!}x^3 + \cdots$$

$$(1 \pm x)^{1/2} = 1 \pm \frac{1}{2}x - \frac{1}{8}x^2 \pm \frac{1}{16}x^3 - \cdots$$

$$(1 \pm x)^{-1/2} = 1 \mp \frac{1}{2}x + \frac{3}{8}x^2 \mp \frac{5}{16}x^3 + \cdots$$

$$\left.\begin{aligned} \sin x &= x - \frac{x^3}{3!} + \frac{x^5}{5!} - \cdots \\ \cos x &= 1 - \frac{x^2}{2!} + \frac{x^4}{4!} - \cdots \\ e^x &= 1 + x + \frac{x^2}{2!} + \frac{x^3}{3!} + \cdots \end{aligned}\right\} \text{for all real } x$$

$$\ln(1 \pm x) = \pm x - \frac{1}{2}x^2 \pm \frac{1}{3}x^3 - \frac{1}{4}x^4 \pm \cdots$$

trigonometric functions

angle (deg)	*sine*	*cosine*	*tangent*	*angle (deg)*	*sine*	*cosine*	*tangent*
0°	0.000	1.000	0.000				
1°	.018	1.000	.018	46°	0.719	0.695	1.036
2°	.035	0.999	.035	47°	.731	.682	1.072
3°	.052	.999	.052	48°	.743	.669	1.111
4°	.070	.998	.070	49°	.755	.656	1.150
5°	.087	.996	.088	50°	.766	.643	1.192
6°	.105	.995	.105	51°	.777	.629	1.235
7°	.122	.993	.123	52°	.788	.616	1.280
8°	.139	.990	.141	53°	.799	.602	1.327
9°	.156	.988	.158	54°	.809	.588	1.376
10°	.174	.985	.176	55°	.819	.574	1.428
11°	.191	.982	.194	56°	.829	.559	1.483
12°	.208	.978	.213	57°	.839	.545	1.540
13°	.225	.974	.231	58°	.848	.530	1.600
14°	.242	.970	.249	59°	.857	.515	1.664
15°	.259	.966	.268	60°	.866	.500	1.732
16°	.276	.961	.287	61°	.875	.485	1.804
17°	.292	.956	.306	62°	.883	.470	1.881
18°	.309	.951	.325	63°	.891	.454	1.963
19°	.326	.946	.344	64°	.899	.438	2.050
20°	.342	.940	.364	65°	.906	.423	2.145
21°	.358	.934	.384	66°	.914	.407	2.246
22°	.375	.927	.404	67°	.921	.391	2.356
23°	.391	.921	.425	68°	.927	.375	2.475
24°	.407	.914	.445	69°	.934	.358	2.605
25°	.423	.906	.466	70°	.940	.342	2.747
26°	.438	.899	.488	71°	.946	.326	2.904
27°	.454	.891	.510	72°	.951	.309	3.078
28°	.470	.883	.532	73°	.956	.292	3.271
29°	.485	.875	.554	74°	.961	.276	3.487
30°	.500	.866	.577	75°	.966	.259	3.732
31°	.515	.857	.601	76°	.970	.242	4.011
32°	.530	.848	.625	77°	.974	.225	4.331
33°	.545	.839	.649	78°	.978	.208	4.705
34°	.559	.829	.675	79°	.982	.191	5.145
35°	.574	.819	.700	80°	.985	.174	5.671
36°	.588	.809	.727	81°	.988	.156	6.314
37°	.602	.799	.754	82°	.990	.139	7.115
38°	.616	.788	.781	83°	.993	.122	8.144
39°	.629	.777	.810	84°	.995	.105	9.514
40°	.643	.766	.839	85°	.996	.087	11.43
41°	.658	.755	.869	86°	.998	.070	14.30
42°	.669	.743	.900	87°	.999	.052	19.08
43°	.682	.731	.933	88°	.999	.035	28.64
44°	.695	.719	.966	89°	1.000	.018	57.29
45°	.707	.707	1.000	90°	1.000	.000	∞

logarithms to the base ten

numbers	0	1	2	3	4	5	6	7	8	9	proportional parts								
											1	2	3	4	5	6	7	8	9
10	0000	0043	0086	0128	0170	0212	0253	0294	0334	0374	4	8	12	17	21	25	29	33	37
11	0414	0453	0492	0531	0569	0607	0645	0682	0719	0755	4	8	11	15	19	23	26	30	34
12	0792	0828	0864	0899	0934	0969	1004	1038	1072	1106	3	7	10	14	17	21	24	28	31
13	1139	1173	1206	1239	1271	1303	1335	1367	1399	1430	3	6	10	13	16	19	23	26	29
14	1461	1492	1523	1553	1584	1614	1644	1673	1703	1732	3	6	9	12	15	18	21	24	27
15	1761	1790	1818	1847	1875	1903	1931	1959	1987	2014	3	6	8	11	14	17	20	22	25
16	2041	2068	2095	2122	2148	2175	2201	2227	2253	2279	3	5	8	11	13	16	18	21	24
17	2304	2330	2335	2380	2405	2430	2455	2480	2504	2529	2	5	7	10	12	15	17	20	22
18	2553	2577	2601	2625	2648	2672	2695	2718	2742	2765	2	5	7	9	12	14	16	19	21
19	2788	2810	2833	2856	2878	2900	2923	2945	2967	2989	2	4	7	9	11	13	16	18	20
20	3010	3032	3054	3075	3096	3118	3139	3160	3181	3201	2	4	6	8	11	13	15	17	19
21	3222	3243	3263	3284	3304	3324	3345	3365	3385	3404	2	4	6	8	10	12	14	16	18
22	3424	3444	3464	3483	3502	3522	3541	3560	3579	3598	2	4	6	8	10	12	14	15	17
23	3617	3636	3655	3674	3692	3711	3729	3747	3766	3784	2	4	6	7	9	11	13	15	17
24	3802	3820	3838	3856	3874	3892	3909	3927	3945	3962	2	4	5	7	9	11	12	14	16
25	3979	3997	4014	4031	4048	4065	4082	4099	4116	4133	2	3	5	7	9	10	12	14	15
26	4150	4166	4183	4200	4216	4232	4249	4265	4281	4298	2	3	5	7	8	10	11	13	15
27	4314	4330	4346	4362	4378	4393	4409	4425	4440	4456	2	3	5	6	8	9	11	13	14
28	4472	4487	4502	4518	4533	4548	4564	4579	4594	4609	2	3	5	6	8	9	11	12	14
29	4624	4639	4654	4669	4683	4698	4713	4728	4742	4757	1	3	4	6	7	9	10	12	13
30	4771	4786	4800	4814	4829	4843	4857	4371	4886	4900	1	3	4	6	7	9	10	11	13
31	4914	4928	4942	4955	4969	4983	4997	5011	5024	5038	1	3	4	6	7	8	10	11	12
32	5051	5065	5079	5092	5105	5119	5132	5145	5159	5172	1	3	4	5	7	8	9	11	12
33	5185	5198	5211	5224	5237	5250	5263	5276	5289	5302	1	3	4	5	6	8	9	10	12
34	5315	5328	5340	5353	5366	5378	5391	5403	5416	5428	1	3	4	5	6	8	9	10	11
35	5441	5453	5465	5478	5490	5502	5514	5527	5539	5551	1	2	4	5	6	7	9	10	11
36	5563	5575	5587	5599	5611	5623	5635	5647	5658	5670	1	2	4	5	6	7	8	10	11
37	5682	5694	5705	5717	5729	5740	5752	5763	5775	5786	1	2	3	5	6	7	8	9	10
38	5798	5809	5821	5832	5843	5855	5866	5877	5888	5899	1	2	3	5	6	7	8	9	10
39	5911	5922	5933	5944	5955	5966	5977	5988	5999	6010	1	2	3	4	5	7	8	9	10

numbers	0	1	2	3	4	5	6	7	8	9	*proportional parts*								
											1	2	3	4	5	6	7	8	9
40	6021	6031	6042	6053	6064	6075	6085	6096	6107	6117	1	2	3	4	5	6	8	9	10
41	6128	6138	6149	6160	6170	6180	6191	6201	6212	6222	1	2	3	4	5	6	7	8	9
42	6232	6243	6253	6263	6274	6284	6294	6304	6314	6325	1	2	3	4	5	6	7	8	9
43	6335	6345	6355	6365	6375	6385	6395	6405	6415	6425	1	2	3	4	5	6	7	8	9
44	6435	6444	6454	6464	6474	6484	6493	6503	6513	6522	1	2	3	4	5	6	7	8	9
45	6532	6542	6551	6561	6571	6580	6590	6599	6609	6618	1	2	3	4	5	6	7	8	9
46	6628	6637	6646	6656	6665	6675	6684	6693	6702	6712	1	2	3	4	5	6	7	7	8
47	6721	6730	6739	6749	6758	6767	6776	6785	6794	6803	1	2	3	4	5	5	6	7	8
48	6812	6821	6830	6839	6848	6857	6866	6875	6884	6893	1	2	3	4	4	5	6	7	8
49	6902	6911	6920	6928	6937	6946	6955	6964	6972	6981	1	2	3	4	4	5	6	7	8
50	6990	6998	7007	7016	7024	7033	7042	7050	7059	7067	1	2	3	3	4	5	6	7	8
51	7076	7084	7093	7101	7110	7118	7126	7135	7143	7152	1	2	3	3	4	5	6	7	8
52	7160	7168	7177	7185	7193	7202	7210	7218	7226	7235	1	2	2	3	4	5	6	7	7
53	7243	7251	7259	7267	7275	7284	7292	7300	7308	7316	1	2	2	3	4	5	6	6	7
54	7324	7332	7340	7348	7356	7364	7372	7380	7388	7396	1	2	2	3	4	5	6	6	7
55	7404	7412	7419	7427	7435	7443	7451	7459	7466	7474	1	2	2	3	4	5	5	6	7
56	7482	7490	7497	7505	7513	7520	7528	7536	7543	7551	1	2	2	3	4	5	5	6	7
57	7559	7566	7574	7582	7589	7597	7604	7612	7619	7627	1	2	2	3	4	5	5	6	7
58	7634	7642	7649	7657	7664	7672	7679	7686	7694	7701	1	1	2	3	4	4	5	6	7
59	7709	7716	7723	7731	7738	7745	7752	7760	7767	7774	1	1	2	3	4	4	5	6	7
60	7782	7789	7796	7803	7810	7818	7825	7832	7839	7846	1	1	2	3	4	4	5	6	6
61	7853	7860	7868	7875	7882	7889	7896	7903	7910	7917	1	1	2	3	4	4	5	6	6
62	7924	7931	7938	7945	7952	7959	7966	7973	7980	7987	1	1	2	3	3	4	5	6	6
63	7993	8000	8007	8014	8021	8028	8035	8041	8048	8055	1	1	2	3	3	4	5	5	6
64	8062	8069	8075	8082	8089	8096	8102	8109	8116	8122	1	1	2	3	3	4	5	5	6
65	8129	8136	8142	8149	8156	8162	8169	8176	8182	8189	1	1	2	3	3	4	5	5	6
66	8195	8202	8209	8215	8222	8228	8235	8241	8248	8254	1	1	2	3	3	4	5	5	6
67	8261	8267	8274	8280	8287	8293	8299	8306	8312	8319	1	1	2	3	3	4	4	5	6
68	8325	8331	8338	8344	8351	8357	8363	8370	8376	8382	1	1	2	2	3	4	4	5	6
69	8388	8395	8401	8407	8414	8420	8426	8432	8439	8445	1	1	2	2	3	4	4	5	6
70	8451	8457	8463	8470	8476	8482	8488	8494	8500	8506	1	1	2	2	3	4	4	5	6
71	8513	8519	8525	8531	8537	8543	8549	8555	8561	8567	1	1	2	2	3	4	4	5	5
72	8573	8579	8585	8591	8597	8603	8609	8615	8621	8627	1	1	2	2	3	4	4	5	5
73	8633	8639	8645	8651	8657	8663	8669	8675	8681	8686	1	1	2	2	3	4	4	5	5
74	8692	8698	8704	8710	8716	8722	8727	8733	8739	8745	1	1	2	2	3	4	4	5	5
75	8751	8756	8762	8768	8774	8779	8785	8791	8797	8802	1	1	2	2	3	3	4	5	5
76	8808	8814	8820	8825	8831	8837	8842	8848	8854	8859	1	1	2	2	3	3	4	5	5
77	8865	8871	8876	8882	8887	8893	8899	8904	8910	8915	1	1	2	2	3	3	4	4	5
78	8921	8927	8932	8938	8943	8949	8954	8960	8965	8971	1	1	2	2	3	3	4	4	5
79	8976	8982	8987	8993	8998	9004	9009	9015	9020	9025	1	1	2	2	3	3	4	4	5

numbers	0	1	2	3	4	5	6	7	8	9	*proportional parts*								
											1	2	3	4	5	6	7	8	9
80	9031	9036	9042	9047	9053	9058	9063	9069	9074	9079	1	1	2	2	3	3	4	4	5
81	9085	9090	9096	9101	9106	9112	9117	9122	9128	9133	1	1	2	2	3	3	4	4	5
82	9138	9143	9149	9154	9159	9165	9170	9175	9180	9186	1	1	2	2	3	3	4	4	5
83	9191	9196	9201	9206	9212	9217	9222	9227	9232	9238	1	1	2	2	3	3	4	4	5
84	9243	9248	9253	9258	9263	9269	9274	9279	9284	9289	1	1	2	2	3	3	4	4	5
85	9294	9299	9304	9309	9315	9320	9325	9330	9335	9340	1	1	2	2	3	3	4	4	5
86	9345	9350	9355	9360	9365	9370	9375	9380	9385	9390	1	1	2	2	3	3	4	4	5
87	9395	9400	9405	9410	9415	9420	9425	9430	9435	9440	0	1	1	2	2	3	3	4	4
88	9445	9450	9455	9460	9465	9469	9474	9479	9484	9489	0	1	1	2	2	3	3	4	4
89	9494	9499	9504	9509	9513	9518	9523	9528	9533	9538	0	1	1	2	2	3	3	4	4
90	9542	9547	9552	9557	9562	9566	9571	9576	9581	9586	0	1	1	2	2	3	3	4	4
91	9590	9595	9600	9605	9609	9614	9619	9624	9628	9633	0	1	1	2	2	3	3	4	4
92	9638	9643	9647	9652	9657	9661	9666	9671	9675	9680	0	1	1	2	2	3	3	4	4
93	9685	9689	9694	9699	9703	9708	9713	9717	9722	9727	0	1	1	2	2	3	3	4	4
94	9731	9736	9741	9745	9750	9754	9759	9763	9768	9773	0	1	1	2	2	3	3	4	4
95	9777	9782	9786	9791	9795	9800	9805	9809	9814	9818	0	1	1	2	2	3	3	4	4
96	9823	9827	9832	9836	9841	9845	9850	9854	9859	9863	0	1	1	2	2	3	3	4	4
97	9868	9872	9877	9881	9886	9890	9894	9899	9903	9908	0	1	1	2	2	3	3	4	4
98	9912	9917	9921	9926	9930	9934	9939	9943	9948	9952	0	1	1	2	2	3	3	4	4
99	9956	9961	9965	9969	9974	9978	9983	9987	9991	9996	0	1	1	2	2	3	3	3	4

periodic table of the elements

The values listed are based on $_{6}C^{12}$ = 12 amu exactly. For artificially produced elements, the approximate atomic weight of the most stable isotope is given in brackets.

period	series	I	II	III	IV	V	VI	VII	VIII	0
1	1	1 H 1.00797								2 He 4.003
2	2	3 Li 6.939	4 Be 9.012	5 B 10.81	6 C 12.011	7 N 14.007	8 O 15.9994	9 F 19.00		10 Ne 20.183
3	3	11 Na 22.990	12 Mg 24.31	13 Al 26.98	14 Si 28.09	15 P 30.974	16 S 32.064	17 Cl 35.453		18 Ar 39.948
4	4	19 K 39.102	20 Ca 40.08	21 Sc 44.96	22 Ti 47.90	23 V 50.94	24 Cr 52.00	25 Mn 54.94	26 Fe 55.85 · 27 Co 58.93 · 28 Ni 58.71	
4	5	29 Cu 63.54	30 Zn 65.37	31 Ga 69.72	32 Ge 72.59	33 As 74.92	34 Se 78.96	35 Br 70.909		36 Kr 83.80
5	6	37 Rb 85.47	38 Sr 87.62	39 Y 88.905	40 Zr 91.22	41 Nb 92.91	42 Mo 95.94	43 Tc [98]	44 Ru 101.1 · 45 Rh 102.905 · 46 Pd 106.4	
5	7	47 Ag 107.870	48 Cd 112.40	49 In 114.82	50 Sn 118.69	51 Sb 121.75	52 Te 127.60	53 I 126.90		54 Xe 131.30
6	8	55 Cs 132.905	56 Ba 137.34	57-71 Lanthanide series*	72 Hf 178.49	73 Ta 180.95	74 W 183.85	75 Re 186.2	76 Os 190.2 · 77 Ir 192.2 · 78 Pt 195.09	
6	9	79 Au 196.97	80 Hg 200.59	81 Tl 204.37	82 Pb 207.19	83 Bi 208.98	84 Po [210]	85 At [210]		86 Rn [222]
7	10	87 Fr [223]	88 Ra [226]	89-103 Actinide series†						

*Lanthanide series	57 La 138.91	58 Ce 140.12	59 Pr 140.91	60 Nd 144.24	61 Pm [147]	62 Sm 150.35	63 Eu 152.0	64 Gd 157.25	65 Tb 158.92	66 Dy 162.50	67 Ho 164.93	68 Er 167.26	69 Tm 168.93	70 Yb 173.04	71 Lu 174.97
†Actinide series	89 Ac [227]	90 Th 232.04	91 Pa [231]	92 U 238.03	93 Np [237]	94 Pu [242]	95 Am [243]	96 Cm [247]	97 Bk [247]	98 Cf [251]	99 E [254]	100 Fm [253]	101 Md [256]	102 No [254]	103 Lw [257]

conversion factors

Conversions which are exact are signified by an asterisk *. For brevity, the conversion factors are written in a dimensionless form. To use them, notice that the symbolism 2.54 cm/in means there are 2.54 centimeters in one inch. A quantity multiplied by any one of these factors changes only the units of the quantity. For example,

$$30 \text{ in} = (30 \text{ in})\ (2.54 \frac{cm}{in}) = 76.2 \text{ cm}$$

and

$$5 \text{ cm} = (5 \text{ cm})\ (\frac{1}{2.54\ cm/in}) = 1.97 \text{ in}$$

LENGTH

* 2.54 cm/in

* 0.3048 m/ft

* 1.609344 km/mi

9.461 X 10^5 m/light year

FORCE

* 10^5 dyne/N

4.45 N/lb

0.225 lb/N

lkg weighs 2.21 lb at g=9.80 m/sec^2

TIME

* 86400 sec/day

3.16 X 10^7 sec/yr

MASS

1.6605 X 10^{-27} kg/amu

6.0222 X 10^{26} amu/kg

SPEED

* 0.3048 (m/sec)/(ft/sec)

60 (mi/hr)/88(ft/sec)

1.47 (ft/sec)/(mi/hr)

0.447 (m/sec)/(mi/hr)

1.609 (km/hr)/(mi/hr)

PRESSURE

* 1.01325 X 10^5 (N/m^2)/atm

* 1.01325 bar/atm

* 0.10 (N/m^2)/(dyne/cm^2)

6.895 X 10^3 (N/m^2)/psi

133.32 (N/m^2)/mm of Hg at 0°C

76 cm of Hg/atm

14.7 psi/atm

1 torr/mm of Hg

WORK and ENERGY

* 10^7 erg/J
* 4.184 J/cal
* 3.60×10^6 J/kW-hr
* 1,054 J/BTU

1.6022×10^{-19} J/eV

6.242×10^{18} eV/J

0.239 cal/J

0.738 ft-lb/J

23.06 (kcal/g-mole)/(eV/molecule)

1 amu $\longrightarrow$ 931.48 MeV

POWER

746 W/hp

550 (ft-lb/sec)/hp

ELECTRICAL

1.6022×10^{-19} C/electron charge

96487 C/faraday

* 10^4 gauss/tesla

physical constants and data

Speed of light	$c = 2.997925 \times 10^{8}$ m/sec
Gravitational constant	$G = 6.67 \times 10^{-11}$ N-m^2/kg^2
Avogadro's number	$N_A = 6.0222 \times 10^{26}$ particles/kg-atom
Boltzmann's constant	$k = 1.3806 \times 10^{-23}$ J/K
Gas constant	$R = 8314$ J/kg-mole-K
	$= 1.9872$ kcal/kg-mole-K
Planck's constant	$h = 6.6262 \times 10^{-34}$ J-s
Electron charge	$e = 1.60219 \times 10^{-19}$ C
Electron rest mass	$m_e = 9.1096 \times 10^{-31}$ kg
	$= 5.4859 \times 10^{-4}$ amu
Proton rest mass	$m_p = 1.67261 \times 10^{-27}$ kg
	$= 1.0072766$ amu
Neutron rest mass	$m_n = 1.67492 \times 10^{-27}$ kg
	$= 1.0086652$ amu
Permittivity constant	$\epsilon_0 = 8.85419 \times 10^{-12}$ C^2/Nm^2
Permeability constant	$\mu_0 = 4\pi \times 10^{-7}$ N/A^2
Std gravitational accel	$g = 9.80665$ m/sec^2 = 32.17 ft/sec^2
Mass of earth	5.98×10^{24} kg
Avg radius of earth	6.37×10^{6} m
Avg density of earth	5.57 g/cm^3
Avg earth-moon distance	3.84×10^{8} m
Avg earth-sun distance	1.496×10^{11} m
Mass of sun	1.99×10^{30} kg
Radius of sun	7×10^{8} m
Sun's radiation intensity at the earth	0.032 cal/cm^2-sec = 0.134 J/cm^2-sec.